Soul

Soul

A CHEF'S CULINARY EVOLUTION IN 150 RECIPES

TODD RICHARDS

FOREWORD BY SEAN BROCK

Oxmoor
House®

©2018 Time Inc. Books
Published by Oxmoor House, an imprint of Time Inc. Books
225 Liberty Street, New York, NY 10281

Executive Editor: Katherine Cobbs

Project Editor: Melissa Brown

Design Director: Melissa Clark

Photo Director: Paden Reich

Designer: Matt Ryan

Assistant Production Director:
  Sue Chodakiewicz

Assistant Production Manager:
  Diane Rose Keener

Copy Editors: Rebecca Brennan,
  Ashley Strickland Freeman

Proofreader: Donna Baldone

Indexer: Mary Ann Laurens

Fellows: Kaitlyn Pacheco, Holly Ravazzolo,
  Hanna Yokeley

ISBN-13: 978-0-8487-5441-9

Library of Congress Control Number:
  2017960063

First Edition 2018
Printed in China
10 9 8 7 6 5 4 3 2 1

We welcome your comments and
suggestions about Time Inc. Books.
Time Inc. Books
Attention: Book Editors
P.O. Box 62310
Tampa, Florida 33662-2310

Time Inc. Books products may be purchased
for business or promotional use.
For information on bulk purchases, please
contact Christi Crowley in the Special Sales
Department at (845) 895-9858.

I dedicate this book to all cooks who utilize our art to bring people closer together: my mother, Valoria Viola Richards, who insisted that every holiday and birthday was a celebration; my dad, Willis Richards Jr., who ensured that technique was essential to a delicious meal; my grandmother, who would make the most delicious powdered milk when all of my cousins would spend the night at her house; and my sister Kea, who is the gatekeeper of family pictures. They taught me to be the gatekeeper of family food, smoking food in particular. I hope my sons, Todd Jr., Graham, and Tedric Simon August, pass it on to their sons as my dad did me.

To my wife, Melissa, who has been my mirror of love, joy, honesty, and "astral plane" traveler, you have restored my voice in the world through your grace, power, and all things wonderful—my soul mate.

CONTENTS

FOREWORD

SOUL: My favorite four-letter word. I've known Todd for over a decade now. When I met him, he was cooking very creative and modern renditions of Southern food in Kentucky. We became fast friends; plus, he liked fine bourbon as much as I did.

I've followed his career and eaten his food ever since, and we've managed to keep in close touch. One of the great pleasures of being a chef and having a friend like Todd is watching how a perspective can change. Over the years we have had a lot of opportunities to cook together at various events. We always sit down and speak about what has us excited at the moment, whether it's a technique or a new country ham source. We have always shared our discoveries with each other and never hesitated to text a question when something has us stumped.

It's a privilege to be sitting here penning the foreword to his first book, Soul. I've read every word in this book and drooled over the photos. Flipping through these pages made me want to hop in the car and go see Todd just to talk food and catch up. My most treasured books make me feel like I'm spending time with that person and getting to know their soul. Todd is very passionate and has a wide array of interests. One minute he'll hand you a bite of perfectly cooked BBQ, and the next, he's artfully plating a modern dish—always striving to be a better craftsman no matter what.

I think a lot about the label "Soul food." To me, each individual person applies his or her own meaning or definition to it. Perhaps it's the food of your grandmother's table or a historic dish from your hometown. It could be a salted slice of tomato that you grew in your backyard. All of these share one thing in common, and that's how you feel when you eat something prepared with love. Soul food is medicine: It can heal a cold or a hangover, or provide comfort when you're missing a loved one. Food can swell the heart and rest a worried mind. Food prepared with love can be a respite and offer healing. I believe that every culture has its own Soul food, whether it's tortellini en brodo in Italy, gumbo from the bayou, or warm apple pie that reminds you of family gatherings.

Soul food also has the power to bring us together, welcoming us all to the table. After reading this book, I was pleased to realize Todd's idea of Soul food isn't "supposed to be" anything but delicious. It feels like Soul food knows no physical boundaries, but rather it manifests as an internal feeling that covers you up like a grandmother's quilt. Within these pages is the story of a chef's journey to define his cuisine and the food that fills his heart. I'm so glad Todd has shared his journey with us. My wish for readers of this book is that you will want to visit a loved one and share a meal, just as I did.

— **SEAN BROCK**

INTRODUCTION

I remember standing on Rainbow Beach in Chicago looking out over the lake and wondering where I came from. It was never a thought of who my parents and family were. It was more to the point of "who are my people?" In my classroom, I had friends from the Philippines and Haiti. They had a strong sense of their heritage and place. Staring into the water, I questioned, what and where was mine?

When we visited my dad's family in Hot Springs, Arkansas, we traded Chicago's Midwestern fare and ethnic restaurants for classic Southern and Soul food made with the freshest ingredients. In the South, playing in the thick red clay replaced staring into the water. Both were exercises for wondering, which I was prone to do. I wondered, if people all came from the same place, why did we shy away from certain parts of Arkansas at night? I wondered why we ate on different sides of the room in a restaurant? I wondered why it was when I was having fun playing with a boy of a different race, his parents told him he couldn't play with me too long? "Don't want people to think we're Negro lovers" was the comment I overheard his dad say to him. And why, I wondered, couldn't I share my McDonald's French fries with him? What I learned was that in some situations in life you just don't share.

Those experiences shaped my soul and cemented my belief that we are socially divided. We live in a world where one would rather not eat than accept an offering of food from someone who is different. This did not jibe with what I was taught in Catholic grammar school or in Baptist Sunday school where it was always about sharing and being humble. So I grew up conflicted.

I was shaped by religion in other ways. I took on a certain humility in understanding the teachings of the Catholic Church, but I always wondered: How could they give you something to eat that tastes so terrible? The Communion cracker was so bland, like sawdust. I contrasted this with Baptist meals, where all things fried and barbecued were the flavorful norm. Yet with the Catholics, on the first Sunday of every month, I got a glass of wine. I'm a kid; am I supposed to be drinking this? Sure, Mom let me sip her Michelob now and then, but why is God okay with wine? Curiously, I liked how well that wine washed down that bland cracker.

PREACHERS OF CUISINE

Today I know a certain truth: Food is a religion of its own. Different regions have produced great preachers of cuisine.

Chefs often tie their parables and menu scribes to a sense of cooking that serves as a reminder of their homes and upbringing. The first time I was in a kitchen with Jacques Pépin, he amazed me with his stories of France and French food. He knew exactly where each dish originated and ingredient came from, who crafted the cheese, and who grew the beets. How could listening to him speak have so much of an influence on me? I wanted to be French! But then I tasted sushi for the first time and I wanted to be Japanese!

While I was cooking the cuisines of many people I dearly admired, I didn't know their stories as innately as Jacques Pépin knew the stories of his own people. I was simply a convert to these cuisines. Sure, I could cook French, Chinese, and Japanese food. I could make the best matzo balls you have ever tasted,

but what was my French food? After all, the foods of my people—my parents and grandparents—were not being highlighted on the menus of fine dining restaurants or fancy hotels. The dishes they grew up eating and I grew up eating were considered lowly and not deserving of the price.

My ancestors were slaves. Like our grits, they ate fufu, like our air-dried meats they made biltong, and, as we do, they used salt and vinegar as a means of preservation. Those intersections weave the fabric that forms the motley quilt of Southern cuisine—and much of American cuisine—so I am called to celebrate and share it. Because my slave ancestors could not read or write, there is little historical record crediting them as the founders of Southern cuisine, unless of course "Soul food" becomes the sole qualifier for what is their accepted contribution.

Soul food is the original cuisine of the South, born from an involuntary collision of cultures. It made its way North and around the country with the Great Migration, as freed slaves sought out the comforting dishes they craved from back home—cornbread, black-eyed peas, a heap of smoky collards, or spicy fried chicken. The flavors used in Soul cooking remain an expression of where we came from. Equally important, how we cook today defines where we want to go.

MY SOUL FOOD

This book is my homage to the cuisine of my family and ancestors. These are the ingredients of my people. This is my sermon about my Soul food. The chapters are short and organized by ingredient. That way, if you get a bumper crop of greens, you can flip to the Collards chapter or if it's peach season, you can find something delicious in the Stone Fruit chapter. Each chapter kicks off with a recipe that's relatively traditional in the African-American culinary repertoire. The recipes progress in my exploration of different flavor combinations and techniques. Even though the recipes are grouped by ingredient, I provide ways to round out a meal time and time again. I encourage you to set a table with a few different dishes to enjoy, even if you're only cooking for two. My suggestions for what to drink, and notes for other serving suggestions, help you master your own pairings. To give you even more inspiration for putting it all together, I include menus throughout to highlight some of my favorite Soul meals, like my mom's home-style Fish Fry or a more avant-garde Chef's Table menu I might serve at an event.

This book is a testament to what I've discovered on my journey and in my practice as a chef. Creating and sharing are both spiritual acts. I happen to create and share food. The cuisine I serve at Richards' Southern Fried is rooted in African-American cooking traditions, which form the very foundation of Southern cuisine. You'll see that I also explore, experiment, and draw inspiration from around the world. When I look at my experiences growing up surrounded by cooks like my mom, dad, and grandmother and creating in the kitchen with chefs like Pépin along the way, it's crystal clear to me that food brings people together if we choose to use it that way. It starts with honoring our culinary heritage, like Chef Pépin does his, and which took me some time to embrace. The next step is acknowledging one another's. Doing so enriches our lives, our communities, and, hopefully, opens minds so that we can begin to appreciate what we all bring to the table.

"Today I know a certain truth:
Food is a religion of its own. Different regions
have produced great preachers of cuisine."

11AM - 7PM TUE - SUN

PEN TOMATOES
HELLED PEAS & BEANS
GA. PEACHES
OILED PEANUTS

FRESH Peas & Beans

VINE RIPE

TOMATOE

FRESH OKRA

COLLARDS

Collard greens didn't come to the New World with the African slave trade, yet it's a common misconception. Collards were grown in the Americas and then incorporated into the cooking and daily meals of slaves and plantation owners. A one-pot meal of greens, accented with bits of meat simmered in broth, was a way to stretch the daily rations and very much in keeping with the traditional long-simmered stews of West Africa. Smoked pork is traditionally incorporated to enhance flavor while its rendered fat carries it. As the greens cool, fat rises to the top of the broth and settles, forming a protective cap that also preserves them for a time. Sturdy collard leaves stand up to braising with whatever fatty cut you prefer—salt pork, ham hock, bacon, or pork jowl—bolstered by aromatics and seasonings. After all of the greens from the pot are eaten, the rich broth (potlikker) makes a delicious base for soups or protein-rich restorative for sipping. The classic trifecta of greens, pork, and broth is a soulful dish that I not only crave but am also compelled to reinterpret in my cooking in myriad ways, as with my Collard Green Ramen and Pickled Collard Green Stems.

Collard Greens with Smoked Ham Hocks and Pickled Collard Green Stems

Is there a more harmonious marriage of deliciousness than ham hock broth and collard greens? Despite a dubious reputation as everyman's fare, collards are quite versatile and can be used in sophisticated and complex dishes.

Cook the greens low and slow to keep them tender but not mushy. Serve with Fried Chicken and Sweet Potato Waffles (page 256). Leftovers keep well. Just reheat them with a touch of water or reserved cooking liquid. Save leftover greens and potlikker to make the Bacon, Collard, and Fried Egg Sandwich (page 26).

Serves 6

4 smoked bacon slices

3 bunches collard greens (1 ½ to 2 pounds)

1 tablespoon olive oil

2 small yellow onions, thinly sliced

4 garlic cloves, thinly sliced

1 pound smoked ham hocks, at room temperature

4 cups (32 ounces) cold water

1 cup (8 ounces) bourbon or whiskey

½ cup (4 ounces) apple cider vinegar (5% acidity)

2 teaspoons kosher salt

½ teaspoon black pepper

½ teaspoon red pepper flakes

Pickled Collard Green Stems (page 21)

1. Freeze the bacon 25 minutes. Remove and cut the bacon crosswise into ⅛-inch pieces.

2. Fill a sink with cold water. Place a cutting board near the sink. Stack 4 collard green leaves on top of each other. Remove the stems with a sharp knife, and reserve for Pickled Collard Green Stems recipe. Cut the leaves into 2-inch squares. Repeat with remaining collard green leaves, and rinse in cold water. Drain.

3. Heat the olive oil in a 4-quart stockpot over medium. Add the bacon. Cook until crisp, about 10 minutes. Remove from the heat. Transfer the bacon to paper towels to drain, reserving the drippings in pot. Reserve the bacon pieces for garnish.

4. Return the pot to medium. Cook the onions and garlic in the hot bacon drippings 2 minutes, stirring often. Add the ham hocks, and cook 5 minutes, turning every 45 seconds or so. Pour 4 cups cold water over the ham hocks, and add the bourbon and vinegar. Bring to a simmer over medium, and cook 25 minutes.

5. Stir in one-fourth of the collards. Continue adding the collards, one-fourth at a time, stirring after each addition. After all collards have been added, simmer 2 minutes.

6. Sprinkle the collards with the salt and black pepper, and cook until the greens are tender, 1 hour to 1 hour and 30 minutes. Remove from the heat, and stir in the red pepper flakes. Let stand 30 minutes before serving.

7. Meanwhile, remove the ham hocks; cool slightly. Pull the meat from the bone. Chop the meat and add it to the collards. Discard the bones. Return the meat to the pot with the greens, and stir. Discard the bones.

8. To serve, sprinkle the collard greens with the reserved bacon. Garnish with the Pickled Collard Green Stems.

Note: One bunch of large collard greens is 8 to 10 large leaves or 1 ½ to 2 pounds. One bunch of baby collard greens is 12 to 16 leaves, about 1 ¼ pounds. Don't use a bunch that's larger than 2 pounds or the leaves will be tough and bitter and the stems woody.
To Drink: Sauvignon Blanc, sparkling wine, Carmenere, Cabernet Sauvignon, Shiraz, amber beers, IPAs, or hard ciders
Serve with: Onion, rice, or pork dishes

pickled collard green stems

Throwing food away is the most bitter pill for me to swallow. Collard stems have, for the most part, been discarded as trash, so this recipe allows you to use the collard stems instead of discarding them. It's important for me to show my chefs that they can turn food that is usually discarded into a delicious part of any meal.

2 pounds collard green stems

8 cups (64 ounces) water

48 cups distilled water

¼ cup pickling salt

¼ cup (2 ounces) apple cider vinegar (5% acidity)

¼ cup (2 ounces) white wine vinegar

1 teaspoon black peppercorns

8 bay leaves

1 poblano chile, cut into 2-inch squares

1 serrano chile, cut into 8 rings

½ teaspoon pink peppercorns

6 garlic cloves, crushed

1. Fill a 2-gallon stockpot half-full with water. Place 8 (1-quart) jars and their lids in the water bath. Bring to a boil and boil 5 minutes to sterilize the jars and lids. Remove the jars and lids using tongs or a jar lifter. Reduce heat to low and maintain a simmer.

2. Fill a sink with cold water. Place a cutting board near the sink. Cut the collard green stems into 2-inch pieces and rinse in cold water. Drain.

3. Bring the 8 cups water to a boil in a separate stockpot over medium-high. Blanch the stems, 2 cups at a time, in the boiling water, 2 to 3 minutes. Meanwhile, fill a medium bowl with ice and water. Transfer the blanched stems to the ice bath.

4. Bring the distilled water to a boil in a 2-gallon stockpot over medium. Add the pickling salt, vinegars, peppercorns, and bay leaves, and cook until the salt is dissolved.

5. Transfer the collard green stems to the hot sterilized jars; top evenly with the chiles, pink peppercorns, and crushed garlic.

6. Pour the pickling salt mixture through a fine wire-mesh strainer into a liquid measuring cup, reserving the peppercorns. Discard the remaining solids. Divide the black peppercorns evenly among the jars. Pour enough of the pickling liquid evenly into the jars to cover the collard green stems, filling to ½ inch from the top of each jar.

7. Wipe jar rims; cover at once with metal lids, and screw on bands (snug but not too tight). Place jars in simmering water in the stockpot. Add additional boiling water as needed to cover by 1 to 2 inches. Simmer about 20 minutes or until jar lids are set. (Follow the jar manufacturer's instructions for a good seal.)

8. Remove from heat. Cool jars in the water bath for 15 minutes. Transfer the jars to a cutting board; let stand at least 3 days before using. Store in a cool, dry place at room temperature. Refrigerate after opening. Makes 8 (1-quart) jars

⊰ TRADITIONAL ⊱

My grandmother Mary Wilson's cooking was where my Soul journey began. We spent hours watching the cooking shows on TV in the '70s and '80s and then we'd cook together. At first, she cooked more traditional Soul dishes, but then she and my great-aunt Viola began experimenting with techniques and flavor combinations they'd seen on TV. They would serve all the dishes they'd made without giving much thought to the menu. Usually it was a heap of side dishes, but it was always delicious and never, ever boring.

Collard Greens with Smoked Ham Hocks
(page 18)

Candied Bacon with Turnip Hash
(page 267)

Smoked Fingerling Sweet Potatoes
(page 332)

Cornbread (page 149)

Pound Cake and Whipped Cream
(page 241)

ON THE RADIO

"Fall In" — *Esperanza Spalding*
"The One-Eye Two-Step" — *The Blackbyrds*
"I'm Your Captain (Closer to Home)" —
Grand Funk Railroad
"Beach Dr." — *Oddisee*

Candied Bacon
(page 267)

Pickled Collard
Green Stems
(page 21)

Cornbread
(page 149)

Roasted Sweet Potatoes
with Collard Green Butter
(page 338)

Turnip Hash
(page 267)

Pound Cake and
Whipped Cream
(page 241)

Collard Greens with
Smoked Ham Hocks
(page 18)

Bacon, Collard, and Fried Egg Sandwich

Poached, soft-scrambled, or fried—egg dishes are an essential part of a chef's repertoire. Cooking eggs correctly requires organizational skill, finesse, and passion; otherwise, the result can be dry, cold, and flavorless. Assemble 80 percent of the dish before adding the egg so it cooks properly and can be served immediately.

Serves 1

¼ cup Pickled Collard Green Stems
  (page 21)
1 small red bell pepper, thinly sliced
1 jalapeño chile, thinly sliced
1 tablespoon pickling liquid from
  Pickled Collard Green Stems (page 21)
1 tablespoon vegetable oil
3 bacon slices
2 sourdough bread slices

1 duck egg or extra-large chicken egg
½ teaspoon kosher salt
¼ teaspoon black pepper
1 cup cooked collard greens,
  roughly chopped
2 cups potlikker from
  cooked collard greens
¼ cup mayonnaise
2 teaspoons hot sauce

1. Stir together the Pickled Collard Green Stems, bell pepper, jalapeño, and pickling liquid in a small bowl. Let stand at least 5 minutes before serving.

2. Heat ½ tablespoon of the oil in a medium sauté pan or skillet over medium. Add the bacon; cook 6 minutes. Turn and cook until crisp, about 4 minutes. Drain the bacon on a plate lined with paper towels. Discard the drippings. Add the bread slices to the pan. Toast over medium to desired degree of doneness. Remove from the pan, and wipe the pan clean with paper towels.

3. Heat the remaining ½ tablespoon oil in the pan. Break the egg into the pan. Cook 4 minutes, shaking the pan occasionally to ensure the egg does not stick. Season with the salt and black pepper. Turn the egg and cook 2 more minutes. Transfer to a plate.

4. Combine the collards and potlikker in a saucepan over medium heat, and cook until warmed through, 2 to 3 minutes. Drain collards, reserving potlikker for another use.

5. Meanwhile, stir together the mayonnaise and hot sauce in a small bowl. Spread mayonnaise mixture onto each slice of toast.

6. Transfer the collards to 1 piece of the sourdough toast using tongs. Top with half of the relish, bacon, and fried egg. Reserve remaining relish for a second sandwich or another use. Top with the remaining piece of toast, spread side down. Secure with skewers or toothpicks, and cut the sandwich in half.

Note: Duck eggs may be found at Whole Foods Market or at Asian markets.

To Drink: Sauvignon Blanc, Chardonnay, rosé, Gamay, Cabernet Sauvignon, amber beers, IPAs, hard ciders, or Bloody Marys

Serve with: Onion, potato, or tomato dishes, green salads, tomato salads

Smoked Turkey and Collard Greens

Smoked turkey has "gobbled" its way into braised dishes, replacing pork as the smoked meat of choice. Some may see it as a healthier alternative to pork. I am one to fall on the side of what's delicious. Both have their merits. Which one I choose really depends on the time of the year.

In late spring and early fall, I like broths to be lighter in texture as well as in overall clarity of flavor, so I turn to smoked turkey. The greens should be the star, and turkey broth lets the collard flavor shine through. Also during these seasons, the greens are younger and less stout in flavor, so a milder broth is preferred.

Using lots of potlikker, this can be a wonderful springtime soup. A heaping spoonful of yellow rice makes it a meal. The pickled collard stem garnish yields bold crunch and a vinegary note that enlivens the collard flavor as well.

Serves 6

3 bunches collard greens (1 ½ to 2 pounds)

1 tablespoon olive oil

1 tablespoon grapeseed oil

2 small yellow onions, thinly sliced

4 garlic cloves, thinly sliced

1 pound smoked turkey wings, at room temperature

4 cups (32 ounces) cold water

1 cup (8 ounces) apple cider vinegar (5% acidity)

1 cup (8 ounces) bourbon or whiskey

2 teaspoons kosher salt

½ teaspoon freshly ground black pepper

½ teaspoon red pepper flakes

Pickled Collard Green Stems (page 21)

Cooked yellow rice (optional)

1. Fill a sink with cold water. Place a cutting board near the sink. Stack 4 collard green leaves on top of each other. Remove the stems with a sharp knife, and reserve for Pickled Collard Green Stems recipe. Cut the leaves into 2-inch squares; rinse in cold water. Repeat with the remaining collard green leaves. Drain.

2. Heat the oils in a 4-quart stockpot over medium. Add the onions and garlic. Cook, stirring often, 2 minutes. Add the turkey wings, and cook 5 minutes, turning every 45 seconds or so. Add 4 cups cold water, vinegar, and bourbon. Bring to a simmer, and cook 15 minutes. Remove the turkey wings from the cooking liquid using tongs.

3. Add the collard leaves to cooking liquid, in 4 batches, stirring after each addition, and simmer 2 minutes. Return the turkey wings to the collard green mixture. Stir in the salt and black pepper. Cook until the greens are tender, 1 to 1 ½ hours. Stir in the red pepper flakes. Remove from the heat, and let stand 30 minutes before serving. Serve with Pickled Collard Green Stems and cooked yellow rice, if desired.

To Drink: Sauvignon Blanc, sparkling wine, Carmenére, Cabernet Sauvignon, Shiraz, amber beers, IPAs, or hard ciders

Serve with: Onion, rice, pork, braised dishes, or potato dishes

Collard Green Ramen

When I was a kid, there was a small Chinese restaurant near our house that served yakamein. *The noodles were always cooked perfectly, the egg cooked to medium, and the freshest scallions topped the bowl. The broth was clear and invigorating. One of my fondest childhood memories was being given permission to slurp my food. That sound of broth and noodles being pulled into the mouth, coupled with silence in the room—no one talks when there are bowls of yakamein—is imprinted in my mind. This recipe pays homage to that dish, but with accents of Southern culture. It's not a replication, but my interpretation and "thank you" to that restaurant for inspiring me to be a chef.*

Serves 4

Collard Greens with Smoked Ham Hocks (page 18)

¼ cup (2 ounces) rice wine vinegar

11 quarts water

4 teaspoons kosher salt

4 large eggs

12 ounces ramen noodles

¼ cup (2 ounces) reduced-sodium soy sauce

4 Pickled Collard Green Stems (page 21), chopped

8 scallions, thinly sliced

4 teaspoons black sesame seeds

Red pepper flakes (optional)

2 limes, each cut into 8 wedges or slices

1 to 2 (2-ounce) packages nori chips (seaweed snacks)

1. Prepare the Collard Greens with Smoked Ham Hocks. (Don't chop the bacon.) Keep the bacon and chopped ham hock meat separate after cooking. Set aside.

2. Bring the vinegar, 12 cups water, and 1 teaspoon salt to a boil in a stockpot over high. Slip the eggs into the water. Cover; boil exactly 5 minutes. Remove the eggs with a slotted spoon. Let stand 5 minutes; peel and set aside. Discard the water from the pot.

3. Add the remaining 8 quarts of water and 1 tablespoon salt to the stockpot, and bring to a boil over high. Add the ramen noodles, and stir to ensure the noodles do not stick together. Boil about 4 minutes or until tender. Drain.

4. Place 1 tablespoon of the soy sauce in each of 4 ramen bowls. Divide ramen noodles evenly among bowls. Arrange about 2 tablespoons of the chopped ham hock meat in each bowl beside the noodles. Place about ¼ cup of the collard greens on top of the noodles in each bowl using tongs. Ladle 1 to 1½ cups potlikker from Collard Greens with Smoked Ham Hocks into each bowl.

5. Cut the eggs in half. Place 2 halves on each bowl. Top with the bacon slices from Collard Greens with Smoked Ham Hocks and chopped Pickled Collard Green Stems.

6. Garnish bowls with sliced scallions. Sprinkle each with about 1 teaspoon sesame seeds and red pepper flakes, if desired. Serve with the lime wedges and nori chips.

To Drink: Sauvignon Blanc, sparkling wine, Cabernet Sauvignon, Shiraz, amber beers, IPAs, Japanese beer, or hard ciders

Serve with: Green salads, poultry, pork, potato, or braised dishes

Oysters Poached in Collard Green Pesto on Cheese Crisps with Caviar

Caviar is a luxury. Here it takes the place of pork to lend salinity to the dish and accentuate the briny flavor of the oysters. These ingredients gave me a choice: celebrate collards in a new way or write yet another recipe on slow-cooked greens. I appreciate Soul classics but strive to reinterpret them again and again.

Serves 4

2 red radishes with green tops

4 ounces aged Cheddar cheese

2 cups Collard Green Pesto (page 35)

16 large shucked oysters, liquor reserved

1 cup Italian-seasoned breadcrumbs

Freshly ground black and pink pepper

1 jalapeño chile, very thinly sliced

1 lemon, cut into 8 wedges

¼ cup mayonnaise

2 teaspoons hot sauce

1 ounce paddlefish caviar

1. Fill a sink with cold water. Trim stems from radish tops and rinse the leaves and radishes with cold water. Drain. Cut the leaves into ⅛-inch-thick strips. Thinly slice the radishes with a mandoline or sharp knife. Place the radish slices in a bowl of cold water.

2. Preheat the oven to 375°F. Line a baking sheet with parchment paper. Grate the Cheddar cheese onto the baking sheet, and spread in an even layer. Bake in the preheated oven 9 minutes. Remove from the oven, and let stand 1 minute. Carefully turn the cheese over using tongs. Bake 8 more minutes or until the cheese begins to brown. Remove from the oven. Let stand 30 minutes. Increase the oven temperature to 400°F.

3. Heat a medium-size ovenproof sauté pan over medium. Remove from heat. Spread the pesto evenly in the pan. Make 16 small wells in the pesto with the back of a spoon. Place 1 oyster in each well. Spoon 1 tablespoon of the oyster liquor over each oyster; sprinkle evenly with breadcrumbs. Bake in the preheated oven 8 minutes. Increase the oven temperature to broil. Broil 3 inches from the heat until the breadcrumbs are browned, about 1 minute. Remove from the oven. Season with peppers to taste.

4. Break the cheese crisp into bite-size pieces. Place the cheese crisps, jalapeño slices, lemon wedges, and radish leaves in separate small serving bowls. Stir together the mayonnaise and hot sauce in a separate small serving bowl. Drain the radish slices, and place in another small serving bowl.

5. To serve, spoon about ⅛ teaspoon caviar on top of each oyster. Spoon the oysters on the cheese crisps, and squeeze lemon juice on top. Garnish the oysters with desired toppings.

To Drink: Sauvignon Blanc, sparkling wine, Champagne, Chardonnay, rosé, Gamay, Cabernet Sauvignon, amber beers, IPAs, hard ciders, or Bloody Marys

Serve with: Green salads, potato, tomato, rice, or spicy dishes

collard green pesto

This is one of my favorite condiments to use on dishes such as pizza, grilled fish, grilled pork chops, and pasta.

8 cups (64 ounces) water

½ pound collard greens, stemmed, leaves cut into 2-inch squares (about 6 cups)

2 tablespoons pecan oil

⅓ cup pecan halves (do not use pieces)

1 teaspoon kosher salt

¼ teaspoon freshly ground black pepper

½ cup (4 ounces) olive oil

2 white anchovies

6 garlic cloves, coarsely chopped

2 ounces Parmesan cheese, grated (about ½ cup)

1. Combine ice and water in a medium bowl.

2. Bring 8 cups of water to a boil in a stockpot over high. Add the collard greens to the boiling water, 2 cups at a time, and cook, 2 to 3 minutes. Transfer the collards to the ice bath using a slotted spoon. Let the collards stand in the ice bath until cold. Drain the collards, and squeeze out excess moisture. Set aside.

3. Heat the pecan oil in a medium sauté pan or skillet over medium-low. Add the pecans, and cook, stirring occasionally, until toasted, 3 to 4 minutes. Sprinkle with the salt and pepper, and remove from the heat.

4. Place the olive oil in a blender. With the blender running on low speed, add the anchovies and garlic; process until smooth. Add the collards, 1 cup at a time, and process until fully chopped, stopping to scrape down the sides of the blender after each addition.

5. Add the pecan mixture, any oil from the pan, and Parmesan to the blender; process just until incorporated. Serve immediately, or store in an airtight container in the refrigerator. Makes 2 cups

Young Collard Greens with Bacon, Calamari, Tomatoes, Olives, and Mint

Often when I'm doing cooking demos, I'm asked what I cook at home. Typically, my answer is anything that takes less than 20 minutes. All I need is some fresh vegetables, olive oil, and protein cooked in a cast-iron skillet with salt and pepper.

The reason I love this particular dish is because the collard greens and calamari force me to keep cooking to a minimum. With calamari, the rule is 30 seconds or 30 minutes; meaning if you sauté it, cook it for 30 seconds to keep it tender, otherwise braise it for 30 minutes to make it tender. Anything in between equals rubbery fail.

The same rule applies to the young collards. They just need to be sautéed for a few seconds or braised for a long period of time, like their more mature counterparts. So, if you think you've sautéed too long, just braise them in chicken stock until tender. Some of the greatest dishes I've ever made were born of mistakes.

Serves 1 as an entrée or 2 as an appetizer

4 bacon slices

4 cleaned squid tubes (about 4 ounces), rinsed

1 bunch young collard greens (½ pound)

1 tablespoon olive oil

1 tablespoon grapeseed oil

4 cherry tomatoes, halved

2 garlic cloves, very thinly sliced

2 tablespoons sherry vinegar

2 tablespoons apple cider

12 pitted mixed olives (about 2 ounces)

1 tablespoon lemon zest (from 1 lemon)

1 teaspoon kosher salt

½ teaspoon black pepper

¼ teaspoon red pepper flakes

1 mint sprig, leaves removed and chopped

8 frisée leaves

1 ounce Parmesan cheese, grated (about ⅔ cup)

1. Freeze the bacon and squid tubes for 30 minutes. Remove the bacon and the squid from the freezer. Cut the bacon slices in half lengthwise. Rotate the bacon 45°, and cut slices into ¼-inch pieces. Cut the squid tubes lengthwise into ¼-inch rings.

2. Fill a sink with cold water. Place a cutting board near the sink. Stack 4 collard green leaves on top of each other. Remove the collard green stems with a sharp knife, and cut the leaves in half lengthwise. If the leaves are longer than 6 inches, cut in half lengthwise again. Repeat the process with the remaining collard green leaves. Rinse the collard greens in cold water, and drain.

3. Heat the olive oil and grapeseed oil in a large sauté pan or skillet over medium. Add the bacon to the hot oil, and cook, stirring often with a spoon or spatula, until the bacon is crisp, about 7 minutes. Transfer the bacon with a slotted spoon to a plate lined with paper towels. Pour the drippings into a bowl, and reserve. Return the pan to heat.

4. Pat the squid dry with a paper towel. Add the squid to the pan, and cook, stirring constantly, for 3 minutes. Add the sliced collard green leaves to the pan, and stir to

combine. Stir in the cherry tomatoes and garlic. Stir in the vinegar and apple cider, and cook 2 minutes. Remove from the heat. Stir in the olives, lemon zest, salt, black pepper, red pepper flakes, and 1 tablespoon of the reserved bacon drippings.

5. Just before serving, stir in the chopped mint. Transfer the collard greens to a serving bowl, and garnish with the frisée. Sprinkle with Parmesan cheese.

To Drink: Sauvignon Blanc, sparkling wine, Champagne, Chardonnay, rosé, Gamay, Pinot Noir, amber beers, IPAs, or hard ciders

Serve with: Grilled seafood, grilled meats, potato, pasta, or cold egg dishes

COLLARDS

I often wonder why food gets categorized in such sweeping terms. Chinese Food is so broad a category it ignores regional uniqueness. Is the dish from Shanghai or was it born in Hong Kong? Where did the person who created it come from? What is their story?

When I was developing recipes for this book, like the Oysters Poached in Collard Green Pesto on Cheese Crisps with Caviar, I admit I got hung up on labels. I started by trying to create dishes that were stereotypically Southern or Soul in category but soon realized that approaching a dish based on preconceived notions limits creativity. So I chose to toss limitations aside.

Caviar came into the dish after exhausting the gamut of supposed-tos: Greens are "supposed to" have pork; greens are "supposed to" be cooked forever; greens are "supposed to" have potlikker. The reality is that the only thing greens are "supposed to" be is delicious.

Limit the labels. You'll liberate yourself in the kitchen, grow as a cook, and your taste buds will have better dining experiences.

Ginger and Collard Green Fried Rice

Soy sauce has become a universal ingredient that provides exceptional flavor to dishes. As with most any ingredient, there are inexpensive substitutions for the real deal. Authentic soy sauce is fermented and aged over time, and there is no substitute for time. The time required for premium soy sauce to brew and age is essential to its quality. It makes all the difference in this classic fried rice with a soulful infusion of collard greens.

Serves 2

1 bunch young collard greens (½ pound)

2 tablespoons vegetable oil

1 duck egg or extra-large chicken egg

1 teaspoon kosher salt

½ teaspoon freshly ground black pepper

1 shallot, thinly sliced

2 garlic cloves, smashed and very thinly sliced

1 (1-inch) piece fresh ginger, peeled and grated (about 2 teaspoons)

3 tablespoons rice wine vinegar

2 tablespoons reduced-sodium soy sauce

1 tablespoon mirin

2 cups cooked white rice

1 teaspoon sesame oil

4 scallions, thinly sliced

1 jalapeño chile, very thinly sliced

1 teaspoon sesame seeds

1 lime, cut into 8 wedges

Red pepper flakes (optional)

1. Fill a sink with cold water. Place a cutting board nearby. Stack 4 collard green leaves on top of each other. Remove the stems with a sharp knife, and trim 2 inches from the bottoms of each stem. Cut the stems into ⅛-inch pieces. Cut the leaves into 2-inch squares. Repeat with remaining leaves. Rinse the leaves and stems in cold water. Drain.

2. Heat 1 tablespoon of the vegetable oil in a medium sauté pan or skillet over medium. Break the egg into the pan, and cook 4 minutes, gently shaking the pan occasionally to ensure the egg does not stick. Sprinkle with the salt and pepper. Turn the egg, and cook 2 more minutes. Transfer to a plate, and keep warm.

3. Heat the remaining 1 tablespoon vegetable oil in the sauté pan over medium. Add the shallot, garlic, and ginger. Cook, stirring occasionally, until shallot is translucent. Add the collard leaves and stems to the pan; cook, stirring constantly, 1 minute. Stir in the vinegar. Stir in the soy sauce and mirin. Stir in the rice, and cover. Simmer until the rice is heated through, about 2 minutes. Uncover and drizzle with sesame oil. Remove from heat, and let stand 2 minutes.

4. Transfer the fried rice to a serving bowl. Cut the fried egg into ⅛-inch-thick strips. Top the rice evenly with the egg strips. Garnish with the scallions, jalapeño slices, sesame seeds, lime wedges, and red pepper flakes, if desired.

To Drink: Sauvignon Blanc, sparkling wine, Champagne, Chardonnay, rosé, Gamay, Pinot Noir, amber beers, IPAs, or hard ciders

Serve with: Grilled seafood, grilled meats, poultry; spicy or citrus dishes

Collard Waffles with Brined Trout and Maple Hot Sauce

Brining fish is not a new technique…just an underutilized one. Most recipes call for curing the fish to reduce moisture content. Brining not only raises the moisture content but provides flavor in a less time-consuming manner. While both techniques are great, I think brining is the way to go for this recipe.

In this recipe the collard greens factor in in a surprising way. The cooked collard greens get finely chopped and folded into the waffle batter for a savory surprise.

Serves 4

TROUT:
4 cups (32 ounces) cold water
2 tablespoons light brown sugar
2 tablespoons smoked salt
2 tablespoons soy sauce
1 lemon
16 ounces skin-on sea trout fillets
½ cup (about 2 ⅛ ounces) all-purpose flour
½ teaspoon kosher salt

¼ teaspoon freshly ground black pepper
2 tablespoons olive oil

ADDITIONAL INGREDIENTS:
½ cup (4 ounces) pure maple syrup
2 tablespoons hot sauce
Collard Waffles (page 44)
½ cup packed micro greens

1. Prepare the Trout: Combine 4 cups cold water, brown sugar, smoked salt, and soy sauce in a 2-quart saucepan. Cut the lemon in half, squeeze the juice, and stir into the mixture. Add the lemon halves. Bring the mixture to a simmer over medium, and simmer until the salt and sugar are completely dissolved. Remove from the heat, and let stand 30 minutes. Add the trout fillets, and let stand in the brine 45 minutes at room temperature or 4 hours in the refrigerator.

2. Remove the fish from the brine; discard brine. Pat fillets dry with paper towels. Stir together the flour, kosher salt, and pepper in a medium bowl. Dredge fish in the flour mixture, shaking off any excess flour.

3. Heat the oil in a 10- to 12-inch nonstick skillet over medium-high. Add the fish fillets, skin side down, and cook until the skin is crispy, 3 to 4 minutes. Turn the fish, and cook until the fish is flaky, 2 to 3 minutes. Drain the fish on a plate lined with paper towels.

4. Stir together the maple syrup and hot sauce in a small bowl. Divide the waffles evenly among 4 plates. Top evenly with trout, and drizzle each with 2 tablespoons of the maple syrup mixture. Sprinkle with micro greens, and serve immediately.

To Drink: Sauvignon Blanc, sparkling wine, Champagne, Chardonnay, rosé, Vouvray, Pinot Noir, Banyuls, sherry, amber beers, IPAs, or hard ciders
Serve with: Grilled seafood or meats, poultry, or spicy dishes

collard waffles

2 ounces (¼ cup) unsalted butter, at room
  temperature
1 ½ cups (12 ounces) whole buttermilk
½ cup collard green potlikker
2 large eggs
1 cup (about 4 ¼ ounces) all-purpose flour
1 cup (about 4 ¼ ounces) stone-ground
  yellow cornmeal

2 teaspoons baking powder
½ teaspoon baking soda
¼ teaspoon kosher salt
¼ teaspoon freshly ground black pepper
½ cup cooked collard greens, cut into
  ¼-inch pieces

1. Microwave the butter in a small microwave-safe bowl on HIGH until melted, about
30 seconds. Stir together the buttermilk, potlikker, melted butter, and eggs in a
medium bowl. Whisk together the flour, cornmeal, baking powder, baking soda, kosher
salt, and pepper in a separate bowl. Add the buttermilk mixture to the flour mixture,
and stir until well incorporated and no lumps remain. Fold in the collard greens.

2. Lightly coat a preheated waffle iron with cooking spray. Pour ½ cup batter into hot
waffle iron. Cook according to a standard waffle maker's manufacturer's instructions
until waffles are cooked through. (Don't let the collards burn.) Makes about 8 (7-inch)
round waffles

Note: It may seem strange to require butter to be at room temperature before melting it, but
it's an important step. Cold butter melts differently—some of the butter may start to brown
before the rest of it is completely melted—and that browning can impact the flavor of the
final dish. Bringing the butter to room temperature before you melt it helps it melt consistently.

ONIONS

Members of the allium family, onions grow pretty much everywhere around the globe with perhaps a few exceptions. The pungent flavor we associate with them comes from the sulfate content of the soil. The more sulfur, the stronger the bulb's characteristic oniony-ness. Cooking mellows the bite with savory-sweet, almost meaty, results. Onions are a backbone of Soul cuisine. They are both cheap, readily available building blocks for cooks forced to make do with meager rations, and a tool for developing rich, complex flavors. I love how onions hold up in low-and-slow simmered dishes but I also use them in raw form to add a dose of crisp heat. In most of my recipes, white and yellow onions are interchangeable. Red onions are not a suitable substitute, so use them only if called for in an ingredient list. Shallots are an extremely versatile exception to that rule. Not to be left out, leeks, ramps, and spring onions infuse dishes with their distinctive, aromatic essences, only with much less of a bite.

Onion Broth with Onion Dumplings and Braised Chicken Wings

I prefer sweet yellow onions in the summertime and white onions in the fall and winter. Cool-season yellow onions tend to be watery and have a souring effect in the dish. Look for yellow onions with longer root stems for best flavor.

Serves 4

¾ cup finely crushed saltine crackers (about 12 crackers)

3 large eggs, lightly beaten

1 cup thinly sliced scallions, plus more for garnish

⅛ teaspoon cayenne pepper

⅛ teaspoon ground nutmeg

¼ cup melted duck fat

5 ½ teaspoons kosher salt

6 cups plus 3 tablespoons chicken stock

2 tablespoons blended olive oil

24 chicken wings and drumettes

1 teaspoon coarsely ground black pepper

4 yellow onions (about 8 ounces), julienned

2 bay leaves

1 thyme sprig

2 tablespoons dry white wine

2 tablespoons apple cider vinegar

2 tablespoons (1 ounce) rye whiskey

1. Combine the saltines, next 5 ingredients, 1 teaspoon of the salt, and 3 tablespoons of the stock in a medium bowl. Cover and refrigerate for 1 hour.

2. Heat the oil in a Dutch oven over medium. Season the wings with 3 teaspoons of the salt and the black pepper. Brown the chicken on all sides, in batches, about 3 minutes per batch. Drain on paper towels. (Chicken will not be fully cooked.)

3. Add the onions and remaining 1 ½ teaspoons salt to the Dutch oven, and cook, stirring often, until caramelized, about 10 minutes. Add the bay leaves, thyme, white wine, vinegar, and rye whiskey; cook for 4 minutes. Return the wings to the Dutch oven, and cook 2 more minutes. Add the remaining 6 cups chicken stock to the Dutch oven, cover, reduce heat to low, and cook 20 minutes or until the wings are fork-tender and cooked through. Remove from the Dutch oven, reserving the stock in the Dutch oven.

4. Spoon the saltine mixture into the hot broth by tablespoonfuls. (Do not overcrowd.) Cover and cook until firm, about 15 minutes.

5. Return the chicken wings to the Dutch oven, and let stand for 10 minutes before serving. Sprinkle each serving with additional scallions.

Note: This recipe calls for large wings. If using small wings, reduce the cooking time.

To Drink: White Burgundy, Chardonnay, Gewürztraminer, Pinot Noir, dry Riesling, light beers, hard ciders, IPAs

Serve with: Green or raw tomato salads, rice dishes, or potatoes

Sausage-Stuffed Onions

Perhaps one of the best-kept chef secrets for striking presentations is to use ingredients in their most natural form. The shape of an onion makes it an ideal vessel for stuffing. Best of all, it gives people the impression you spent painstaking hours in the kitchen preparing the meal when in fact it was quite simple.

Serves 6

2 tablespoons blended olive oil

6 large yellow onions, cut in half crosswise

½ pound hot Italian sausage, casings removed

1 Korean sweet potato or small sweet potato (about 8 ounces), peeled and diced

1 celery stalk, finely chopped

1 shallot, finely chopped

1 cup uncooked wild rice, cooked according to package directions

½ cup panko (Japanese-style breadcrumbs)

¼ cup chopped pecans

¼ cup golden raisins

2 tablespoons sherry vinegar

½ teaspoon kosher salt

¼ teaspoon black pepper

1. Preheat the oven to 400°F. Heat the oil in a skillet over medium.

2. Place the onion halves, cut sides down, in the skillet and cook, in batches, until caramelized, about 5 minutes. Remove from the heat, and transfer the onions, cut sides down, to a baking sheet. Bake in the preheated oven until just slightly tender, 10 to 15 minutes. Let cool, about 20 minutes.

3. Scoop out 2 to 3 inches in the center of each onion with a spoon. Dice the scooped-out onion (about 1 ½ cups), and set aside.

4. Return the skillet to medium. Cook the sausage, stirring constantly, until browned and crumbly (some pink will remain), about 5 minutes. Stir in the reserved diced onions, sweet potato, celery, and shallot. Cover, reduce the heat to medium-low, and cook until the sausage is browned and the potatoes are tender, about 20 minutes.

5. Remove from the heat, and stir in the wild rice, panko, pecans, raisins, sherry vinegar, salt, and pepper; let stand for 10 minutes.

6. Spoon the sausage stuffing into the onion centers, about ¾ cup per onion half. Bake in the preheated oven on the bottom rack until the onions are tender, 10 to 12 minutes. Remove from oven, and let stand for 5 minutes before serving.

Note: Many different types of sausage can be used. For best results, be sure the fat to meat content of the sausage is equal.

To Drink: White Burgundy, Chardonnay, Pinot Noir, red blends, vintage Zinfandel, amber beers, hard ciders, IPAs

Serve with: Grilled buttered bread, mixed greens salads, compotes and jams, grilled steaks or pork chops

Fermented Ramps
(page 54)

Fried Chicken Gizzards
with Honey Mustard
(page 54)

Fried Chicken Gizzards with Honey Mustard and Fermented Ramps

Don't dismiss these tasty morsels of crispy goodness. Gizzards have the flavor of chicken thighs with the mineral qualities of liver. After braising, serve them over rice with the pan jus.

Ramps are one of the most sought-after types of spring onions and appear fleetingly during spring. They have a distinctively sweet yet pungent flavor well suited to many different cuisines. Don't be afraid to purchase ramps still covered in soil. The soil protects the leaves from bruising prior to washing and cooking.

Serves 4 as an appetizer

1 pound chicken gizzards, trimmed of all silver skin and gristle

2 cups (16 ounces) whole buttermilk

½ cup (about 2 ⅛ ounces) all-purpose flour

2 tablespoons cornstarch

1 ½ teaspoons kosher salt

1 teaspoon coarsely ground black pepper

1 teaspoon ground coffee

½ teaspoon granulated garlic

½ teaspoon granulated onion

½ teaspoon celery salt

½ teaspoon ground ginger

¼ teaspoon cayenne pepper

3 cups blended olive oil

Honey Mustard (recipe follows)

Fermented Ramps (recipe follows)

1. Combine the gizzards and buttermilk in a medium bowl. Let stand 30 minutes.

2. Combine the flour, cornstarch, salt, black pepper, ground coffee, granulated garlic, granulated onion, celery salt, ginger, and cayenne pepper in a shallow dish.

3. Heat the oil to 325°F in a deep skillet over medium-high.

4. Dredge the chicken gizzards in the seasoned flour, turning to coat completely. Shake off any excess flour. Discard the buttermilk.

5. Fry the gizzards, in batches, until crispy and cooked through, about 10 minutes.

6. Drain on paper towels. Serve the chicken gizzards with the Honey Mustard and Fermented Ramps.

To Drink: Grenache, Pinot Noir, rosé, sparkling rosé, IPAs, amber beers, dark beers, or hard ciders

Serve with: Rice, onion, or root vegetable dishes; green salads; fruit salads

honey mustard

1 cup sour cream

¼ cup Dijon mustard

¼ cup honey

Combine all ingredients in a medium bowl. Makes about 1½ cups

fermented ramps (ramp kimchi)

½ cup (4 ounces) rice wine vinegar

½ cup Asian chili garlic sauce

¼ cup granulated sugar

2 tablespoons reduced-sodium soy sauce

1¼ teaspoons kosher salt

40 ramps (about 1½ pounds), cut into 1-inch pieces

1. Stir together the vinegar, chili garlic sauce, sugar, soy sauce, and salt in a large bowl. Let stand for 10 minutes.

2. Add the ramps to the mixture, and toss to coat. Massage the mixture until the ramps become juicy.

3. Pack the ramps in a sterilized 1-quart glass jar, and press down until the liquid covers the ramps. Cover with cheesecloth, and secure with a rubber band. Let stand at room temperature for 3 to 5 days, stirring every 12 hours to ensure the ramps are covered with liquid. Makes 1 quart

Hot and Spicy
Zucchini Slaw
(recipe opposite)

Smoked Oysters
on Deviled Egg
Toast (recipe
opposite)

Caramelized
Onion Tart
(recipe opposite)

Caramelized Onion Tart, Hot and Spicy Zucchini Slaw, and Smoked Oysters on Deviled Egg Toast

Caramelizing onions requires patience. Start them on medium heat and then reduce the heat to low to let the natural sugars concentrate and moisture evaporate. This is key for even cooking. Rush the process and you'll have pan-fried onions instead.

When it comes to slaw, crunchy cabbage comes to mind, but often a softer vegetable is better suited to a dish. Zucchini is a perfect example.

Serves 12

CRUST:

3 ounces (6 tablespoons) unsalted butter

2 tablespoons water

1 ½ tablespoons sorghum syrup

1 tablespoon blended olive oil

½ teaspoon kosher salt

1 ¼ cups (about 5 ⅜ ounces) all-purpose flour, plus more for dusting

½ cup (about 2 ounces) whole-wheat flour

FILLING:

4 teaspoons blended olive oil

4 bacon slices

3 medium-size yellow onions, thinly sliced (about 5 cups)

4 garlic cloves, thinly sliced

½ cup (4 ounces) sherry

2 tablespoons sherry vinegar

2 teaspoons kosher salt

1 teaspoon coarsely ground black pepper

1 thyme sprig

4 ounces Gruyère cheese, shredded (about 1 cup)

Hot and Spicy Zucchini Slaw (page 58)

Smoked Oysters on Toast (page 142)

Deviled Egg Spread (page 143)

1. Prepare the Crust: Preheat the oven to 375°F. Heat a saucepan over medium. Add the first 4 ingredients and whisk until the butter melts. Remove from the heat. Stir in the salt. Add both flours; stir until combined. Let the dough stand for 5 minutes.

2. Turn out the dough onto a well-floured surface, and roll to a ⅛-inch thickness. Fit the dough into a 9-inch pie pan, allowing the dough to overlap the sides. Trim the sides of the dough to within ¼ inch of the sides. Line the crust with parchment paper, and fill with pie weights or dried beans.

3. Bake in preheated oven until lightly browned and set, about 10 minutes. Remove the pan from the oven, and remove the pie weights. Set crust aside.

4. Prepare the Filling: Heat 2 teaspoons of the oil in a sauté pan or deep skillet over medium. Add the bacon, and cook until crisp. Remove the bacon from the pan with a slotted spoon, reserving the drippings in the pan.

5. Add the remaining 2 teaspoons oil to the pan. Add the onions and cook over medium, stirring often, until the onions reduce in volume by half, about 10 minutes.

6. Add the garlic, and cook, stirring often, 2 minutes. Add the sherry, vinegar, salt,

continued

pepper, and thyme. Cook until the liquid is reduced to almost a syrup-like consistency, about 10 minutes. Remove from the heat, and let stand for 10 minutes.

7. Remove and discard the thyme sprig. Fold in half of the cheese. Chop the bacon, and fold into the onion mixture. Spoon the mixture into the crust.

8. Top the tart with the remaining cheese, and bake in the preheated oven until the cheese begins to form a crust (like baked macaroni and cheese), about 10 minutes. Remove the tart from the oven; Let stand 15 minutes before cutting into wedges.

9. Serve with Hot and Spicy Zucchini Slaw, Smoked Oysters, and Deviled Egg Toast.

hot and spicy zucchini slaw

2 large zucchini (about 10 ounces each)

2 tablespoons aged red wine vinegar

1 tablespoon sambal oelek

1 ½ teaspoons kosher salt

1 teaspoon granulated sugar

1 teaspoon blended olive oil

1. Cut each zucchini lengthwise into 4 slices. Remove and discard the seeds, and cut into ⅛-inch matchstick slices.

2. Combine the zucchini, vinegar, sambal oelek, salt, sugar, and olive oil in a medium bowl. Serves 8

⤙ YOUTHFUL ⤚

This hodgepodge of dishes is the sort of meal I would expect on my birthday or for big holiday celebrations when all our Chicago neighbors would come to the party with a covered dish of their own making. There was always something sweet, something piping hot, something chilled, and plenty of spice and unique flavors. At a glance, the dishes rarely seemed to go together. Once you tasted everything, you realized that there is often perfection in potluck and there is always something delicious for everyone.

Fried Chicken Gizzards with Honey
Mustard and Fermented Ramps (page 54)

Ginger and Collard Green Fried Rice
(page 40)

Hot and Spicy Zucchini Slaw
(page 58)

Blueberry Fried Pies with Meyer Lemon Glaze
(page 89)

ON THE RADIO

"I Can't Help It" — *Michael Jackson*
A Love Supreme album —*John Coltrane*
"Fresh" — *Kool & The Gang*
"Look Closer (Can't You See the Signs?)" — *Saun & Starr*

Fried Chicken
Gizzards with
Honey Mustard
(page 54)

Blueberry Fried Pies
with Meyer Lemon
Glaze (page 89)

Hot and Spicy
Zucchini Slaw
(page 58)

Ginger and Collard
Green Fried Rice
(page 40)

The onion-averse are afraid of two things: the pungency that sticks with you an entire day, or the surprising heat of raw ones. Once you familiarize yourself with the nuances of the wide variety of onions, you realize that their unique flavors and textures tell you how to use them. Mild green onions and wild ramps are tender shoots that turn brown and lose flavor when overcooked. Cut into a heavy white onion, and its firm texture and eye-watering aroma let you know it can stand up to longer cooking, like braising or roasting. Sweet yellow onions are truly versatile. Simmered a long time in the lightest of broths, a Vidalia or Maui sings with sweetness yet expresses the distinctive oniony-ness you want in a dish. Shallots hum a similar tune, while bulb onions and leeks offer options: Preserve the tops to use as an accent in different dishes and use the white parts in a long-simmered braise or stew.

"Once you familiarize yourself with the nuances of the wide variety of onions, you realize that their unique flavors and textures tell you how to use them."

Liver and Spring Onions with Crispy Shallots and Potato Puree

When you buy livers, they usually come frozen. Rarely do you find fresh ones. I prefer them frozen. Freezing and thawing leaches impurities for cleaner flavor. The mild potato puree works as a delicious textural counterpoint to the onions and a creamy vehicle for enjoyment of the complex pan jus.

Serves 4

1 cup (8 ounces) whole buttermilk

2 (8-ounce) calf's livers (about ¾-inch thick)

1 ½ cups plus 2 tablespoons blended olive oil

4 spring onion bulbs (about 5 ounces)

3 ½ teaspoons kosher salt

1 teaspoon freshly ground black pepper

½ cup (4 ounces) chicken stock

2 tablespoons dry white wine

1 thyme sprig

2 cups (about 8 ½ ounces) all-purpose flour

½ tablespoon granulated onion

½ tablespoon granulated garlic

½ teaspoon curry powder

½ teaspoon ground coffee

⅛ teaspoon cayenne pepper

Potato Puree (page 68)

Crispy Shallots (page 68)

1. Combine the calf's livers and buttermilk in a bowl and let stand at least 30 minutes.

2. Heat 2 tablespoons of the oil in a large sauté pan or skillet over medium-high.

3. Season the spring onion bulbs with ½ teaspoon each of the salt and black pepper. Place the bulbs, cut sides down, in the pan. Sear until golden brown, about 2 minutes. Turn the onions over, and continue to cook until browned, about 2 minutes.

4. Add the chicken stock, white wine, and thyme to the pan. Cover, reduce heat to medium-low, and simmer until the spring onions are just tender, 6 to 8 minutes.

5. Meanwhile, combine the flour, granulated onion and garlic, curry powder, ground coffee, cayenne, and remaining salt and black pepper in a shallow dish.

6. Heat the remaining 1 ½ cups oil in a sauté pan or skillet over medium-high.

7. Remove the livers from the buttermilk. Dredge in the seasoned flour. Shake off excess and fry until crispy and browned, 2 to 3 minutes on each side. (Do not overcook.)

8. Serve the liver with the spring onions, Potato Puree, and Crispy Shallots.

To Drink: White Burgundy, Champagne, vintage Champagne, Chardonnay, Gewürztraminer, Pinot Grigio, dry Riesling, sparkling rosé, light beers, hard ciders, IPAs

Serve with: Mixed green salads

potato puree

8 cups (64 ounces) water
2 bay leaves
1 thyme sprig
2 garlic cloves
1 tablespoon plus 2 teaspoons kosher salt
6 medium Yukon Gold potatoes, unpeeled
  (about 3 ¾ pounds)

8 ounces (1 cup) high-quality unsalted butter,
  cubed and softened
1 cup (8 ounces) heavy cream
¾ teaspoon ground white pepper

1. Bring 8 cups water, bay leaves, thyme, garlic, and 1 tablespoon of salt to a boil in a stockpot over high heat.

2. Add the potatoes, making sure they are covered with water. Cover and cook until the potatoes are tender but not mushy, 20 to 25 minutes.

3. Remove the potatoes from the water, and reserve the liquid. Process the potatoes with a food mill into a medium bowl until smooth.

4. Stir in the butter, cream, pepper, ¼ cup of the cooking liquid, and the remaining 2 teaspoons salt into the potatoes. Stir in additional cooking liquid, 1 tablespoon at a time to reach desired consistency. Cover and keep warm until ready to serve. Makes about 7 ½ cups

Note: The potato puree can be garnished with shaved truffles or roasted garlic puree.

crispy shallots

I use these crunchy, flavorful morsels as a garnish on my Baked Quail Eggs in Green Pea Soup with Ham Hocks, Crispy Shallots, and Parmesan (page 311), but they are also delicious on top of mashed potatoes, green salads, or in a burger.

2 large shallots, thinly sliced into rings
⅓ cup whole buttermilk
1 cup (about 4 ¼ ounces) all-purpose flour
½ tablespoon kosher salt
¾ teaspoon granulated onion
¾ teaspoon granulated garlic

¾ teaspoon coarsely ground black pepper
¼ teaspoon curry powder
¼ teaspoon ground coffee
⅛ teaspoon cayenne pepper
1 ½ cups blended olive oil

1. Combine the shallots and buttermilk in a small bowl and let stand 30 minutes.

2. Stir together the flour, salt, granulated onion, granulated garlic, black pepper, curry powder, coffee, and cayenne pepper in a small bowl.

3. Heat the oil in a large, heavy-bottomed sauté pan or skillet over medium-high.

4. Drain the shallots, and toss in the flour mixture to coat, shaking off any excess.

5. Fry the shallot rings in the hot oil until crispy, 2 to 3 minutes. Transfer the fried shallots to a paper towel-lined plate to drain. Makes about 1 ½ cups

Short Ribs with Ramps
Sautéed in Beef Drippings
(page 72)

Green Pea Salad
(page 73)

Short Ribs with Ramps Sautéed in Beef Drippings

Salt is a flavor enhancer that can destroy an onion's texture. Using the pan drippings as the seasoning brings out the delicious goodness of the onion in a way that complements the meat.

Green peas are often shunned as frostbitten things from the freezer. While I am partial to fresh peas in peak season, when unavailable, quality frozen peas are fine.

Serves 4

1 bunch radishes with green tops (about 6 ounces)

1 orange, zest removed, cut into 8 wedges

1 cup reduced-sodium soy sauce

½ cup apple cider vinegar

3 tablespoons sorghum syrup

1 (1 ½-inch) piece fresh ginger, peeled and coarsely chopped

2 garlic cloves, thinly sliced

1 teaspoon black peppercorns

2 pounds Korean-cut (flanken cut) beef short ribs

2 tablespoons blended olive oil

1 teaspoon coarsely ground black pepper

½ pound ramps or scallions

½ teaspoon smoked salt

1. Rinse the radishes and tops with cold water. Remove the green tops and chop. Reserve the radishes for the Green Pea Salad (recipe follows).

2. Combine the chopped green tops and the orange pieces in a medium bowl. Add the soy sauce, cider vinegar, sorghum, ginger, garlic, and peppercorns to the bowl, and stir to combine. Add the short ribs to the marinade, and refrigerate for 4 hours.

3. Preheat the broiler with 1 oven rack 5 ½ inches from the heat and 1 oven rack 3 inches from the heat. Line a rimmed baking sheet with heavy-duty aluminum foil. Place the baking sheet on the lower oven rack for 2 minutes. Remove from the oven, and carefully add the oil, tilting the pan to spread evenly.

4. Remove the short ribs from the marinade, reserving the marinade. Arrange in 1 layer on the hot baking sheet; sprinkle with the ground black pepper.

5. Broil the ribs on the lower rack for 6 minutes. Remove from the oven, and turn over.

6. Remove the ginger and radish tops from the marinade using a slotted spoon. Place them on top of the ribs. Broil the ribs on the top rack until very lightly charred, 2 to 4 minutes. Remove from the oven and transfer ribs and toppings to a serving dish.

7. Arrange the ramps in the beef drippings on the pan, and sprinkle with the smoked salt. Broil the ramps on the top rack until they start to blister, about 4 minutes. Remove the pan from the oven, and place the ramps on top of the short ribs. Spoon any remaining drippings over the short ribs, and serve hot.

To Drink: Cabernet Sauvignon, Pinot Noir, red blends, Southern French reds, vintage Zinfandel, amber beers, dark beers, hard ciders, IPAs

Serve with: Green salads, rice or peanut dishes

green pea salad

8 cups (64 ounces) water

2 tablespoons kosher salt

½ pound fresh green peas (about 1 ½ cups)

4 ¼ teaspoons red pepper flakes

¼ cup raw or roasted unsalted peanuts

2 tablespoons sour cream

1 tablespoon bacon drippings or short rib drippings

1 teaspoon apple cider vinegar

½ teaspoon coarse-grain mustard

½ teaspoon smoked salt

¾ cup diced radishes (about 3 ounces)

1 tablespoon torn mint leaves

4 ounces pea tendrils (about 5 cups)

1 tablespoon olive oil

½ teaspoon lemon zest (from 1 lemon)

½ teaspoon orange zest (from 1 orange)

1. Fill a large bowl with ice and water. Bring 8 cups water to a boil in a saucepan over high. Add the salt, and continue to boil for 2 minutes.

2. Add the peas to the boiling water, and cook until tender, about 2 minutes. Transfer the peas from the boiling water to the ice water with a fine wire-mesh strainer. Let stand for 5 minutes to stop the cooking process. Reserve the cooking water in the pan.

3. Add the red pepper flakes and peanuts to the water in the pan. Cook over medium-low until peanuts are tender, about 5 minutes. Drain the peanuts on paper towels and let cool.

4. Combine the sour cream, bacon or short rib drippings, vinegar, mustard, and smoked salt in a small bowl.

5. Transfer the peas from the ice bath to a large bowl; stir in the diced radishes and peanuts.

6. Add the sour cream mixture, and stir to coat the peas. Sprinkle with the mint.

7. Place the pea tendrils in a bowl, and drizzle with the olive oil. Add the zests, and gently toss to coat. Top the pea and sour cream salad with the pea tendrils, and serve. Serves 4

Note: Thawed frozen peas can be used in place of fresh. The dish can be served with soy sauce on the side.

BERRIES

Berry varieties abound during Southern summers. Dewberries, blackberries, strawberries, scuppernongs, and muscadines are foraged favorites during the fleeting seasons in which they make an appearance. Eaten off the vine they provide energy and nutrition. Cooked and preserved they sustain during lean times. Mashed and fermented with sugar, berries become wine. Ranging in flavor from the mouth-puckering tart to eye-opening sweet, berries are a Soul food staple—beyond the expected cobblers and pies. When I cook meats, I often incorporate berries to accentuate the rich, umami flavors of the protein while tempering any strong gamey notes. In desserts, I think berries shine just as they come, but their sweetness is always complemented by a spoonful or two of fresh or whipped cream. Cooked, berries become something nuanced and entirely different. Because they are terrific for digestion, berries are an ideal ending to any meal.

Strawberries with Champagne Aspic, Whipped Cream, and Honey

My grandma went from using a little whisk to make whipped cream, to Cool Whip in its plastic tub, Reddi-wip for whiskey coffee, and back to whipping cream by hand for freshly baked cakes that her sister would bring. Powdered milk was used to satisfy hungry mouths, the whipped mixture producing silver dollar-sized bubbles we called "money" as we stood in line to get a spoonful. Food can be—and should be—fun to eat.

There is a substantial difference between wild strawberries and cultivated strawberries. Wild ones tend to be smaller and more delicate. Conventional strawberries are firm and take longer to ripen. It's best not to wash them until just before using, since moisture breaks down the fruit quickly.

Serves 8

1 tablespoon raw sugar

½ teaspoon lemon zest (from ½ lemon)

3 black peppercorns

2 fresh basil leaves

1 ¼ cups (10 ounces) Champagne or sparkling white wine

1 tablespoon unflavored gelatin

1 cup (8 ounces) heavy cream

½ teaspoon bourbon vanilla paste

32 ripe strawberries (about 1 ½ pints), hulled and sliced

¼ cup honey

Basil flowers or mint sprigs (optional)

1. Bring the sugar, lemon zest, peppercorns, basil leaves, and ¾ cup of the Champagne to a simmer over medium heat.

2. Meanwhile, pour the remaining ½ cup Champagne into a medium bowl, and sprinkle with the gelatin. Let stand 10 minutes.

3. Pour the hot Champagne mixture through a fine wire-mesh strainer into the gelatin mixture, and whisk until the gelatin dissolves. Discard the solids in the strainer. Cover and let stand 20 minutes. Transfer the mixture into an 8-inch square baking dish. Cover and refrigerate until set, at least 1 hour.

4. Place the heavy cream and vanilla paste into a chilled metal bowl, and beat with an electric mixer fitted with whisk attachment on high speed until soft peaks form, about 2 minutes.

5. Remove the aspic from the refrigerator, and cut into ¼-inch cubes.

6. Divide the strawberries evenly among 8 bowls, and top with 1 tablespoon aspic and 2 tablespoons whipped cream. Drizzle each serving with 1 ½ teaspoons honey. Garnish with basil flowers or mint sprigs, if desired.

To Drink: Champagne and Champagne cocktails; white Burgundy; Pilsners; IPAs
Serve with: Green salads; soft or hard cheeses; smoked turkey or chicken; quick breads; whipped cream

Pickled Strawberry Salad with Champagne Vinaigrette, Black Pepper Créme Fraîche, and Smoked Pecans

The beauty of Soul food is that it is enriched through celebration and the gathering together of people. Though the host typically provides most of the food, guests bring dishes that are either a personal favorite to eat or showcase their own skill in the kitchen. This salad is one of my favorites to share. The ingredients may sound familiar, but the green strawberries are a bit of a surprise. Champagne-spiked vinaigrette adds a dose of party to the mix.

Serves 4

1 cup (8 ounces) heavy cream

2 tablespoons (1 ounce) whole buttermilk

1 teaspoon coarsely ground black pepper

Pinch of gray sea salt

2 cups Pickle Brine (page 354)

16 unripe strawberries

Champagne Vinaigrette (page 80)

¼ cup créme fraîche

2 teaspoons cracked black pepper

Smoked Pecans (page 80)

¼ cup packed micro greens

1. Combine the cream, buttermilk, pepper, and sea salt in a glass jar.

2. Cover the jar with cheesecloth, and secure with rubber bands. Let stand at room temperature until thickened, 12 to 16 hours. Refrigerate until ready to use.

3. Bring the Pickle Brine to a simmer in a saucepan over medium. Add the strawberries, and remove from the heat. Cover and let stand for 15 minutes.

4. Transfer the pickled strawberries and Pickle Brine to a jar or dish, making sure the strawberries are completely covered with liquid. Refrigerate until chilled completely, about 30 minutes.

5. To serve, slice the strawberries, and place 4 sliced strawberries onto each of 4 plates. Drizzle 1 tablespoon Champagne Vinaigrette over each serving. Stir together the créme fraîche and cracked black pepper. Top each serving with 1 tablespoon black pepper crème fraîche, 2 tablespoons chopped Smoked Pecans, and micro greens.

Note: Conventional strawberries may be used for this recipe. Be sure they are fully ripe before serving.

To Drink: Blanc de blancs Champagne, Moscato, dry prosecco, rosé, sparkling rosé, white Zinfandel, amber beers, light beers, IPAs

Serve with: Green salads, light poultry dishes, cakes, pies, peppered bacon, candied dishes

champagne vinaigrette

¼ shallot, minced (about 1 tablespoon)

1 tablespoon Champagne vinegar

2 teaspoons Dijon mustard

½ teaspoon honey

1 splash Champagne or sparkling white wine

¼ teaspoon kosher salt

3 tablespoons blended olive oil

Combine the shallot, vinegar, Dijon, honey, and Champagne in a small bowl. Whisk in the salt and blended olive oil. Makes ¼ cup

smoked pecans

1 tablespoon blended olive oil

½ cup pecan halves

1 ounce (2 tablespoons) unsalted butter

1 tablespoon raw sugar

1 teaspoon smoked salt

Pinch of red pepper flakes

Pinch of coarsely ground black pepper

1 thyme sprig

1. Heat the blended oil and pecans in a skillet over medium-low. Cook the pecans, stirring occasionally, until toasted, 10 to 15 minutes. Stir in the butter, sugar, smoked salt, red pepper flakes, black pepper, and thyme. Increase heat to medium-high, and cook until the butter is browned, stirring constantly.

2. Remove skillet from heat. Cover and let stand for 5 minutes. Spread the pecan mixture in an even layer on paper towels.

3. Let stand for 30 minutes. Remove and discard thyme sprig. Coarsely chop the pecans if using them in a salad. Makes ½ cup

Strawberry-
Rum Coolers
(page 84).

Turkey Wings Glazed with
Strawberry BBQ Sauce
(page 85)

Strawberry-Rum Coolers

The joyful laughter that comes from sitting around the BBQ pit, under the sun, wiping your brow, sipping a refreshing drink is all about the love of food, family and friends, and reverence for the cook. It's hard not to be dutiful to the person cooking for you, "Is there anything you need?" When I'm the one wearing the cook's hat, I want something cold, boozy, and delicious. And delicious is what this drink is. It's the kind of drink that upon first sip seems to stop the sun's rays in their tracks and makes the breeze feel somehow cooler. That's called refreshment.

Serves 8

Strawberry-Rum Cooler Base (recipe follows)	Orange bitters
	Crushed ice
1 cup (8 ounces) white rum	2 cups (16 ounces) ginger beer
1 cup (8 ounces) dark rum	1 orange, cut into 8 wedges

For each cooler, combine ¼ cup Strawberry-Rum Cooler Base, 2 tablespoons (1 ounce) white rum, 2 tablespoons (1 ounce) dark rum, and 6 dashes of bitters in a mixing glass, and top with ice. Stir mixture until ice dilutes the liquid into a smooth puree. Pour over crushed ice, and top with ¼ cup ginger beer. Garnish with an orange wedge.

Serve with: This is a seasonal beverage and can be served with any seasonal item spring and summer.

strawberry-rum cooler base

2 ½ cups very ripe strawberries, hulled and sliced	2 tablespoons fresh lime juice (from 1 lime)
	2 tablespoons agave syrup
1 cup (8 ounces) water	¼ teaspoon ground ginger

1. Bring the strawberries, 1 cup water, lime juice, agave syrup, and ginger to a simmer in a saucepan over medium-low. Cook until mixture is fragrant and strawberries are tender, about 5 minutes. Remove from the heat, and cool completely, about 1 hour.

2. Transfer the strawberry mixture to a blender. Process until smooth, about 30 seconds. Refrigerate for at least 1 hour or up to 5 days. Makes about 2 cups

Turkey Wings Glazed with Strawberry BBQ Sauce

The sweet, meaty quality of turkey is highlighted when it is smoked or grilled. Frying protects the meat's moisture content while smoking and grilling concentrates the flavors. The turkey wing has the best skin for smoking. It crisps rapidly and holds firm under longer cooking times. The skin also reheats very well and gives adequate protection to keep the meat from drying out.

The strawberries in the barbecue sauce are unexpected and add a complex sweetness to the usual players.

Serves 8

8 turkey wings
4 quarts Sweet Tea Brine (page 355)
Strawberry BBQ Sauce (page 86)
¼ cup blended olive oil
2 tablespoons kosher salt
1 tablespoon coarsely ground black pepper

1 teaspoon onion powder
1 teaspoon poultry seasoning
½ teaspoon garlic powder
½ teaspoon smoked paprika
¼ teaspoon chili powder

1. Combine the turkey wings and the Sweet Tea Brine in a large container and refrigerate at least 8 hours or up to 24 hours.

2. Meanwhile, prepare the Strawberry BBQ Sauce.

3. Preheat the oven to 350°F with the oven rack about 10 inches from the heat. Remove the wings from the brine, and pat dry with a paper towel. Place the wings on a large baking sheet, and rub with the olive oil. Discard the brine.

4. Stir together the salt, pepper, onion powder, poultry seasoning, garlic powder, paprika, and chili powder in a small bowl. Sprinkle the spice mixture evenly over the turkey wings.

5. Bake the turkey wings in the preheated oven until a meat thermometer inserted in the thickest part of the meat registers 165°F, 45 to 55 minutes. Remove from the oven.

6. Increase oven temperature to broil, and spoon 2 tablespoons of the Strawberry BBQ Sauce over the turkey wings. Broil until the sauce starts to caramelize, 5 to 7 minutes.

7. Remove from the oven, and let stand for 10 minutes before serving. Serve with Strawberry BBQ Sauce and Strawberry-Rum Coolers (previous page).

Note: The turkey wings can also be grilled or smoked.
To Drink: Blanc de blancs Champagne, Moscato, dry prosecco, rosé, sparkling rosé, white Zinfandel, amber beers, light beers, IPAs, stout
Serve with: Green salads; sweet potatoes; egg or bean dishes

strawberry bbq sauce

1 tablespoon canola oil

1 medium-size yellow onion, finely chopped

1 cup (8 ounces) dark rum

1 ½ pounds fresh strawberries, hulled and
  quartered

¾ cup (6 ounces) apple cider vinegar

½ cup raw sugar

½ cup ketchup

¼ cup (2 ounces) Worcestershire sauce

2 tablespoons blended olive oil

2 tablespoons sorghum syrup

2 teaspoons kosher salt

1 teaspoon coarsely ground black pepper

6 garlic cloves, thinly sliced

4 bay leaves

1 serrano chile

1. Heat the oil in a saucepan over medium-high. Add the onion, and cook, stirring often, until caramelized, about 5 minutes. Remove from the heat. Add the rum and stir for 2 minutes. Add the strawberries and place over medium-high. Cook, stirring occasionally, until the strawberries are tender, about 5 minutes.

2. Add the vinegar, sugar, ketchup, Worcestershire sauce, oil, syrup, salt, black pepper, garlic, bay leaves, and serrano chile, and cook until the mixture reduces slightly and is thick enough to coat a spoon, about 15 minutes.

3. Remove and discard the bay leaves. Process the sauce until smooth using a handheld blender, about 1 minute.

4. Let stand for 30 minutes before serving. Store any leftover sauce in an airtight container in the refrigerator for up to 2 weeks. Makes 5 ½ cups

As a city kid playing outside, it was a great respite to stumble upon honeysuckle vines in bloom or blackberry canes heavy with fruit. People don't think rabbits run around or wild things grow on the southside of Chicago. Growing up, foraging was never a planned thing. Running around all day in the neighborhood, you just knew where the good stuff was growing. We always had to venture a bit farther out to find wild strawberries...and strawberries were considered a luxury food then. Many of the recipes here reflect the strawberry-and-Champagne culture of my '70s youth. My mom would make gallons of blueberry-infused tea but it was never just for chugging. That tea found its way into marinades and sauces, braising liquids, and brines. In our house, we used up every last bit of something in the most novel ways. Tossing nothing was an inspired exercise in creativity.

Blueberry Fried Pies with Meyer Lemon Glaze

For me, peaches are for cobbler and blueberries are for fried pies. I savor the flavor of a tart berry, butter, and sugar combo, whether it's an elevated recipe like this or the star-wrapped pies in the candy store (which I'd pass up everything in the store for as a kid). Leftover filling is great on pancakes, waffles, or ice cream.

Makes about 20 pies

1 cup granulated sugar

2 tablespoons cornstarch

¾ cup (6 ounces) water

¼ cup (2 ounces) dark rum

1 teaspoon orange zest (from 1 orange)

¼ teaspoon vanilla bean paste

Pinch of kosher salt

1 thyme sprig

4 cups fresh blueberries (about 1 ¼ pounds)

Erika Council's Piecrust (page 352)

All-purpose flour, for dusting

1 large egg

4 cups (32 ounces) vegetable oil

Meyer Lemon Glaze (recipe follows)

1. Whisk together the sugar and cornstarch in a saucepan. Add ½ cup of the water, and whisk until combined. Whisk in the rum, orange zest, vanilla bean paste, and salt. Add the thyme sprig. Cook over medium, whisking constantly, until the mixture is thickened, 12 to 14 minutes. Remove from the heat, and fold in the blueberries. Let stand for 30 minutes. Remove and discard the thyme sprig.

2. Cut the piecrust in half. Refrigerate 1 portion until ready to use. Roll out remaining portion to ⅛-inch thickness on a lightly floured surface. Cut the dough into 10 circles with a 4 ½-inch round cookie cutter, re-rolling scraps once. Repeat with remaining dough half.

3. Spoon about 1 tablespoon of filling into the center of each dough circle. Whisk together the egg and remaining ¼ cup water. Brush the edges of the pies, and fold over so the edges meet. Press the edges together with a fork to seal. Repeat the process with the remaining dough, filling, and egg wash.

4. Heat the oil in a skillet over medium to 375°F. Fry the pies until golden brown, about 4 minutes. Turn and cook about 2 more minutes. Drain on paper towels, and let cool 20 minutes. Drizzle with Meyer Lemon Glaze.

To Drink: Sparkling wine, Champagne, Chardonnay, rosé, Shiraz, Moscato, hard ciders
Serve with: Ice cream, lemon sorbet

meyer lemon glaze

1 cup (about 4 ounces) powdered sugar

2 tablespoons Meyer lemon juice

1 to 3 teaspoons heavy cream

Whisk together the powdered sugar and lemon juice in a small bowl. Whisk in the heavy cream, 1 teaspoon at a time, until desired consistency is reached. Makes ½ cup

Blueberry Sweet Tea
(page 92)

Blueberry Sweet
Tea-Brined Roasted
Chicken Thighs with
Golden Beet Hash
(page 93)

Blueberry Sweet Tea

Sweet tea brewed in a commercial kitchen is great but doesn't have the same pitch and hue as the sweet sun tea my aunt would make in the hot sun outside her Hot Springs, Arkansas, home. She would put the tea bags in the jar, fill it with water and sugar, and place it in the sun to brew. It seemed like there was a sort of purity in tea brewed this way—at least in my rose-colored remembrance of it. I was always mindful of bees buzzing around the jar, attracted by the sticky drips. My aunt never allowed us to open the jar on the outside table because any sugary spills would attract ants too. This version of sweet tea is infused with the distinctive summertime sweetness that comes from Blueberry Simple Syrup spiced with black pepper and star anise.

Makes about 2 quarts

2 quarts (8 cups) water

12 regular-size orange pekoe black tea bags

Blueberry Simple Syrup (recipe follows)

Orange wedges (optional)

Fresh blueberries (optional)

Bring 2 quarts of water to a boil in a medium saucepan over high heat. Add the tea bags, and remove from the heat. Cover and let stand 7 minutes. Stir in the Blueberry Simple Syrup, and cool completely, about 20 minutes. Serve over ice. Garnish with orange wedges and skewers of blueberries (about 3 per skewer), if desired.

Serve with: Summer dishes, smoked meats, smoked poultry, fried meats, game meats, smoked vegetables, cheeses, salads with cheese

blueberry simple syrup

1 cup granulated sugar

1 tablespoon lemon zest (from 1 lemon)

6 black peppercorns

1 star anise pod

2 cups (16 ounces) water

1 cup fresh blueberries

1. Bring the sugar, lemon zest, peppercorns, star anise, and 2 cups water to a boil in a saucepan over medium.

2. Add the blueberries, and reduce the heat to low. Cover and simmer about 8 minutes.

3. Remove from heat, and let stand 30 minutes. Mash the blueberries in the syrup using a potato masher or the back of a slotted spoon. Pour the syrup through a fine wire-mesh strainer into a bowl; discard solids. Store in an airtight container in the refrigerator up to 2 weeks. Makes 2 cups

Note: The tea and simple syrup can be made year-round with various seasonal fruits.

Blueberry Sweet Tea-Brined Roasted Chicken Thighs with Golden Beet Hash

The dark meat of chicken thighs naturally has a good amount of moisture. Brining accentuates the juiciness of the thigh and also coaxes out the prized natural flavors in the chicken that make it such a popular favorite. Know that the brine may give the chicken a bluish or red hue. Be sure to regulate the cooking temperature well. Thighs, by nature, take some time to cook. With the sugar content being elevated from the brine, a pan too hot will cause the skin to caramelize faster than the meat can reach its ideal internal temperature. Until you master doneness of different cuts of chicken, a meat thermometer is useful for making sure the chicken is ready.

Serves 4

8 chicken thighs
Blueberry Sweet Tea (recipe at left)
2 tablespoons blended olive oil

1 teaspoon coarsely ground black pepper
Golden Beet Hash (page 320)

1. Combine the chicken thighs and the Blueberry Sweet Tea in a large bowl and refrigerate 4 hours or up to overnight.

2. Preheat broiler with oven rack 6 inches from heat.

3. Remove the chicken from the brine, and pat dry with paper towels. Let stand at room temperature 1 hour. Rub with the oil, and sprinkle with the pepper.

4. Line a rimmed baking sheet with aluminum foil, and top with a wire rack. Place chicken, skin side up, on rack, and broil until skin is golden brown and crisp, about 15 minutes. Turn chicken over, and broil until chicken starts to pull away from the bone, about 10 minutes. Let stand for 10 minutes, and serve with Golden Beet Hash.

Note: All chicken parts can be used in making this recipe.
To Drink: White Burgundy, Chardonnay, Merlot, Pinot Noir, red blends, rosé, sparkling rosé, sparkling Shiraz, full hoppy beers, bourbon cocktails
Serve with: Summer dishes, smoked vegetables, cheeses, salads with cheese, tomatoes

Blackberry-Balsamic Roasted Venison

Game meats are best paired with accompaniments that balance the strong flavors of the meat. It is the same yin and yang approach to putting hot sauce on boldly flavored items like canned sardines; it helps to quiet the in-your-face, stronger flavor in order to realize the delicious nuanced flavors underneath.

Maple syrup is a terrific way to quiet gamey flavors, provided it's not just sweetness you're going for. Utilizing herbs such as thyme, the brightness of lemon zest, and the smokiness of bourbon makes the blackberry-infused maple syrup a catalyst of flavor and not just a sweet component of the dish.

Serves 4

2 tablespoons blended olive oil

1 pound venison loin or 2 (8-ounce) venison loin steaks

2 teaspoons coarsely ground black pepper

½ teaspoon kosher salt

1 shallot, cut into ⅛-inch-thick rings (about ¼ cup)

½ medium-size orange, sliced

1 oregano sprig

2 garlic cloves

3 tablespoons Blackberry-Balsamic Vinegar Reduction (page 96)

1 tablespoon Blackberry Maple Syrup for Game Meats (page 96)

1 teaspoon sea salt

1. Heat oil in a skillet over medium.

2. Sprinkle the venison with the pepper and kosher salt. Sear the venison in hot oil until golden brown, about 4 minutes per side.

3. Add the shallot to the skillet. Cook until the shallot is golden brown, about 2 minutes. (Transfer the shallot to the top of the meat if it starts to burn.)

4. Arrange the orange slices, oregano, and garlic around the meat in the skillet, and cook 4 minutes, turning the oranges after 2 minutes. Spoon the Blackberry-Balsamic Vinegar Reduction over the venison, and cook, basting with reduction mixture in the skillet until venison is medium-rare, about 4 minutes. Transfer the venison to a cutting board, and let stand 10 minutes.

5. Meanwhile, add the Blackberry-Maple Syrup for Game Meats to the drippings in the skillet, and stir until combined, about 1 minute. Slice venison, and sprinkle with the sea salt.

Note: Lean meat, such as pork tenderloin, can be substituted for the venison. When using high-fat meats, pour off the excess oil before adding the vinegar reduction.

To Drink: White Burgundy, Chardonnay, Merlot, Pinot Noir, red blends, rosé, sparkling rosé, sparkling Shiraz, full hoppy beers, bourbon cocktails

Serve with: Summer dishes, roasted meats or game meats, smoked game meats, poultry, roasted or smoked vegetables, biscuits, spicy mixed green salads

blackberry-balsamic vinegar reduction

2 cups (16 ounces) balsamic vinegar

½ cup packed light brown sugar

1 tablespoon orange zest (from 1 orange)

1 thyme sprig

1 pint plus 12 whole fresh blackberries

1. Bring balsamic vinegar, brown sugar, orange zest, thyme sprig, and 1 pint of the blackberries to a simmer in a saucepan over medium heat. Cook until mixture is reduced by half, about 20 minutes.

2. Remove saucepan from heat, and let stand 15 minutes. Cut remaining 12 blackberries in half.

3. Pour syrup through a fine wire-mesh strainer into a 1-pint glass; discard solids. Add the halved blackberries to the jar. Serve immediately, or cover with a lid and store at room temperature up to 3 days. Makes about 3 cups

blackberry maple syrup for game meats

1 pint fresh blackberries

2 cups (16 ounces) pure maple syrup

2 cups (16 ounces) bourbon

1 cup firmly packed light brown sugar

1 ½ tablespoons lemon zest (from 1 lemon)

1 tablespoon orange zest (from 1 orange)

8 black peppercorns

1 thyme sprig

1. Bring all ingredients to a simmer in a saucepan over medium. Cook until the syrup is reduced by about half, about 20 minutes.

2. Remove the saucepan from the heat, and let stand for 1 hour.

3. Pour the syrup through a fine wire-mesh strainer into a 1-pint glass jar; discard solids. Serve immediately, or cover with a lid and store at room temperature up to 3 days. Makes about 2 cups

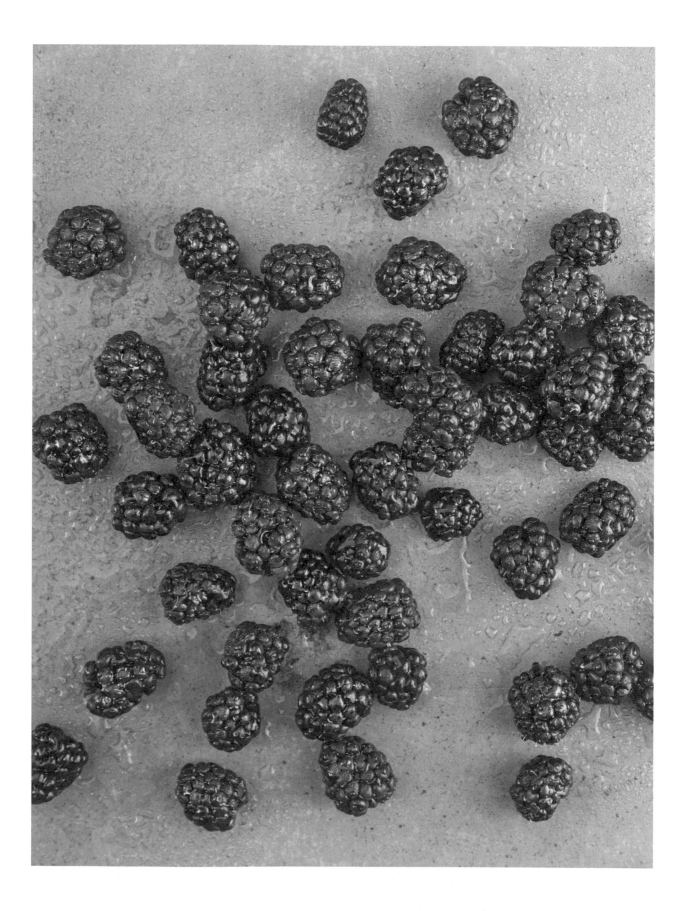

LAMB

In the colonial South, aristocratic landowners craved Old World dishes. Since the ingredients were procured and prepared by African slaves, the resulting dishes were a culinary patois of European and African cuisine. Many West African dishes are built on lamb or goat meat, so slaves understood how to balance the pronounced flavor of the meat of older sheep using traditional techniques and available spices. Soul food was born of black cooks' reinterpretation of French and English dishes and inspired by the ingredients available to them in the South. It was a pidgin cuisine until it stood firmly on its own. While pork is typically identified as the most common meat used in Soul food, lamb remains a staple that cannot be discounted. Whether smoked as in traditional barbecue, simmered in hearty stews and curries, ground for burgers, or cut into steaks and chops, lamb's versatility offers me countless opportunities to showcase my creativity and skill in the kitchen.

Leg of Lamb Steak with
Pepper and Olive Relish
(page 102)

Cheese Rice
(page 295)

Leg of Lamb Steak with Pepper and Olive Relish and Cheese Rice

Leg of lamb steak is as delicious as a beef rib eye. The way the meat draws to the bone is very similar in flavor and texture to rib eye but with more grassy, earthy flavors. If the butcher requires you to purchase an entire leg of lamb to slice in steaks, don't fret. Leg of lamb freezes very well and thaws rapidly.

Like nutty risotto, Cheese Rice (page 295) is comfort food that's as delicious on its own as it is a complement to other dishes. The creaminess of the rice works well with the meat and the tang of the relish.

Serves 2

2 (8- to 10-ounce, ½-inch-thick) leg of lamb steaks	2 bay leaves
3 tablespoons blended olive oil	Strips of peel of 1 orange (reserve the juice for the Pepper and Olive Relish)
1 tablespoon Curried Coffee Rub (page 351)	2 ounces (¼ cup) unsalted butter
8 blanched walnuts	1 cup (8 ounces) chicken stock
2 thyme sprigs	¼ cup (2 ounces) dry red wine
1 mint sprig	Pepper and Olive Relish (recipe follows)
2 garlic cloves	Cheese Rice (page 295)
8 black peppercorns	

1. Pat the lamb dry with paper towels. Rub with 2 tablespoons of the oil and the Curried Coffee Rub. Let the lamb stand until it comes to room temperature.

2. Heat the remaining 1 tablespoon oil in a sauté pan or skillet over medium-high. Sear the lamb steaks in the hot oil until golden brown, about 6 minutes. Turn the steaks. Add the walnuts, thyme sprigs, mint sprig, garlic, peppercorns, bay leaves, orange peel, and 2 tablespoons of the butter. Cook, basting the lamb often with the butter mixture, 4 minutes. Remove the lamb steaks from the pan, and set aside.

3. Reduce the heat to medium-low to maintain a simmer. Add the stock and wine, and cook until reduced by half. Whisk in the remaining 2 tablespoons butter. Pour mixture through a fine wire-mesh strainer into a gravy boat for serving. Remove the walnuts from the solids, and chop them. Fold the walnuts into the Pepper and Olive Relish. Discard the remaining solids.

4. Place 1 steak onto each of 2 plates. Pour the sauce evenly over steaks, and spoon some of the Pepper and Olive Relish on each steak. Serve with Cheese Rice.

Note: Lamb can be grilled and roasted under the broiler.

To Drink: Bordeaux, Cabernet Sauvignon, Chianti Classico, honey wine, Northern Rhône red, Rioja Reserva, red blends, amber beers, light beers, hard ciders, coffee beverages, IPAs

Serve with: Green salads, braised or roasted vegetable dishes, nut dishes

pepper and olive relish

1 teaspoon blended olive oil

4 red bell peppers, diced (about 4 cups)

1 small red onion, diced (about 1 cup)

1 jalapeño chile, seeded and diced (about ¼ cup)

8 large pitted green olives, cut into ⅛-inch-thick slices

½ cup (4 ounces) red wine vinegar

⅓ cup fresh orange juice (from 1 orange) (reserve the peel for the Leg of Lamb Steak recipe)

1 teaspoon orange blossom or wildflower honey

8 blanched walnuts (reserved from the Leg of Lamb Steak recipe) or 8 walnuts, chopped

1 oregano sprig

Heat the oil in a saucepan over medium. Add the bell peppers, onion, jalapeño, and olives; cook, stirring often, 5 minutes. Add the vinegar, orange juice, and honey. Simmer 2 minutes. Fold in the walnuts and oregano, and remove from the heat. Let stand until cool. Store the relish in an airtight container in the refrigerator up to 1 week. Remove and discard the oregano sprig before serving. Makes 5 cups

Country-Fried Lamb Steak, Hot Chicken Style

Frying leg of lamb is a delicious approach. Hot sauce cuts the meat's strong flavors and pays homage to the American South as well as Africa.

Knowledge of the region where a protein is regularly eaten is a good way to inform your flavor pairings. This recipe takes its cue from the Mediterranean with sweet onions and figs and the sweet-tart acidity of balsamic. It's a magical trio.

I'm so fond of radishes that I have a tattoo of them. The assertiveness of the Radish Slaw brings this dish all together.

Serves 4

½ cup sour cream

⅛ teaspoon caraway seeds

1 teaspoon apple cider vinegar

2 teaspoons coarsely ground black pepper

3 ½ teaspoons kosher salt

1 cup (about 4 ¼ ounces) all-purpose flour

1 teaspoon granulated onion

1 teaspoon granulated garlic

¼ teaspoon ground cumin

¼ teaspoon chili powder

½ cup (4 ounces) water

2 large eggs

4 (6-ounce) cubed lamb steaks

½ cup plus 3 tablespoons (5 ½ ounces) blended olive oil

4 potato bread slices

Hot Chicken Sauce (page 106)

Radish Slaw (page 106)

Fig, Bacon, and Onion Chutney (page 106)

1. Stir together the sour cream, caraway seeds, vinegar, 1 teaspoon of the pepper, and ½ teaspoon of the salt in a small bowl. Set aside.

2. Stir together the flour, granulated onion, granulated garlic, cumin, chili powder, 1 teaspoon of the salt, and remaining 1 teaspoon pepper in a medium bowl. Whisk together ½ cup water and eggs in a separate bowl. Dip each steak into the egg mixture, then dredge in the flour mixture, shaking off any excess.

3. Heat ¼ cup of the oil in a large skillet over medium-high. Add 2 of the lamb steaks to the skillet, and fry until golden brown, 3 to 4 minutes per side. Drain on paper towels. Repeat procedure with ¼ cup of the oil and remaining 2 lamb steaks.

4. Discard the drippings in skillet. Heat the remaining 3 tablespoons oil in skillet, and add the potato bread slices. Toast until golden brown, about 1 minute per side. Spread each toast with 2 tablespoons of the sour cream mixture. Top each with 1 lamb steak. Spoon about 1 tablespoon Hot Chicken Sauce on each lamb steak. Top with Radish Slaw. Serve with Fig, Bacon, and Onion Chutney and remaining Hot Chicken Sauce.

To Drink: Bordeaux, Cabernet Sauvignon, Chianti Classico, honey wine, Northern Rhône red, Rioja Reserva, red blends, amber beers, light beers, hard ciders, coffee beverages, IPAs
Serve with: Green salads; braised or roasted vegetable dishes

hot chicken sauce

2 tablespoons light brown sugar

2 tablespoons Worcestershire sauce

1 tablespoon cayenne pepper

1 teaspoon red pepper flakes

1 teaspoon paprika

¾ teaspoon kosher salt

½ teaspoon chili powder

¼ teaspoon ground ginger

¼ cup (2 ounces) blended olive oil

Whisk together the brown sugar and Worcestershire sauce in a small bowl until the sugar dissolves. Stir in the cayenne pepper, red pepper flakes, paprika, salt, chili powder, and ginger until well combined. Whisk in the oil, or process in a blender, until combined. Store in an airtight container in the refrigerator up to 1 week. Makes about ½ cup

fig, bacon, and onion chutney

2 tablespoons blended olive oil

2 small yellow onions, diced (about 9 ounces)

¼ cup (2 ounces) apple cider

3 tablespoons fig balsamic vinegar or regular balsamic vinegar (do not use aged)

1 star anise pod

1 dried fig, finely chopped (about 4 ½ ounces)

4 cooked bacon slices, finely chopped

1 tablespoon orange zest (from 1 orange)

1 tablespoon lemon zest (from 1 lemon)

½ teaspoon kosher salt

Pinch of red pepper flakes

1. Heat oil in a saucepan over medium. Add onions and cook, stirring often, until onions are very tender and caramelized, about 10 minutes.

2. Add cider, vinegar, and star anise; cook until liquid is reduced slightly, 30 seconds to 1 minute. Remove from the heat. Stir in the fig, bacon, orange zest, lemon zest, salt, and red pepper flakes. Let stand 15 minutes before serving. Makes ¾ cup

radish slaw

6 red radishes, thinly sliced (about 3 ounces)

1 small carrot, peeled and grated (about 2 ounces)

1 jalapeño chile, halved lengthwise

1 tablespoon kosher salt

½ cup (4 ounces) white wine vinegar

2 tablespoons granulated sugar

1. Combine the radishes, carrot, jalapeño, and salt in a medium bowl. Let stand 45 minutes. Transfer the mixture to a fine wire-mesh strainer, and rinse with cold water.

2. Heat the vinegar and sugar in a saucepan over medium. Cook until the sugar dissolves, about 3 minutes. Remove from the heat.

3. Combine the radish mixture and the hot vinegar mixture in a heatproof, airtight container. Cover and refrigerate until ready to serve. Serves 4

My mentor, Chef Daryl E. Evans, taught me the art of preparing lamb. He stressed the importance of clean, pearly white bones on a perfectly tied rack of lamb. He exalted the critical necessity of basting to ensure the meat would not be dry. And while we worked side by side, he often reminded me not to forget where I came from.

Chef Evans was all about simplicity—a very hard lesson to learn for any eager new chef on the bottom of the totem pole. Focusing on the basics was tedious, because as far as I was concerned it was my time to prove myself to the culinary world. To be honest, I couldn't even put my hat on straight and didn't have a clue that being given a hard time by the other cooks was a restaurant-kitchen rite of passage…a test of my mettle and resilience.

Over time, bone by bone and baste by baste, I found my way. Focusing on the task at hand was meditative. It provided me an opportunity to reflect on my craft and, as Chef Evans urged, where I came from…as well as where I hoped to go through delicious means.

Merguez Sausages with Preserved Lemon and Pickled Carrots and Turnips

Lamb sausage is often made from many cuts of the animal and the spices used are key. As lamb ages, its flavors intensify. Sweet carrots are a classic accompaniment that when pickled help cut through the rich flavors of the sausage with each bite.

An ancient grain, farro is also sold as wheat berries. Folding whipped cream into cooked farro adds velvety smoothness to its toothsome texture. Enjoy farro as cereal like you would oatmeal or Cream of Wheat.

Serves 4

1 preserved lemon

1 tablespoon blended olive oil

8 (2-ounce) Merguez sausages

2 cups (16 ounces) chicken stock

1 tablespoon sherry vinegar

1 ounce (2 tablespoons) unsalted butter

1 tablespoon coarse-grain mustard

1 tablespoon chopped fresh oregano

¼ teaspoon kosher salt

¼ teaspoon freshly ground black pepper

3 cups Creamed Farro (page 110)

½ cup Pickled Carrots and Turnips (recipe follows)

1. Peel the preserved lemon. Finely dice the peel to equal 1½ tablespoons; set aside.

2. Heat the oil in a large skillet over medium-high. Add the sausages. Brown on all sides, 6 to 8 minutes. Add the stock and the vinegar. Bring to a boil; reduce heat to medium. Simmer until cooked through and barely firm, 4 to 5 minutes. Remove the sausages from the skillet; set aside. Continue to simmer until the sauce is reduced to ¼ cup, 3 to 4 minutes. Whisk in the butter, mustard, oregano, salt, and pepper.

3. Spoon about ¾ cup Creamed Farro onto each of 4 plates. Top each with 2 sausages and the Pickled Carrots and Turnips.

To Drink: Bordeaux, Cabernet Sauvignon, Chianti Classico, honey wine, Northern Rhône red, Rioja Reserva, red blends, amber beers, light beers, hard ciders, coffee beverages, IPAs

Serve with: Green salads, braised or roasted vegetable dishes

pickled carrots and turnips

4 cups Pickle Brine (page 354)

2 carrots, peeled

1 small turnip, peeled

1. Bring the Pickle Brine to a boil in a saucepan over medium. Add the carrots and turnip; reduce heat to low. Simmer about 15 minutes. Remove from the heat; let stand 30 minutes. Remove the vegetables, reserving the brine in the saucepan.

2. Dice the vegetables and place in a sterilized glass jar. Pour the brine through a fine wire-mesh strainer into the jar. Cover with lid. Refrigerate up to 1 month. Makes 2 cups

creamed farro

Serves 4

1 tablespoon blended olive oil
1 large shallot, diced (about ½ cup)
1 ½ cups uncooked farro
3 cups (24 ounces) chicken stock
¼ cup (2 ounces) dry sherry
1 ½ teaspoons kosher salt

1 cup (8 ounces) heavy cream, whipped until
   soft peaks form
3 tablespoons Collard Green Pesto (page 35)
1 ounce (2 tablespoons) unsalted butter
½ teaspoon freshly ground black pepper

1. Heat the oil in a saucepan over medium. Add the shallot, and cook, stirring often, 2 minutes. Add the farro, and cook, stirring often, 2 minutes. Stir in the stock, sherry, and salt. Bring to a boil. Reduce heat and simmer until farro has the texture of cooked rice but is not mushy, 25 to 30 minutes.

2. Remove the farro mixture from the heat, and pour through a fine wire-mesh strainer into a bowl. Discard the liquid, and return the farro to the saucepan. Fold in the cream, Collard Green Pesto, and butter just until incorporated. Sprinkle with pepper.

Lamb Meatball Skewers with Fig Yogurt Sauce

Meatballs are a wonderful way to use ground meats. Forming them around skewers is a practical way of serving them. I prefer this method because you can dip them into the yogurt sauce without needing another utensil. I also enjoy these skewers with Baked Eggs in Tomato Sauce (page 192).

Serves 4 as an appetizer

2 cups plain Greek yogurt

2 tablespoons Fig, Bacon, and Onion Chutney (page 106)

2 teaspoons lemon zest plus 1 teaspoon juice (from 1 lemon)

3 tablespoons (1 ½ ounces) water

1 large egg

2 tablespoons panko (Japanese-style breadcrumbs)

1 pound ground lamb

½ cup diced poblano chile

½ cup finely chopped fresh flat-leaf parsley

¼ cup diced white onion

¼ cup finely chopped fresh cilantro

1 garlic clove, smashed and chopped

1 teaspoon light brown sugar

1 teaspoon kosher salt

½ teaspoon ground cumin

½ teaspoon coarsely ground black pepper

¼ teaspoon ancho chile powder

⅛ teaspoon red pepper flakes

16 to 20 wooden skewers, soaked in water

2 tablespoons blended olive oil

1. Combine the yogurt, chutney, and lemon juice in a small bowl. Let stand 15 minutes.

2. Whisk together the 3 tablespoons water and egg in a large bowl. Add the panko; let stand 10 minutes. Add the lamb, poblano chile, parsley, onion, cilantro, garlic, brown sugar, salt, cumin, black pepper, ancho chile powder, red pepper flakes, and lemon zest. Stir just until incorporated.

3. Shape about 2 ounces of the lamb mixture (about the size of a small Yukon Gold potato) into a ball. Insert 2 skewers parallel in the meatball, and press the meatball to flatten slightly into a disk shape. Repeat with remaining lamb mixture and skewers.

4. Preheat a grill to medium (400° to 450°F). Brush meatballs evenly with oil. Grill the lamb until browned on 1 side, 5 to 6 minutes. Turn and cook until browned and done, about 4 minutes. Let stand at least 5 minutes before serving. Serve with the fig yogurt sauce.

Note: If you don't soak the panko in water, the meatballs will become brittle in spots.

To Drink: Bordeaux, Cabernet Sauvignon, Chianti Classico, honey wine, Northern Rhône red, Rioja Reserva, red blends, amber beers, light beers, hard ciders, coffee beverages, IPAs

Serve with: Green salads; braised or roasted vegetable dishes

Curried Lamb Ribs with Crawfish Butter-Boiled Potatoes

Spring lamb is mellow compared to its fall counterpart or older sibling, mutton. The complex flavors of curry accentuate the richness of lamb while muting any gamey qualities.

When serving intense spices and game meats, simple potatoes can be one of the most important parts of the meal. Your taste buds need a break from the assertive flavors on the plate. I first understood this when my dad made pot roast (one of his dishes I long for the most). I often asked for seconds of the potatoes, because they were a sponge for the delicious meat jus that should never be left behind.

Serves 4

2 pounds lamb ribs (Denver or baby back)
¼ cup blended olive oil
3 tablespoons Curried Coffee Rub (page 351)
8 Red Bliss potatoes or Grade A new potatoes
8 cups (64 ounces) water

2 tablespoons kosher salt
6 tablespoons Crawfish Butter (page 346)
½ bunch fresh flat-leaf parsley, stemmed and coarsely chopped
½ teaspoon coarsely ground black pepper
Corn Maque Choux (page 162)

1. Preheat the oven to 300°F. Pat lamb dry with paper towels to remove excess moisture. Using a sharp knife, score the back of the ribs on the bone side in a X pattern. Rub lamb with 2 tablespoons of the oil, and rub with the Curried Coffee Rub. Let the lamb stand until it reaches room temperature.

2. Place the lamb in a deep roasting pan, and roast in preheated oven until the bones pull away entirely from the meat, about 3 hours.

3. Meanwhile, bring the potatoes, 8 cups water, and the salt to a boil in a stockpot over medium-high. Cook until a knife can be inserted easily in potatoes, about 12 minutes.

4. Drain the potatoes, and let stand 10 minutes. Freeze the potatoes for 30 minutes.

5. Heat the remaining 2 tablespoons oil in a sauté pan or skillet over medium. Cut the potatoes in half. Arrange the potatoes in a single layer in the sauté pan, and sear until golden brown, about 6 minutes per side.

6. Add the Crawfish Butter, parsley, and black pepper to the pan. Spoon the melted butter mixture evenly over the potatoes until well coated. Remove from the heat.

7. Remove the lamb from oven, and let stand 20 minutes before slicing. Serve with Corn Maque Choux.

Note: Serve with the Corn Maque Choux (page 162).

To Drink: Red Bordeaux, Cabernet Sauvignon or Cabernet/Merlot blend, Rioja Reserva, Chianti Classico, Northern Rhône red, amber beers, IPAs, stouts, hard ciders

Serve with: Green salads; potato, tomato, spicy, or rice dishes; chutneys

SEAFOOD

Seafood is as much a part of West African fare as it is a cornerstone of the countless dishes along the American coasts that drifted inland. Seafood dishes that meld spices with tomato are common in African cookery and made their way into the dishes of the Geechee and Gullah of the Carolina Lowcountry and on into the pantheon of Southern cooking. Seafood's versatility is undeniable: It can be fried, braised, grilled, roasted, smoked or poached...even dried or cured. Poaching fish and shellfish in flavorful bouillon is a common technique that I also employ to gently cook sea urchin in the shell. Instead of traditional batter-fried shrimp or shrimp on a bed of grits, I serve shrimp cloaked in a grits crust. Broiled perch folded in butter lettuce leaves with tomato aspic is my riff on a fish taco. Only your imagination and the ingredients at hand limit you. There are no rules.

Mom's Fried Catfish with Hot Sauce

My mother made catfish on Fridays as part of her weekly rotation of dishes. I was always amazed by the crispiness of her fish. She let it sit in cornmeal for about 5 minutes—a technique I use today.

Serves 4

2 cups (16 ounces) whole buttermilk

2 tablespoons Worcestershire sauce

1 tablespoon Hot Sauce (recipe follows, or use store-bought), plus more for serving

¼ teaspoon granulated garlic

¼ teaspoon granulated onion

4 teaspoons kosher salt

1 ½ teaspoons freshly ground black pepper

1 ½ pounds catfish fillets, cut into 2-inch pieces

2 cups (about 8 ½ ounces) plain yellow cornmeal

¼ teaspoon cayenne pepper

4 cups (32 ounces) vegetable oil

1. Combine the buttermilk, Worcestershire sauce, Hot Sauce, granulated garlic, granulated onion, and 1 teaspoon each of the salt and black pepper in a large bowl or large ziplock plastic freezer bag. Add catfish pieces; cover or seal, and refrigerate for 2 to 8 hours.

2. Whisk together the cornmeal, cayenne, remaining 3 teaspoons salt, and ½ teaspoon black pepper in a shallow dish or pie pan.

3. Heat the oil in a skillet over medium.

4. Remove the catfish from the buttermilk mixture, and dredge in the cornmeal. Let stand 5 minutes.

5. Fry the catfish (large pieces first), in batches, until golden brown 5 to 7 minutes per side. Drain on a plate lined with paper towels. Serve with additional Hot Sauce.

Note: If using boneless catfish, this dish can be served as a sandwich with lettuce and Chive Aioli (page 357).

To Drink: Chardonnay, dry Riesling, Sauvignon Blanc, Sémillon, amber beers, dark beers, hard ciders, IPAs

Serve with: Other fried foods; braised green, breakfast, potato, egg, or bean dishes; green or tomato salads

hot sauce

2 teaspoons blended olive oil

3 red Fresno chiles, stemmed and coarsely chopped

1 jalapeño chile, stemmed and coarsely chopped

½ small yellow onion, diced

3 garlic cloves

½ cup (4 ounces) apple cider vinegar

¼ cup (2 ounces) red wine vinegar

½ teaspoon red pepper flakes

1 tablespoon kosher salt

1. Heat the oil in a stockpot over medium. Add the chiles, onion, and garlic; cook, stirring often, until tender, 6 to 8 minutes.

2. Add the vinegars and red pepper flakes. Bring to a boil; cover, reduce heat to medium-low and simmer until vegetables are tender, about 20 minutes.

3. Stir in the salt, and remove from the heat. Let stand 20 minutes.

4. Process the chile mixture in a blender or food processor until smooth, stopping to scrape down the sides. (Remove the center of the blender top to prevent the mixture from overflowing, and be wary of inhaling pepper vapors.) Makes ¾ cup

⊰ FISH FRY ⊱

This menu exemplifies the way my family ate together and the way my mom, VV, cooked for us. She had this thing for serving fried foods with smoked foods. Her fried fish came doused in hot sauce, and she served smoked oysters from a can on saltine crackers. Everything was on the table—platters of fish, bottles of beer, condiments—ready to be passed and shared. Like a block party or church supper, this meal is all about the fellowship around food, which is the very expression of Soul.

Mom's Fried Catfish with Hot Sauce
(page 118)

Smoked Oysters on Toast
(page 142)

Cheese Rice (page 295)

Radish Slaw (page 106)

ON THE RADIO

"Catfish" — *The Four Tops*
"Some Like It Hot" — *The Power Station*
"Deep Waters" — *Incognito*
"Feelin' Alright" — *Joe Cocker*

Mom's Fried Catfish with Hot Sauce (page 118)

Radish Slaw (page 106)

Cheese Rice
(page 295)

Smoked
Oysters
on Toast
(page 142)

Smoked Catfish Dip with Parmesan Tuiles

This dish embodies my family's tastes: It marries my mother's love for catfish and my dad's love of smoked and grilled meats. It also speaks to Mom's love of fish dips and Dad's love of cheese crackers. It's one of my favorites to share.

Serves 9

2 (8-ounce) skinless catfish fillets

4 cups (32 ounces) Sweet Tea Brine (page 355)

2 tablespoons blended olive oil

1 teaspoon kosher salt

½ teaspoon coarsely ground black pepper

4 ounces cream cheese, softened

½ cup mayonnaise

¼ cup chopped fresh flat-leaf parsley

¼ cup minced shallot (about 1 medium shallot)

¼ cup sour cream

1 tablespoon Dijon mustard

1 teaspoon lemon zest (from 1 lemon)

1 teaspoon hot sauce

¼ cup thinly sliced scallions

8 ounces Parmesan cheese, grated (about 2 cups) (do not use preshredded cheese)

1. Combine the catfish and Sweet Tea Brine in a large container or large ziplock plastic freezer bag. Cover or seal, and refrigerate for 4 to 12 hours.

2. Preheat a grill or smoker to very low (250°F) on 1 side according to manufacturer's instructions. Remove the catfish from brine; discard brine. Rub fish evenly with oil, and sprinkle with the salt and pepper.

3. Place the fish fillets on oiled grates over the unlit side of the grill. Grill, covered, about 15 minutes or until a meat thermometer inserted in thickest part of fish registers 140°F and fish flakes easily. Remove fish from grill, and let stand 1 hour.

4. Stir together the cream cheese, mayonnaise, parsley, shallot, sour cream, mustard, lemon zest, and hot sauce in a medium bowl. Flake the catfish, and fold into the cream cheese mixture. Transfer to a serving dish, and sprinkle with the scallions. Refrigerate at least 15 minutes or until ready to serve.

5. Heat a large nonstick skillet over medium. Sprinkle about ½ tablespoon of the cheese into 6 (2-inch) circles. Cook until cheese is golden brown, 4 to 5 minutes. Turn tuiles, and cook until golden brown throughout, about 2 minutes. Transfer to a plate lined with paper towels. Repeat with remaining cheese. Serve tuiles with the catfish dip.

Note: It is best to use fresh catfish fillets for this recipe. Frozen catfish may lose its essential oils that are of major importance to the texture of the dish. Use wood for smoking that is natural to your home. In Georgia, we use pecan and oak.

To Drink: Champagne, Chardonnay, dry Riesling, Sauvignon Blanc, Sémillon, amber beers, dark beers, hard ciders, IPAs

Serve with: Seafood; braised greens; breakfast, potato, egg, or bean dishes; mixed green or tomato salads

Salmon Croquettes with Grits Croutons and Chive Aioli

I pay close attention to how the textures of foods play together, especially those paired with creamy sauces. Like crunchy oyster crackers on top of creamy chowder, the crisp exterior of a tender fish croquette meets its perfect counterpart in a rich and creamy sauce. That contrast makes this dish enjoyable bite after bite.

Serves 4

1 pound skin-on salmon fillets (about 1 inch thick)

4 cups (32 ounces) Citrus Brine (page 354)

½ cup (4 ounces) blended olive oil

2 teaspoons kosher salt

1 teaspoon coarsely ground black pepper

1 ¼ cups panko (Japanese-style breadcrumbs)

⅓ cup chopped fresh flat-leaf parsley (from 1 small bunch)

⅓ cup mayonnaise

1 small red bell pepper, diced (about 3 ½ ounces)

1 small red onion, diced (about 3 ¼ ounces)

1 celery stalk, diced (about 1 ounce)

2 teaspoons coarse-grain mustard

2 teaspoons hot sauce

1 teaspoon lemon zest (from 1 lemon)

Grits Croutons (page 156)

Chive Aioli (page 357)

1. Combine the salmon fillets and Citrus Brine in a large bowl. Cover and refrigerate 4 hours.

2. Preheat the oven to 400°F. Heat ¼ cup of the oil in an ovenproof saucepan over medium-high. Remove the salmon from the brine; discard brine. Pat the salmon dry with paper towels, and sprinkle both sides with the salt and black pepper. Place fillets in hot oil, skin side down. Transfer saucepan to the preheated oven, and bake until salmon is firm to the touch, about 14 minutes.

3. Remove the pan from oven, and turn salmon fillets. Carefully remove the skin from the fillets. Remove the fillets from the pan, and return the skins to the pan. Bake until the skin is crispy, about 6 minutes. Remove from oven, and let cool 20 minutes.

4. Chop the salmon skin, and place in a medium bowl. Gently flake the salmon fillets, and add to the bowl. Stir in the panko, parsley, mayonnaise, bell pepper, onion, celery, mustard, hot sauce, and lemon zest until thoroughly combined. Scoop the salmon mixture by ½ cupfuls using a 2 ½-inch scoop, and shape into 1-inch-thick patties (about 3 inches in diameter). Cover and refrigerate patties at least 1 hour.

5. Heat the remaining ¼ cup oil in a sauté pan or skillet over medium. Cook the croquettes, in batches, until golden brown, about 3 minutes per side. Drain on a plate lined with paper towels. Serve with Grits Croutons and Chive Aioli.

To Drink: White Burgundy, NV Grand Cru Champagne, unoaked Chardonnay, Chenin Blanc, Pinot Blanc, unoaked Sauvignon Blanc, amber beers, light beers, hard ciders

Serve with: Egg, stewed, breakfast, vegetable, or curry dishes; green salads

Fish Market Scallops with Lemon Aioli

Coating scallops in flour or cornmeal before frying is another example of pairing opposing textures for interest. I prefer cornmeal breading when serving with loose or thin sauces, because the cornmeal will remain crunchy.

Serves 4

2 large eggs

1 cup (8 ounces) water, at room temperature

1 cup (about 4 ½ ounces) plain yellow cornmeal

1 ½ tablespoons kosher salt

1 tablespoon paprika

2 teaspoons coarsely ground black pepper

2 teaspoons granulated onion

1 teaspoon granulated garlic

1 pound U10 large sea scallops (about ½ to 1 ½ ounces each)

½ cup (about 4 ounces) blended olive oil

Lemon Aioli (page 357)

1. Whisk together the eggs and 1 cup water in a shallow dish. Stir together the cornmeal, salt, paprika, black pepper, granulated onion, and granulated garlic in a shallow dish.

2. Dip the scallops in the egg mixture using a slotted spoon, and then dredge in the cornmeal mixture, turning to coat on all sides.

3. Heat ½ cup oil in a sauté pan over medium-high. Fry scallops in hot oil until cornmeal is crispy and coating is golden brown, about 2 minutes per side. Transfer to paper towels to drain. Serve with Lemon Aioli (page 357).

To Drink: Sauvignon Blanc, sparkling wine, Champagne, Chardonnay, rosé, Pinot Noir, amber beers, IPAs, hard ciders, Bloody Marys

Serve with: Green salads; potato, tomato, spicy, or corn dishes

Shrimp and Grits with Grits Crust and Shrimp Butter

Utilizing grits as a coating for the shrimp speaks to the grain's versatility. Grits used in this manner are a great coarse substitute for cornmeal in most dishes. Where cornmeal is finely milled, grits add toothsome crunch to a dish and are a better-suited breading for protecting leaner proteins such as shrimp or mild fish such as flounder.

Serves 4

1 ½ pounds head-on, unpeeled large raw shrimp

1 cup (8 ounces) whole buttermilk

1 tablespoon Worcestershire sauce

¼ teaspoon lemon zest (from 1 lemon)

Pinch of red pepper flakes

½ cup uncooked instant grits or polenta

1 teaspoon kosher salt

¼ teaspoon granulated onion

¼ teaspoon granulated garlic

¼ teaspoon coarsely ground black pepper

1 cup (8 ounces) blended olive oil

Shrimp Butter (page 347)

Lemon wedges

1. Peel and devein the shrimp, leaving the heads on. Reserve the shells to make the Shrimp Butter.

2. Combine the buttermilk, Worcestershire sauce, lemon zest, and red pepper flakes in a medium bowl or large ziplock plastic freezer bag. Add the shrimp. Cover or seal, and refrigerate 15 minutes.

3. Stir together the grits, salt, granulated onion, granulated garlic, and black pepper in a shallow dish.

4. Remove the shrimp from the marinade; discard marinade. Heat the oil in a skillet over medium. Dredge the shrimp in the grits mixture, and toss to coat. Fry shrimp, in 2 batches, until the shrimp are done and the crust is golden brown, about 2 to 3 minutes per side. Drain the shrimp onto a plate lined with paper towels. Serve with Shrimp Butter and lemon wedges.

Note: Using head-on shrimp is essential to providing excellent shrimp flavor to a dish. Some people might find it difficult to see the head on the plate. In that case, cook the shrimp with the heads on and remove them before plating.

To Drink: Champagne, Chardonnay, dry Riesling, Sauvignon Blanc, Sémillon, amber beers, dark beers, hard ciders, IPAs

Serve with: Braised greens; breakfast, potato, egg, bean, and smoked dishes; mixed green and tomato salads

Blue Crab, Apple, and Horseradish Salad

Crab has always been one of my favorite foods. The delicate texture of crabmeat, as well as its sweetness, gives it versatility in dishes. It is a delicious accompaniment with steak or braised meats and is lovely folded into salads. A salad like this one highlights the beauty of fresh crabmeat. It truly is a delicacy.

Serves 4

1 large fresh horseradish root (about 1 pound), peeled

1 tablespoon kosher salt

2 medium-size red apples, peeled and diced

2 tablespoons mayonnaise

1 tablespoon red wine vinegar

1 ½ teaspoons coarse-grain mustard

1 ½ teaspoons Worcestershire sauce

¼ teaspoon coarsely ground black pepper

1 tablespoon lemon zest (from 1 lemon)

1 pound fresh blue crabmeat or jumbo lump crabmeat, drained

8 fresh chives (about ¼ bunch)

1. Grate the horseradish root to equal ½ teaspoon, and set aside. Place the remaining horseradish root in a stockpot. Add water to cover and the salt. Bring to a boil over high. Reduce heat to medium-low, and simmer until the horseradish is tender and a paring knife can be inserted easily into root, 15 to 20 minutes. Drain and let stand 5 minutes. Dice into small pieces.

2. Combine the horseradish, apples, mayonnaise, vinegar, mustard, Worcestershire sauce, pepper, lemon zest, and the grated horseradish in a medium bowl. Pick crabmeat, removing any bits of shell. Gently fold the crabmeat and chives into the diced horseradish mixture. Refrigerate the salad 30 minutes before serving.

Note: Fresh or pasteurized crabmeat is the best to use for this recipe. Frozen crabmeat tends to hold water and often has more bits of shell remaining in the mix after processing. If frozen crabmeat is your only alternative, turn to poached shrimp or lobster instead.

To Drink: Champagne, Chardonnay, dry Riesling, Sauvignon Blanc, Sémillon, amber beers, dark beers, hard ciders, IPAs

Serve with: Braised greens; breakfast, potato, egg, bean, or smoked dishes; mixed green or tomato salads

Broiled Lake Perch and Tomato Aspic in Lettuce Wraps

Lake perch is most often deep-fried. It's a flaky, mild fish that sadly gets overlooked when it comes to other cooking methods. Broiling fish is so simple and it provides the meat an exterior crust and tender center not unlike deep-frying, only without all the trouble. This recipe uses lots of spice for a mild fish.

Serves 2

2 teaspoons ground coffee

1 teaspoon kosher salt

1 teaspoon paprika

½ teaspoon raw sugar

½ teaspoon onion powder

½ teaspoon coarsely ground black pepper

¼ teaspoon cayenne pepper

2 teaspoons blended olive oil

1 pound skin-on lake perch fillets or other flaky mild white fish (such as mullet)

2 teaspoons unsalted butter

1 head butter lettuce

Tomato Aspic (page 182)

1 cup Lemon Aioli (page 357)

2 scallions, sliced (about ¼ cup)

1 lemon

1. Preheat the broiler with the oven rack 6 inches from heat.

2. Stir together the ground coffee, salt, paprika, sugar, onion powder, black pepper, and cayenne pepper in a small bowl.

3. Place a skillet under the broiler for 5 minutes. Remove the skillet, and add the olive oil to the hot skillet.

4. Sprinkle the ground coffee mixture on both sides of the fish. Arrange the fillets in a single layer in the skillet, and broil just until flaky, 5 to 7 minutes.

5. Transfer the fish to a platter. Add the butter to the hot skillet, and stir until melted. Pour the pan sauce over the fish.

6. Trim the end of the lettuce, and separate the leaves. Cut the aspic into narrow slices.

7. Place 1 piece of Broiled Lake Perch and 2 slices of tomato aspic into each of 6 lettuce leaves. Top evenly with Lemon Aioli and scallions.

8. Cut the lemon in half, and squeeze lemon juice over the fish.

To Drink: White Burgundy, Chardonnay, Chenin Blanc, Pinot Noir, Riesling, amber beers, hard ciders

Serve with: Beans and field peas; tomato, grits, or peanut dishes; avocado; buttermilk dressing

Growing up, we had a tight-knit community in Chicago. If a parent wasn't home, you went next door or across the street and ate there. We went to certain houses for certain meals. I can't recall a single time we fried chicken at home. For that, we'd go to Mrs. Arnold's, and she'd come to ours for barbecue. The fence was where we met for conversation or to share an invitation to dinner. Mrs. Arnold always had cornbread on the stove and chocolate mousse pie on the counter—iconic Soul dishes. Another neighbor was Haitian. Between Mrs. Arnold's traditional Southern food and the Bayard's French-influenced Haitian dishes, I came to appreciate the diversity of cuisines. I saw how the same ingredients in the hands of two different cooks yield such different dishes. The stuffed green peppers you'd get in any Soul food joint were entirely different from my Haitian friend's mom's that included chopped hot chiles and spices. On the city's east side, cooks stuffed poblanos instead of bell peppers for Mexican chiles rellenos. I noticed cooks putting spins on traditional foods, too. My grandmother stopped frying catfish. She began steaming, grilling, and smoking it. I didn't understand what she was doing at first. All I knew was I loved those caramelized bits of fish that clung to the tinfoil. Bite by bite, I was sold on my grandmother's new ways with our old recipes.

COOKING SKIN-ON FISH

Cooking skin-on fish is a technique that requires patience, a steady hand, and attention to what you are doing. Skin provides texture, retains moisture, and helps prevent overcooking; plus, crispy skin tastes pretty damn delicious. There are a few basic guidelines for searing skin-on fish.

Buy the freshest fish possible

Buying the freshest fish possible not only guarantees great taste and quality but ensures the essential oils are still in the skin. This helps prevent sticking in the pan and will protect the inner protein.

Utilize the proper pan

Just because a pan may be called nonstick doesn't mean it's the proper pan to cook fish. The best pans to cook skin-on fish are seasoned cast iron and steel. Nonstick pans typically don't give the fish skin the amount of surface contact needed for thorough caramelization.

Cook at the proper temperature

Cooking fish skin at too low a temperature will cause the skin to poach and become rubbery. Cooking at too high a heat can cause the skin to burn before it has adequate time to crisp up properly, which is required to retain the moisture of the flesh.

The thicker the fillet, the more likely scoring may be required

Thin fish, like trout or flounder, don't require scoring of the fish skin to ensure even cooking, but it helps prevent curling in the pan. With thicker fish, like salmon, scoring the skin—though not totally necessary—helps the meat cook while the skin becomes crisp without burning.

Utilize the proper oil

Cooking skin-on fish requires a cooking oil that doesn't burn quickly. Vegetable oil, grapeseed oil, or blended olive oil are all suitable for cooking skin-on fish. Oils or fats such as butter can caramelize far too quickly, which can leave the skin burnt and/or give the fish a sooty taste.

Pan-Fried Skin-On Trout

You can successfully substitute different skin-on fish, such as flounder or snapper, here with terrific results. If the fish is more than about 1 inch in thickness, preheat the oven to 350°F before you begin. After turning over the fish, place the pan in the oven for 4 minutes, remove, and proceed with the basting process.

Serves 2

1 tablespoon blended olive oil

2 (5-ounce) skin-on trout fillets

½ teaspoon kosher salt

½ ounce (1 tablespoon) unsalted butter

8 black peppercorns

Thyme sprigs

1 garlic clove, smashed

¼ lemon, sliced

1. Heat the oil in a cast-iron skillet over medium-high until it shimmers. Sprinkle the fish evenly with the salt. Add fish, skin side down. Gently shake the pan to ensure the oil flows under the fish.

2. Gently press the fish with a spatula so that the skin makes contact with the pan, and hold 15 to 30 seconds per fillet. Cook until the flesh of the fish is almost opaque on top, about 4 minutes. Turn the fish, and reduce heat to medium-low. Add the butter, peppercorns, thyme, and garlic. Cook 30 seconds. Add the lemon. Cook, constantly basting the fish with the butter mixture, 30 seconds.

3. Transfer to a plate lined with paper towels to drain. Serve the fish skin side up.

Note: Even if you have trouble with the fish sticking to the pan, don't despair. Once you remove the fish from the pan, the skin should lift from the pan easily and can be placed on top as part of the garnish, or it can be used as a garnish for the side dish, such as a tomato salad or braised greens.

To Drink: Champagne, Chardonnay, dry Riesling, Sauvignon Blanc, Sémillon, amber beers, dark beers, hard ciders, IPAs

Serve with: Braised greens; breakfast, potato, egg, bean, or smoked dishes; mixed green or tomato salads

Grilled Sardines with Buttered Couscous

I grew up eating oily fish, especially sardines of the canned variety with hot sauce on crackers. Now I like to pair just-caught sardines with unexpected flavors like coffee and paprika. Fennel seeds lend a citrus note that helps cut through the rich fat of these tiny fish, which are always best cooked head-on. The anatomy of the fish keeps the skin intact when the head is left in place. It requires some skill to ensure the skin doesn't pull away from the meat when cooking (see Cooking Skin-On Fish, page 137).

Serves 4

3 teaspoons blended olive oil

1 teaspoon ground coffee

½ teaspoon smoked paprika

½ teaspoon coarsely ground black pepper

¼ teaspoon fennel seeds

1 ½ teaspoons lemon zest (from 1 lemon)

2 teaspoons kosher salt

12 fresh sardines, dressed and scored

1 cup (8 ounces) water

1 cup uncooked couscous

Pinch of red pepper flakes

2 tablespoons unsalted butter, softened

½ cup loosely packed fresh flat-leaf parsley, leaves, coarsely chopped

4 nori (dried seaweed) sheets

½ cup loosely packed fresh cilantro leaves, chopped

Cucumber-Tomato Salad (page 176)

1. Preheat grill to medium (350° to 400°F).

2. Combine the olive oil, ground coffee, smoked paprika, black pepper, fennel seeds, lemon zest, and 1 teaspoon of the kosher salt in a small bowl. Rub the sardines with the spice mixture, and let stand at room temperature for 20 minutes.

3. Meanwhile, bring 1 cup water and the remaining 1 teaspoon salt to a boil in a saucepan over high.

4. Combine the couscous and the red pepper flakes in a large heatproof bowl. Pour the boiling salted water over the couscous. Cover and let stand for 5 minutes. Fluff with a fork, and fold in the butter and parsley.

5. Place the sardines on an oiled grill grate. Cover the fish with nori sheets, and grill, uncovered, until the skin is crisp on 1 side, 3 to 4 minutes. Remove the nori, and set aside. Carefully turn the fish, and grill until the skin is charred and flesh is flaky, 2 to 4 more minutes.

6. Place the nori on serving dish and top with fish. Sprinkle with the chopped cilantro. Serve with the buttered couscous and Cucumber Salad.

Note: Sardines can be substituted with mackerel, trout, salmon, or other oily fish.

To Drink: White Burgundy, Champagne, Chardonnay, Pinot Gris, Pinot Noir, rosé, sparkling rosé, sparkling Shiraz, amber beers, light beers, gin cocktails, vodka cocktails

Serve with: Bean, potato, tomato, or toast and bread dishes

Smoked Oysters on Toast

Smoked oysters are succulent and salty with a creamy texture that pairs beautifully with bright, acidic flavors. The egg spread provides another layer of richness. These may seem like disparate components of a menu, but each one brings something to the meal in terms of flavor, texture, aroma, and appearance to create a memorable experience.

Serves 8

1 ounce (2 tablespoons) unsalted butter, softened

4 spelt or other multigrain bread slices

6 tablespoons Deviled Egg Spread (recipe at right)

½ cup chopped egg whites (reserved from Deviled Egg Spread)

½ stalk blanched celery, diced (reserved from Deviled Egg Spread)

1 (3 ¾-ounce) can smoked oysters

1 ounce smoked trout roe

2 teaspoons chopped fresh chives

1 lemon, cut into 8 wedges

Hot sauce

1. Preheat the broiler with oven rack 5 inches from the heat. Line a baking sheet with heavy-duty aluminum foil.

2. Spread the butter evenly on both sides of the bread, and place on the prepared pan. Broil in preheated oven until deep golden brown, about 2 minutes per side.

3. Spread 1½ tablespoons Deviled Egg Spread onto each toasted bread slice. Sprinkle evenly with chopped egg whites and diced celery. Cut each slice into 4 triangles.

4. Top each triangle with smoked oysters and about ¼ teaspoon of trout roe. Garnish with chopped chives, and serve with lemon wedges and hot sauce.

Note: This dish does not have to be built as a toast. The elements can be arranged on a platter with the toast in the middle.

To Drink: Chablis, sparkling wine, Champagne, prosecco, Chardonnay, dry Riesling, rosé, amber beers, IPAs

Serve with: Green salads; potato, tomato, or egg dishes; grilled vegetables

deviled egg spread

6 cups (48 ounces) water

2 tablespoons plus ½ teaspoon kosher salt

1 celery stalk

½ cup (4 ounces) white vinegar

4 large eggs

½ cup mayonnaise

1 tablespoon Dijon mustard

1 teaspoon aged red wine vinegar

1 teaspoon hot sauce

1 teaspoon sliced fresh chives

½ teaspoon coarsely ground black pepper

1. Fill a large bowl with ice and water.

2. Bring 6 cups water and 2 tablespoons salt to a boil in a deep saucepan over high heat. Add the peeled celery stalk to the boiled water, and cook for 2 minutes. Remove from the pan, and plunge in the ice bath.

3. Remove the outer stringy layer of the celery with a vegetable peeler and discard.

4. Add the vinegar to the water, and return to a boil. Add the eggs to the pan, and cook for 8 minutes. Remove the eggs from the pan, and plunge in the ice bath.

5. When the eggs are cool enough to handle, peel them and separate the whites from the yolks. Chop the egg whites to equal ½ cup, and reserve for Smoked Oysters on Toast. Reserve the remaining whites for another use.

6. Combine the egg yolks, mayonnaise, Dijon, red wine vinegar, and hot sauce in a medium bowl.

7. Dice the celery and fold half into the egg yolk mixture. (Reserve the remaining celery for Smoked Oysters on Toast.) Stir in the chives, black pepper, and remaining ½ teaspoon salt. Makes about 1½ cups

CORN

Long before the first slave ships arrived, Native Americans were growing corn in the New World. Because it had been grown in Africa since the 1500s, it was a familiar crop to slaves. Rice was not readily available in the inland parts of the South, so corn was the staple starch. Cooked kernels were used in salads and pea dishes. Grilled corn became a portable meal that could be kept wrapped in the husk and eaten out of hand when hunger struck. Mature corn was dried and ground into meal for cornbread and grits. From husk to silk and kernel to cob, all parts of the plant were used. The husks were used to smoke meats, roll tobacco, and to stuff mattresses, make dolls, weave chair seats, and brooms. Cobs were fermented for whiskey and used as a readily available fuel source. Stalks, leaves, husks, and cobs were a major food for livestock. Nothing went to waste, which is an idea I take to heart in my cooking today. From seed to stem and nose to tail, I try to use it all. I'm all for having fun with classics like cornbread and maque choux, but I also like to experiment by pickling ears of baby corn for salads and garnishes and using popped corn as a breading that adds crunchy contrast to buttery scallops.

Cornbread

What is authentic cornbread will forever be debated because of different views about sugar in the recipe. What most don't realize is that sugar was used to preserve cornbread for trade when it wouldn't be eaten straightaway. This recipe highlights that use of sugar—though the bread can be eaten right away or reheated to enjoy the next day if it lasts that long. The buttermilk used is significant. Its rich, tangy quality lends balance to the cornmeal and sugar. It is the bridge between.

Serves 10

2 cups (about 11 ½ ounces) plain white
  cornmeal

2 cups (about 8 ½ ounces) all-purpose flour

2 cups (16 ounces) buttermilk

1 cup granulated sugar

8 ounces (1 cup) unsalted butter, melted

1 teaspoon baking soda

1 teaspoon kosher salt

4 large eggs

1 teaspoon blended olive oil

1 ounce (2 tablespoons) unsalted butter,
  softened

1. Preheat the oven to 375°F. Stir together the cornmeal, flour, buttermilk, sugar, melted butter, baking soda, salt, and eggs in a large bowl.

2. Heat a 12-inch cast-iron skillet over medium. Add the oil, and tilt the skillet to spread evenly around skillet. Pour the cornbread batter into the hot skillet.

3. Bake the cornbread in the preheated oven until golden brown, about 40 minutes. Top with the softened butter.

To Drink: White Burgundy, NV Grand Cru Champagne, Chardonnay, Merlot, amber beers, light beers, hard ciders, IPAs

Serve with: Egg, stewed, breakfast, vegetable, curry, or fried dishes; green salads

Hot Water Cornbread

This is a perfect example of how great food can be built upon with just a few basics—cornmeal, hot water, and oil. It's easy to add extras such as chopped cooked bacon, chives, or cooked shrimp to this variation of cornbread. I often tell people to master the basics and then experiment to come up with your own creations.

Serves 10

2 ½ cups (20 ounces) water

2 teaspoons kosher salt

2 cups (about 8 ½ ounces) plain yellow cornmeal

1 teaspoon raw sugar

¾ teaspoon baking soda

¼ teaspoon baking powder

¼ teaspoon ground nutmeg

¼ teaspoon cayenne pepper

1 tablespoon popcorn kernels, popped

⅔ cup (about 6 ounces) whole buttermilk

½ cup (4 ounces) vegetable oil

½ cup (about 2 ⅛ ounces) all-purpose flour

1. Bring 2 ½ cups water and salt to a boil in a stockpot over high.

2. Stir together the cornmeal, sugar, baking soda, baking powder, nutmeg, and cayenne pepper in a medium-size heatproof bowl. Add the boiling water, and stir until combined. Let stand 5 minutes.

3. Fold the popped corn kernels and buttermilk into the cornmeal mixture. Let stand 5 minutes.

4. Heat the oil in a skillet over medium. With floured hands, shape 1 ½ tablespoons of the cornmeal mixture into a 2 ½-inch round, and fry until golden brown, about 2 minutes per side. Repeat with remaining cornmeal mixture to make about 20 pieces. Drain on paper towels. Serve hot.

To Drink: Chardonnay, Shiraz, amber beers, IPAs, hard ciders, stouts

Serve with: As a side to soup or main dishes; croutons for salad

Hoecakes

While cornbread is soft and velvety, hoecakes are a crunchier cousin with all the tender goodness on the inside. I often serve hoecakes in the fall. Corn's distinctive, grassy essence really shines through in the later harvest. Hoecakes make a great base for canapés. A Salmon Croquette (page 126) on top of a hoecake lets you showcase your skill as an accomplished cook through the simplest of dishes.

Serves 8

2 cups (about 8 ½ ounces) plain yellow cornmeal
¼ teaspoon baking soda
¼ teaspoon ground nutmeg
¼ teaspoon cayenne pepper
1 ½ cups (12 ounces) whole buttermilk
½ cup (4 ounces) water

2 teaspoons kosher salt
½ tablespoon popcorn kernels, popped
2 tablespoons vegetable oil
1 ounce (2 tablespoons) unsalted butter, softened
Maple syrup (optional)

1. Combine the cornmeal, baking soda, nutmeg, and cayenne pepper in a large bowl. Add the buttermilk, ½ cup water, and salt, and stir until combined. Let stand 5 minutes.

2. Fold the popped corn kernels into the cornmeal mixture, and let stand 5 minutes.

3. Heat the oil in a skillet over medium. Spoon the batter by 2 tablespoonfuls into the hot oil, and fry, in batches, until golden brown, about 2 minutes per side. Drain on a plate lined with paper towels.

4. Top the hoecakes with butter, and drizzle with maple syrup, if desired. Serve hot.

To Drink: Chardonnay, Shiraz, amber beers, IPAs, hard ciders, stouts
Serve with: As a side to soup or main dishes; croutons for salad

CORN

Cush-cush

Of the four types of cornbread here, the origin of cush-cush is most closely tied to Africa. While basic cornbread is seasoned with just salt or sugar, cush-cush is often accented with spices such as nutmeg or cayenne. Serve it for breakfast with sorghum or cane syrup, or as a savory side with other corn dishes, poultry, or pork. Cush-cush can stand in for rice in seafood dishes like gumbo too.

Serves 8

1 ½ cups (12 ounces) water

2 teaspoons kosher salt

2 cups (about 8 ½ ounces) plain yellow cornmeal

¼ teaspoon baking powder

¼ teaspoon ground nutmeg

¼ teaspoon cayenne pepper

1 tablespoon popcorn kernels, popped

2 tablespoons vegetable oil

1 ounce (2 tablespoons) unsalted butter, softened

Buttermilk

Molasses

1. Preheat the broiler with the oven rack 6 to 8 inches from the heat. Bring 1 ½ cups water and the salt to a boil in a saucepan over medium-high.

2. Combine the cornmeal, baking powder, nutmeg, and cayenne pepper in a heatproof bowl. Add the boiling salted water, and stir until combined. Let stand 5 minutes.

3. Fold the popped corn kernels into the cornmeal mixture. Let stand 5 minutes.

4. Heat oil in a 12-inch cast-iron skillet over medium. Spoon the batter into the hot oil, and spread into a ½-inch-thick circle. Fry until golden brown, about 8 minutes.

5. Transfer the skillet to the preheated oven, and broil until the bread is golden brown, about 8 minutes.

6. Turn out the cush-cush onto a serving dish. Spread with the butter. Let stand 5 minutes. Break into pieces and serve cush-cush in a bowl with the buttermilk and molasses.

To Drink: Prosecco, Chardonnay, amber beers, stouts, chai tea, coffee, cognac

Serve with: Bacon, ice cream, nuts, dried fruit

Stone-Ground Grits

I love how square butter pats turn into a melted pool in hot grits. It gives the grits the creaminess that the corn lost in dehydration. Black pepper is a key to a delicious bowl of grits. It heightens aroma, which transports both the scent of the pepper and the deeper corn essence with each flavorful bite. Cheese brings it all together and helps bond the butter to the grits.

Serves 4 as a side dish

8 cups (64 ounces) water
1 tablespoon kosher salt
2 cups uncooked stone-ground grits
4 ounces aged Cheddar cheese, shredded
  (about 1 cup)

½ cup heavy cream
1 ½ ounces (3 tablespoons) unsalted butter
½ teaspoon coarsely ground black pepper

Bring the water and salt to a boil in a medium stockpot over medium. Add the grits, and stir with a wooden spoon or high-temperature spatula to ensure the grits don't stick to the bottom of the pot. Cover, reduce heat to medium-low, and simmer, stirring occasionally, 30 minutes. Uncover and cook, stirring often, until very thick, about 15 minutes. Remove from the heat, and let stand 5 minutes. Fold in the cheese, cream, butter, and pepper. Let stand 5 minutes before serving.

Note: This dish can be served at any meal. Don't limit it to breakfast.

Grits Croutons

Leftover grits solidify in the pot as they cool and usually get discarded as a round sphere of misfortune. Reheating isn't ideal. Adding water creates a soggy, flavorless mess. Instead, cut cold grits into squares, fry them, and enjoy.

Makes about 50 croutons

Stone-Ground Grits (recipe above), chilled
  until firm
¼ cup (2 ounces) blended olive oil
1 cup (about 4 ¼ ounces) plain
  yellow cornmeal

1 teaspoon kosher salt
1 teaspoon coarsely ground black pepper
1 teaspoon granulated onion

1. Cut the grits into 1-inch squares. Heat the oil in a sauté pan over medium.
2. Combine the cornmeal, salt, pepper, and granulated onion in a shallow dish. Dredge the cubes in the cornmeal mixture. Fry the cubes, in batches, in the hot oil until crispy on all sides, 6 to 8 minutes. (If the grits are very cold, frying will take 8 to 10 minutes.) Drain the croutons on a plate lined with paper towels.

Stone-Ground Grits Soufflés

When you bake grits they tend to transform back into the savory taste of the corn kernel. Eggs bind the deep corn flavors with the flavor of cream. Baking also allows for the cheese to form a crunchy textural crust. Though whipping egg whites and folding them into a grits dish may seem complicated, the act of cooking is really about losing yourself in the process and showing people how much you love them.

Serves 6

2 ⅔ cups (about 21 ounces) water

1 ½ teaspoons kosher salt

⅔ cup uncooked stone-ground grits

2 large egg whites

1 teaspoon granulated sugar

4 ounces aged Cheddar cheese, shredded (about 1 cup)

3 tablespoons unsalted butter, plus more for greasing ramekins

¾ teaspoon coarsely ground black pepper

1. Preheat the oven to 400°F. Bring 2 ⅔ cups water and the salt to a boil in a large saucepan over medium. Whisk in the grits, making sure they do not stick to the bottom of pan. Cover, reduce heat to medium-low, and simmer, stirring often with a wooden spoon or high-temperature spatula, 30 minutes. Remove from the heat, and let stand 5 minutes.

2. Grease 6 (6-ounce) ramekins with butter. Whisk together egg whites and sugar until stiff peaks form. Gently fold the whipped egg white mixture, cheese, butter, and pepper into the grits. Pour the grits mixture evenly into the ramekins. Place the ramekins on a baking sheet. Bake in preheated oven until grits rise slightly and become firm, 10 to 15 minutes.

To Drink: White Burgundy, blanc de blancs Champagne, NV Grand Cru Champagne, Gamay, Grenache, rosé, vintage sparkling rosé, unoaked Sauvignon Blanc, sherry, amber beers, light beers, hard ciders

Serve with: Braised greens, fish or smoked dishes, green salads and slaws, breakfast items

Cornmeal Butter Crackers
(page 160)

Tomato Jam
(page 183)

Chicken Liver Mousse
with Chorizo Butter
(page 161)

Cornmeal Butter Crackers with Chicken Liver Mousse, Chorizo Butter, and Tomato Jam

Fat is essential in baking. With fat as a catalyst, baking develops the fragrant caramelization of spices, salts, and sugar. The aroma of these crackers makes your mouth water and the Chicken Liver Mousse satisfies. It is the lighter side of pâté and cooler side of fried livers. It pairs well with other creamy fats such as butter or pork. Chorizo adds spice to the dish that tempers the mineral tang of chicken liver.

Serves 16 as an appetizer

1 cup (about 5 ¾ ounces) plain white
   cornmeal
¾ cup (6 ounces) warm water
3 tablespoons Chorizo Butter, softened
   (recipe follows)
1 ounce aged Cheddar cheese, shredded
   (about ¼ cup)
1 ½ teaspoons kosher salt

1 teaspoon chopped fresh thyme
1 ¼ cups (about 5 ⅜ ounces) all-purpose flour
1 teaspoon unsweetened cocoa
1 teaspoon coarse sea salt
Chicken Liver Mousse with Chorizo Butter
   (recipe follows)
Tomato Jam (page 183)

1. Combine the cornmeal, ¾ cup water, Chorizo Butter, cheese, salt, thyme, and 1 cup of the flour in the bowl of a food processor; pulse just until combined, about 10 times. Transfer the mixture to a bowl; cover and refrigerate until slightly firm, 1 to 2 hours.

2. Preheat the oven to 375°F. Sprinkle 2 tablespoons of the flour on a work surface. Roll the dough ⅛ inch thick; dust with the remaining 2 tablespoons flour. Sprinkle the dough with the cocoa and sea salt and lightly roll into the dough. Cut the dough into 2-inch squares with a pastry cutter and arrange 1 inch apart on greased baking sheets.

3. Bake in the preheated oven until golden brown, 20 to 22 minutes. Immediately transfer crackers from the baking sheets to a wire rack. Cool completely before serving with Chicken Liver Mousse with Chorizo Butter and Tomato Jam.

To Drink: Nonvintage brut rosé Champagne, amber beers, hard ciders
Serve with: Braised greens; quiches; beans and field peas; tomato, grits, or pork dishes; avocado; buttermilk dressing

chicken liver mousse with chorizo butter

Serves 8 to 10 as an appetizer

1 pound chicken livers

2 cups (16 ounces) whole buttermilk (or 1 cup regular buttermilk and 1 cup heavy cream)

2 teaspoons blended olive oil

2 garlic cloves, thinly sliced

1 thyme sprig

1 cup (8 ounces) apple cider

¼ cup (2 ounces) apple cider vinegar

¼ cup (2 ounces) bourbon

1 pound (2 cups) unsalted butter, softened

1 teaspoon kosher salt

1 teaspoon coarsely ground black pepper

Chorizo Butter (recipe follows)

1. Combine the chicken livers and buttermilk in a large bowl and refrigerate for 2 hours.

2. Heat the oil in a skillet over medium; add the garlic. Cook, stirring often, until lightly browned, about 1 minute. Remove the livers from the buttermilk, and drain on paper towels. Discard the buttermilk. Add the livers and thyme sprig to the pan, and cook, stirring constantly, until firm, about 5 minutes. Remove the livers from the pan, and drain on clean paper towels. Let the livers cool about 15 minutes.

3. Remove the pan from the heat. Add the apple cider, cider vinegar, and bourbon. Return the pan to medium; cook until reduced by two-thirds (to about ½ cup), about 10 minutes. Remove from heat; let stand 5 minutes. Remove and discard the thyme sprig.

4. Process the livers and butter in a food processor until smooth, about 1 minute. Add the reduced cider mixture, salt, and pepper to the puree, and process 30 seconds. Season with salt and pepper to taste.

5. Spread about 1 tablespoon of the Chorizo Butter on the bottom and sides of an 8-inch round baking dish (about 1½ inches deep). Spoon the mousse in the prepared dish, up to ¼ inch of the top. Cover and refrigerate until firm, about 8 hours.

6. Spread about ⅓ cup Chorizo Butter on top of the pâté, and reserve the remaining Chorizo Butter for serving with the Cornmeal Butter Crackers. Refrigerate until set, about 30 minutes. Let stand at room temperature 30 minutes before serving.

chorizo butter

1 ounce dry-cured Spanish chorizo, cut into ¼-inch slices

1 teaspoon blended olive oil

8 ounces (1 cup) unsalted butter, softened

½ teaspoon kosher salt

1. Place the chorizo in the bowl of a food processor, and pulse until finely chopped, about 6 times. (Or finely chop by hand.)

2. Heat a small sauté pan or skillet over medium. Add the oil and chorizo, and cook, stirring often, until the chorizo is reduced in size by about half, 4 to 5 minutes, reducing the heat if necessary to prevent burning. Transfer the chorizo and drippings to a bowl. Cool 10 minutes. Add the butter and salt, and combine. Makes about 1 cup

Corn Maque Choux

Maque choux is a Creole staple. It is served as an appetizer, entrée, or side dish. Adding crawfish is a tribute to maque choux's southern Louisiana heritage. Paying homage to a recipe's origin is a fundamental part of Soul cooking. It allows you to appreciate and savor a dish's history as you re-create it.

Serves 4 as an entrée or 8 as an appetizer

4 ears fresh corn (with husks)

¼ cup (2 ounces) blended olive oil

1 cup (8 ounces) water

1 cup (8 ounces) chicken stock

¼ cup (2 ounces) dry white wine

2 garlic cloves

1 thyme sprig

¼ teaspoon black peppercorns

2 teaspoons kosher salt

1 cup (8 ounces) heavy cream, at room temperature

2 red bell peppers, diced

1 red onion, diced

2 jalapeño chiles, seeded and diced

1 celery stalk, peeled and diced

¼ teaspoon dried oregano

¼ teaspoon paprika

⅛ teaspoon cayenne pepper

1 pound peeled cooked crawfish tails, thawed if frozen

1 bunch fresh flat-leaf parsley, stemmed and coarsely chopped

½ ounce (1 tablespoon) cold unsalted butter

1. Rinse the corn with cold water; pat dry. Shuck the corn, reserving the husks. Cut corn kernels from the cobs. Reserve both the kernels and the cobs.

2. Heat 2 tablespoons of the oil in a stockpot over medium-high. Add the corn cobs. Cook, stirring occasionally, until cobs are caramelized on all sides. Add the corn husks, 1 cup water, stock, wine, garlic, thyme, peppercorns, and ½ teaspoon of the salt. Bring to a simmer, and cook 20 minutes.

3. Stir in heavy cream, and simmer 10 minutes. Pour the mixture through a fine wire-mesh strainer into a large bowl, and discard the solids. Set the liquid aside.

4. Heat the remaining 2 tablespoons oil in a sauté pan or skillet over medium. Add the corn kernels, bell peppers, onion, jalapeños, celery, oregano, paprika, and cayenne. Cook, stirring often, until the corn is cooked through but not mushy, 8 to 10 minutes.

5. Add the corn mixture to the corn liquid, and stir to combine. Fold in the crawfish tails, parsley, butter, and remaining 1½ teaspoons salt.

Note: Serve with Curried Lamb Ribs with Crawfish Butter-Boiled Potatoes (page 114).

To Drink: White Burgundy, NV Grand Cru Champagne, Chardonnay, amber beers, light beers, hard ciders, IPAs

Serve with: Green salads; braised or roasted vegetable dishes

As with so many New World ingredients, corn was incorporated into Soul cooking in ways that replicated the comforting, familiar dishes of Africa. Corn cakes resembled fried yucca and fermented corn whiskey evoked memories of honey wine. When you look closely, you can't help but find parallels. The season in which an ingredient grew also informed how it was cooked and eaten. Crops that were harvested at the same time were often served or cooked together. Think about how well matched a staple crop like corn is with another summer favorite—tomatoes—in salads or soups. Add crisp cucumber to the salad or sliced okra to the stew and the summer flavors just keep giving. Corn was eaten fresh all summer and also dried to preserve it for the leaner times of the cool season. Much of the dried corn was ground for cornmeal and cereal grain to be used year-round. Grits were the inland substitute for the rice that was a key part of West African slaves' native diets. In turn, grits became the foundation of much of Soul and Southern cooking.

Popcorn-Crusted Scallops on Corn Porridge with Pickled Baby Corn and Beet Salad

Growing up near the famous 95th Street Pier in Chicago, we lived off boxes of fried scallops during summer when they were on the market menu. Sauces were on offer, but I liked the scallops by themselves at first...until I figured out that tartar sauce cooled them down quickly. When I peered into an empty box, crunchies that tasted just like buttered popcorn remained. That's the inspiration for this dish.

A popcorn crust reveals the nutty flavors of roasted corn while the scallop is the buttery vehicle. Corn Porridge is a beautiful base that can be eaten any time of day, taken in a savory direction with ingredients like scallops or bacon, or a sweet one with a touch of honey or cane syrup. Thyme is an essential part of either approach; it contributes a floral aroma that complements the corn. Pickled Baby Corn adds a bright note that brings it all together.

Serves 2 as an entrée and 4 as an appetizer

5 tablespoons (2 ½ ounces) blended olive oil

1 tablespoon popcorn kernels

1 teaspoon sorghum kernels

8 (U10) sea scallops (about 1 ½ ounces each)

½ teaspoon kosher salt

¼ teaspoon coarsely ground black pepper

Corn Porridge (page 167)

Pickled Baby Corn (page 166)

Beet Salad (page 319)

1. Heat a saucepan over medium-high. Add 1 teaspoon of the oil, and heat until hot. Add the popcorn kernels. Cover, and cook until all the kernels are popped. Set aside.

2. Add 1 teaspoon of the oil to the pan. Heat until hot. Add the sorghum kernels and cover. Cook until most of the kernels are popped. Discard unpopped kernels.

3. Transfer the popped popcorn to a food processor. Process until coarsely ground. Combine the ground popcorn and popped sorghum in a bowl, and set aside.

4. Heat a sauté pan or skillet over medium-high. Coat the scallops in 2 tablespoons of the oil, and sprinkle with salt and pepper. Dredge the scallops in the popcorn mixture, and toss to coat. Add the remaining oil to the pan, and heat until hot. Sear the scallops until golden brown, 2 to 3 minutes per side. (Do not overcrowd the pan.) Drain on a plate lined with paper towels.

5. Place 2 tablespoons of the Corn Porridge on the center of each plate. Top with scallops and serve with Pickled Baby Corn and Beet Salad.

Note: Sorghum kernels are available from Bob's Red Mill; or replace the sorghum kernels with additional popcorn. Popcorn provides a textural element to the scallops while maintaining their delicate nature. The dish can be made without the popcorn, but the flavors won't be as exciting.

To Drink: White Burgundy, NV Grand Cru Champagne, Chardonnay, amber beers, light beers, hard ciders, IPAs

Serve with: Green salads; vegetable, curry, or fried dishes

Pickled Baby Corn

Makes about 2 cups

4 cups (32 ounces) Pickle Brine (page 354)   1 teaspoon kosher salt
16 ears fresh baby corn (with husks)

1. Bring all of the ingredients to a boil in a saucepan over medium-high. Reduce heat to medium-low, and simmer 15 minutes.

2. Remove from heat, and let stand 10 minutes.

3. Remove the corn from the brine, reserving the liquid in the pan. Let the corn stand 1 hour.

4. Remove and discard the husks from the corn. Place the corn in a sterilized glass jar. Pour the brine through a fine wire-mesh strainer into the jar until the corn is completely covered. Discard remaining liquid. Cover and refrigerate at least 1 hour before serving. Store in the refrigerator up to 1 month.

Note: Find baby corn in season at your local farmers' market. Or, you can buy canned baby corn, rinse it, and use it in place of the baby corn ears.

Corn Porridge

Serves 2 as an entrée or 4 as an appetizer

4 ears fresh corn (with husks)

¼ cup (2 ounces) blended olive oil

1 cup (8 ounces) water

1 cup (8 ounces) chicken stock

¼ cup (2 ounces) dry white wine

¼ teaspoon black peppercorns

2 garlic cloves

1 thyme sprig

1 teaspoon kosher salt

2 cups (16 ounces) heavy cream, at room temperature

½ ounce (1 tablespoon) unsalted butter

¼ teaspoon freshly ground black pepper

⅛ teaspoon cayenne pepper

1. Rinse the corn with cold water; pat dry. Shuck the corn, reserving husks from 2 ears. Cut the corn kernels from the cobs. Reserve both the kernels and the cobs.

2. Heat 2 tablespoons of the oil in a stockpot over medium-high. Add the corn cobs. Cook, stirring occasionally, until cobs are caramelized on all sides. Add the corn husks, 1 cup water, stock, wine, peppercorns, garlic, thyme, and ½ teaspoon of the salt. Bring to a simmer, and cook 20 minutes.

3. Stir in the heavy cream, and simmer 10 minutes. Pour the mixture through a fine wire-mesh strainer into a bowl, and discard the solids. Set aside the liquid.

4. Heat the remaining 2 tablespoons oil in a sauté pan over medium. Add the corn kernels, and cook, stirring often, until corn is cooked through but not mushy, 8 to 10 minutes. Add the corn to corn liquid.

5. Transfer the corn mixture to a blender or food processor, and process until smooth. Add the butter, black pepper, cayenne pepper, and remaining ½ teaspoon salt. Process until combined. Serve warm.

TOMATOES

Native to Central and South America, tomatoes made it to Africa via the slave trade. African cooks used tomatoes for the body and flavor they lent to braised and boldly spiced stews. Tomatoes were enlisted similarly in Soul cuisine, providing a bright base for herbs and aromatics such as onions and garlic and a brothy backdrop for Lowcountry rice dishes like pirlau. Fresh tomatoes tossed with chunks of watermelon or cucumber refresh the palate when paired with fatty meats such as pulled pork or barbecued ribs, while the versatile green tomato adds zing to pickled condiments such as chowchow. Fried green tomatoes have become synonymous with Southern food, but the reality is that Jews immigrating to the States brought that dish with them. Like so many dishes, the recipe was simply co-opted by Soul and Southern cooks who have introduced countless creative spins. I have a thing for bruised, battered, ugly tomatoes and the sweet, juicy essence they impart in my cooking—from eggs baked in tomato sauce to sweet-tart tomato jam. Never scoff at imperfection.

Heirloom Tomato Salad

A great dish is about taking what you have and elevating it to something soulful, prompting everyone to ask, "What's in this?" Lavender has mint- and basil-like qualities but also adds a flavor note most identified with France. If we dismiss the French influence on Soul cuisine, we might as well ignore New Orleans.

Serves 4

2 Brandywine, Black Krim, or other heirloom tomatoes (about 1 ½ pounds)

4 Green Zebra, Cherokee Purple, or other heirloom tomatoes (about 1 pound)

¼ cup (2 ounces) Herb Vinaigrette (recipe follows)

12 dried culinary lavender flowers

8 pea tendrils or baby arugula leaves

¼ teaspoon sea salt

¼ teaspoon freshly ground black pepper

1. Cut the large tomatoes into ¼-inch-thick slices. (Reserve ends for another use, such as making tomato sauce.) Cut the small tomatoes into quarters. Arrange 2 to 4 tomato slices on each of 4 plates. Drizzle with 2 tablespoons of the Herb Vinaigrette.

2. Press the lavender flowers with the edge of a knife until they split. Sprinkle the tomato slices with some of the lavender. Top each salad with 4 to 6 tomato wedges. Drizzle with the remaining vinaigrette. Sprinkle evenly with more lavender.

3. Top the salads with pea tendrils, and sprinkle evenly with the salt and pepper.

To Drink: Barbera, sparkling Lambrusco, rosé, Sancerre, Sauvignon Blanc
Serve with: Fish, pickled fish, shellfish; smoked meats and poultry; grilled meats and poultry; breads; other seasonal vegetables

herb vinaigrette

½ cup (4 ounces) avocado oil or vegetable oil

1 shallot, halved lengthwise

6 tablespoons (3 ounces) aged red wine vinegar

2 tablespoons Dijon mustard

1 tablespoon fresh lemon juice (from 1 lemon)

1 teaspoon wildflower honey

½ teaspoon fresh thyme leaves

¼ teaspoon kosher salt

¼ cup finely chopped fresh flat-leaf parsley

Heat ¼ cup of the oil in a saucepan over medium. Add the shallot. Brown 2 minutes on each side. Remove from the heat. Stir in vinegar. Cover, place over low heat, and cook until the shallot is tender, about 3 minutes. Transfer mixture to a blender. Add the mustard, lemon juice, honey, thyme, and salt. Process on low speed 2 minutes until smooth. Remove center of the blender lid. With blender on low speed, slowly add the remaining ¼ cup oil through the center of the blender lid and process until emulsified. Stir in the parsley. Refrigerate at least 30 minutes before serving. Makes about 3 cups

⊰ BRUNCH ⊱

A Soul brunch is never formal or stuffy. It is often a boisterous gathering after church or a morning spent sleeping in after a late night out. It's the sort of meal that exemplifies the Soul table because it is a fun occasion full of storytelling and laughter. The dishes paired here offer a pleasing balance of flavors and textures. To match the casualness of the occasion, serve this meal family-style and pass platters at the table.

Bacon, Collard, and Fried Egg
Sandwich (page 26)

Heirloom Tomato Salad (page 170)

Oysters and Cucumber Mignonette
(page 207)

Strawberries with Champagne Aspic,
Whipped Cream, and Honey
(page 76)

ON THE RADIO

"Don't Know Why" — *Norah Jones*
"Spread Love" — *Al Hudson and the Soul Partners*
"Feeling Good" — *Nina Simone*
"Cherchez La Femme" — *Dr. Buzzard's Original Savannah Band*

TOMATOES

Bacon, Collard, and
Fried Egg Sandwich
(page 26)

Oysters and
Cucumber
Mignonette
(page 207)

Strawberries with
Champagne Aspic,
Whipped Cream, and
Honey (page 76)

Heirloom Tomato
Salad (page 170)

Cucumber-Tomato Salad

Water-loving plants like tomatoes and cucumbers are naturally a great match. On their own tomatoes have a captivating flavor. They are both sweet and acidic and require salinity for balance. When paired with other water-loving plants, like cucumbers, their natural juices come alive, providing a textured crunch and spark of freshness bite after bite. Both ingredients are dependent on the soil and how it is tended. Loose soil won't hold the roots and stems in place. Firmly packed soil keeps water from percolating down to reach the roots, leaving the plant parched. As in cooking, a happy balance is key.

This dish is my lifeblood. To be exact, it is not mine but my father's. If every dish in my repertoire could be made with four or five ingredients I would be perfectly content to let those ingredients shine. Dad often reminds me to know who I am and stay humble, and there's a quiet humility in the simplicity of this dish.

Serves 4 as a side or 2 as an entrée

2 heirloom cucumbers or small cucumbers (about 1 pound)

2 large Brandywine, Black Krim, or other heirloom tomatoes (about 1 ½ pounds)

1 small Green Zebra, Cherokee Purple, or other heirloom tomatoes (about 3 ounces)

3 tablespoons red wine vinegar

1 teaspoon sea salt

¼ teaspoon freshly ground black pepper

1. Peel ½-inch-wide long strips every ¼ inch on the cucumbers. Cut the cucumbers into ¼-inch-thick slices.

2. Remove stem ends from the tomatoes and reserve for another use. Cut the tomatoes into ¼-inch-thick slices.

3. Arrange the tomatoes and cucumbers alternately in a shallow dish. Drizzle with the red wine vinegar, and sprinkle with the sea salt and black pepper.

4. Let stand at room temperature for at least 30 minutes before serving.

Note: In making this dish throughout the summer, there are many other water-loving vegetables that can be added such as shaved fennel or radishes.

To Drink: Barbera, sparkling Lambrusco, rosé

Serve with: Fish; shellfish; smoked meats and poultry; grilled meats and poultry; lamb; breads; crackers; other seasonal vegetables

Fried Green Tomatillos with Ancho Chile BBQ sauce

If it wasn't for my mother's love of tacos, I wouldn't have been exposed to Mexican food at an early age. Though we lived on the east side of Chicago, I didn't venture to the "far" East Side until my late teens. That's when I discovered the mole sauce I put on everything: ribs, chicken, fried catfish, and even fried green tomatoes. Once Dad got me a car, I would drive to the "far" East Side to pick up tacos and then head to the Queen of the Sea buffet for sweet potatoes, turkey, and fried green tomatoes. As odd as it sounds, something about that combination was special.

I started making Ancho Chile BBQ Sauce early in my career. Anchos provide a depth of smokiness similar to Dad's barbecue sauce that really works here.

Serves 4 as an appetizer

1 ½ cups (12 ounces) whole buttermilk

¼ cup (2 ounces) Worcestershire sauce

2 tablespoons hot sauce

1 teaspoon freshly ground black pepper

3 teaspoons kosher salt

6 large tomatillos, husks removed and cut into ½-inch slices

1 cup (about 4 ¼ ounces) stone-ground yellow cornmeal

½ cup (about 2 ounces) whole-wheat flour

½ cup (2 ounces) masa harina (corn flour)

1 tablespoon granulated onion

1 ½ teaspoons granulated garlic

¼ teaspoon paprika

½ cup (4 ounces) corn oil

Ancho Chile BBQ Sauce (page 180)

1. Whisk together the buttermilk, Worcestershire sauce, hot sauce, black pepper, and 1 ½ teaspoons of the salt in a medium bowl. Add the tomatillo slices to the buttermilk mixture, 1 at a time, ensuring the slices are well coated. Let stand at room temperature 25 minutes before breading.

2. Stir together the cornmeal, flours, granulated onion, granulated garlic, paprika, and remaining 1 ½ teaspoons salt in a shallow dish. Remove the tomatillo slices from the marinade, 1 slice at a time, and dredge in the cornmeal mixture.

3. Heat the oil in a skillet over medium. Arrange the tomatillo slices in the skillet, leaving at least ¼ inch between slices. Fry, in batches, 2 to 3 minutes per side or until golden brown. Drain on a plate lined with paper towels. Serve hot with the Ancho Chile BBQ Sauce.

Note: This dish can accompany many types of dishes. It pairs well with smoked ribs as well as most onion dishes.

To Drink: White Burgundy, Grenache, prosecco, dry Riesling, Sauvignon Blanc, amber beers, mezcal cocktails

Serve with: Braised greens; beans and field peas; tomato, grits, pork dishes; avocado; buttermilk dressing

ancho chile BBQ sauce

2 teaspoons blended olive oil

¼ teaspoon cumin seeds

2 medium-size yellow onions, diced

2 dried ancho chiles, rehydrated in hot water, stemmed and seeded

1 poblano chile, stemmed and cut into ½-inch pieces

1 jalapeño chile, stemmed and halved lengthwise

4 garlic cloves, crushed

½ cup (4 ounces) whiskey

½ cup tomato paste

¼ cup (2 ounces) apple cider vinegar

¼ cup (2 ounces) Worcestershire sauce

2 tablespoons sorghum syrup or dark molasses

1 tablespoon raw sugar

1 teaspoon kosher salt

1. Heat the oil in a medium saucepan over medium. Add the cumin seeds, and cook, stirring constantly to avoid burning, 1 minute. Add the onions, ancho chiles, poblano, jalapeño, and garlic; cook, stirring occasionally, 7 minutes. Remove from heat.

2. Stir in the whiskey, tomato paste, vinegar, Worcestershire sauce, syrup, sugar, and salt. Return the pan to medium, and simmer until the vegetables are tender, 5 to 7 minutes. Remove from the heat, and let stand 10 minutes.

3. Process the mixture with an immersion blender or standard blender until smooth. (If using a standard blender, remove the center of the blender lid to allow steam to escape and to prevent overflowing.) For a thinner sauce, pour the mixture through a fine wire-mesh strainer, and discard the solids. Store sauce in an airtight container in the refrigerator up to 1 month. Makes about 1 cup

We often look for perfection in tomatoes, searching for those of a similar size, round and firm, hoping that an unblemished facade somehow guarantees ripe perfection and streams of juicy tomato nectar. In seeking uniformity, we fail to appreciate the unique wonders of imperfection. Aiming to make each snowflake the same is futile, so why do we attempt it with ingredients? There is romance in bruised-and-battered tomatoes. They have a story to tell. A tomato that grows pressed up against the vine may be misshapen, but its nooks and crannies give it character that does nothing to diminish flavor. Yet people disregard it. Diversity, wherever it exists, should be exalted. One bite of that misshapen tomato with a bit of salt, pepper, and a splash of vinegar and I have no doubt you'll agree.

Tomato Aspic

Aspic concentrates flavors into one bite. The flavors are bound by gelatin, providing a smooth texture that melts across the tongue and spreads the taste of the aspic evenly. Aspic is a surprising component of my spin on a fish taco: Broiled Lake Perch and Tomato Aspic in Lettuce Wraps (page 134).

Serves 4

10 ½ cups (84 ounces) water

3 ½ tablespoons kosher salt

3 large beefsteak tomatoes (about 1 ⅔ pounds)

2 teaspoons blended olive oil

½ cup diced yellow onion (about 2 ounces)

1 celery stalk, diced (about 1 ½ ounces)

1 cup (8 ounces) Madeira

1 tablespoon hot sauce

1 tablespoon Worcestershire sauce

2 (¼-ounce) envelopes unflavored gelatin

1 radish, diced (about 1 ounce)

½ tablespoon lemon zest (from 1 lemon)

½ tablespoon chopped fresh mint

½ tablespoon chopped fresh oregano

1 teaspoon coarsely ground black pepper

1. Combine ice and water in a large bowl.

2. Bring 10 cups water and 3 tablespoons of the salt to a boil in a large stockpot over high.

3. Cut an X on the bottom of each tomato. Cook tomatoes in the boiling water until the skin starts to split and separate, 30 to 60 seconds. Transfer the tomatoes to the ice bath. Let stand until cold, 2 minutes. Remove from the ice bath, and peel away the skin. (Reserve the tomato skins for another use.) Cut the tomatoes into ½-inch pieces, and set aside.

4. Heat the oil in a large saucepan over medium. Add the diced onion and celery. Cook, stirring occasionally, until translucent, 4 to 5 minutes. Add the Madeira, hot sauce, Worcestershire sauce, and half of the tomatoes to the pan. Bring to a simmer, and cook until the tomatoes are cooked down, about 10 minutes. Remove from heat.

5. Whisk together the gelatin and remaining ½ cup water in a bowl until gelatin dissolves. Whisk the gelatin mixture into the tomato mixture. Stir in the radish, lemon zest, and remaining tomatoes. Stir in the mint, oregano, pepper, and remaining salt.

6. Transfer the tomato aspic mixture to an 8-inch square baking dish, and refrigerate until set, at least 3 hours before serving. Refrigerate any leftover aspic. (Do not cover; covering with plastic wrap can distort the appearance.)

To Drink: Sauvignon Blanc, Pinot Gris, Chardonnay, rosé, Sangiovese, Barbera, Pinot Noir, amber beers, Bloody Mary

Serve with: Broiled Lake Perch in Lettuce Leaves (page 134)

Tomato Jam

Using tomatoes in jam is fascinating to me. Yes, they are technically a fruit but are used far more in savory preparations than in sweet ones. The addition of serrano or jalapeño chiles adds an intense heat that brightens the jam and cuts the richness of the tomato reduction. This jam can stand alone as a spread for bread or elevate rich dishes such as chicken livers.

Serves 16

2 teaspoons blended olive oil

1 ½ pounds plum tomatoes (about 7 tomatoes), cut into ½-inch pieces (about 4 cups)

2 garlic cloves, thinly sliced

1 medium-size yellow onion, chopped (about 1 ¼ cups)

1 jalapeño or serrano chile, stemmed and cut into ¼-inch pieces (about ¼ cup)

1 poblano chile, stemmed, seeded, and cut into ¼-inch pieces (about ½ cup)

1 cup raw sugar or packed light brown sugar

1 tablespoon aged red wine vinegar

1 tablespoon sherry vinegar

1 medium-size red bell pepper, diced (about 1 cup)

1 teaspoon kosher salt

1 teaspoon coarsely ground black pepper

¼ teaspoon ground coriander

1 ½ teaspoons chopped fresh mint

Cornmeal Butter Crackers (page 160) (optional)

Chicken Liver Mousse with Chorizo Butter (page 161) (optional)

Heat oil in a medium saucepan over medium. Add the tomatoes, garlic, onion, jalapeño, and poblano. Cook, stirring often, until tomatoes begin to soften, about 7 minutes. Add the sugar, red wine vinegar, sherry vinegar, bell pepper, salt, black pepper, and coriander. Simmer, stirring often, until the mixture is slightly thickened, 20 minutes. Fold the mint into the jam. Remove from the heat, and let stand 20 minutes before serving. Store the jam in an airtight container in the refrigerator for up to 1 month. Serve with Cornmeal Butter Crackers and Chicken Liver Mousse with Chorizo Butter, if desired.

Shrimp, Field Peas, and Andouille in Smoked Tomato Broth (page 186)

Shrimp, Field Peas, and Andouille in Smoked Tomato Broth

I love ugly tomatoes. Bumps and bruises give them character unlike their unblemished, anemic, hybridized-for-transport cousins. I look for ugly tomatoes at the farmers' market to make this dish. Bruised tomatoes give up their juices rapidly without losing their fragrance or subtle acidity. Ugly tomatoes, especially when smoked, deliver a smoky, distilled tomato essence that the most perfect tomato cannot.

Serves 6

8 ounces andouille sausage

1 leek, cut in half lengthwise

3 ½ tablespoons blended olive oil

1 tablespoon plus 1 ¼ teaspoons kosher salt

¾ teaspoon freshly ground black pepper

1 pound oak, pecan, or hickory wood chips, soaked in water for 30 minutes

8 partially soft medium tomatoes, halved

24 jumbo raw shrimp, peeled and deveined, shells reserved

1 cup (8 ounces) dry white wine

¼ cup (2 ounces) sherry vinegar

¼ teaspoon red pepper flakes

2 bay leaves

2 thyme sprigs

10 cups (80 ounces) water

1 cup fresh field peas (such as pink-eyed peas, lady peas, or black-eyed peas)

8 ounces baby salad greens (such as spinach, arugula, or watercress)

1 tablespoon toasted peanut oil or extra-virgin olive oil

1 lemon, halved and seeded

Freshly ground black pepper

1. Preheat a charcoal grill to medium-high (about 450°F). Place the sausage on the grill grate. Grill, uncovered, on 1 side until the skin starts to slightly blister, about 6 minutes. Turn the sausage over, and cook on the other side until slightly blistered, about 2 more minutes; remove from the grill. Cool 10 minutes, and cut the sausage into ¼-inch-thick slices. Reserve for finishing the dish.

2. Rub cut sides of the leek with 1 tablespoon of the olive oil. Sprinkle with ¼ teaspoon each of the salt and pepper. Place the leek halves, cut side down, on the grill grates. Grill 2 minutes on each side. Remove from the grill, and set aside.

3. Prepare the wood chips in the grill according to manufacturer's instructions. Place grate back on the grill. Rub the tomatoes with 1 tablespoon of the olive oil, and sprinkle with 1 teaspoon of the salt and ½ teaspoon of the pepper. Place the tomatoes, cut side down, on the grill grates over the wood chips. Grill, covered with the grill lid, until the tomatoes begin to release their juices, about 6 minutes. Remove from the grill.

4. Heat a large Dutch oven over medium. Cut the leeks into ⅛-inch-thick pieces. Add the remaining 1 ½ tablespoons olive oil to the Dutch oven. Add the shrimp shells, leeks, and tomatoes. Cook, stirring occasionally, until the tomatoes begin to break down, about 4 minutes.

5. Add the white wine and sherry vinegar. Cook, stirring occasionally, until the leeks are softened and shrimp shells are bright orange, about 6 minutes.

6. Add the red pepper flakes, bay leaves, thyme, and 2 cups of the water. Bring to a simmer, and remove from the heat, and let stand 10 minutes. Remove the bay leaves, and set aside. Remove and discard the shrimp shells and thyme sprigs with a slotted spoon. Process the tomato mixture with an immersion blender or standard blender until smooth. (If using a standard blender, remove the center of the blender lid to prevent overflowing.) Return tomato mixture to the Dutch oven.

7. Bring remaining 8 cups water to a boil in a large saucepan over high. Add the reserved bay leaves and remaining 1 tablespoon salt. Boil for 2 minutes. Reduce heat to medium; add the peas, and simmer until the peas are just tender, about 15 minutes. (Skim and discard any froth from the top.) Remove from the heat; let stand 5 minutes. Remove the peas from the Dutch oven with a slotted spoon, and spread on a baking sheet to cool. Reserve cooking liquid.

8. Bring the tomato broth to a simmer over medium-high. Stir ½ cup of the field pea cooking liquid into the tomato broth. At this point the broth may be used for other recipes like Sea Urchin with Smoked Tomato Broth and West African Spices (page 188) or cooled and refrigerated for later use.

9. Add the shrimp to the tomato broth in a single layer. Cover and simmer the shrimp 4 minutes. Uncover and turn the shrimp over. Place the grilled sausage and field peas on top of the shrimp. Remove the Dutch oven from the heat; cover and let stand 2 minutes.

10. To serve, top the servings with salad greens, peanut oil, a squeeze of fresh lemon juice, and freshly ground black pepper to taste.

To Drink: Barbera, sparkling Lambrusco, rosé, Sancerre, Sauvignon Blanc
Serve with: Fish, pickled fish, shellfish; smoked meats and poultry; grilled meats and poultry; breads; other seasonal vegetables

Sea Urchin with Smoked Tomato Broth and West African Spices

Most people would never consider sea urchins Soul food and are more likely to lump them with sushi. However, along the West Africa coast the simple grilling of fish, shellfish, and sea urchins is common. This may not be the most fashionable way to prepare it, but I find it to be one of the most delicious.

Serves 4 as an appetizer or 2 as an entrée

4 live medium sea urchins (about 5 ounces each)

1 tablespoon blended olive oil

1 teaspoon kosher salt

½ teaspoon smoked paprika

¼ teaspoon granulated sugar

¼ teaspoon ground thyme

⅛ teaspoon chili powder

⅛ teaspoon ground cumin

Pinch of red pepper flakes

2 cups Smoked Tomato Broth (page 186)

4 fresh okra pods

1 tablespoon sesame seeds

1 tablespoon roasted peanuts, coarsely chopped

1. Preheat a grill to medium-high (450°F).

2. Cut out the top of the sea urchin shells with scissors, and carefully pierce the bottom. Let drain. Carefully remove the membrane around the roe (uni), if necessary. Drizzle olive oil on the roe, and place the sea urchins, roe side up, on the grill grates. Grill, covered, until the roe begins to slightly pull away from the shell, about 10 minutes. Remove the sea urchins from the grill.

3. Combine the salt, paprika, sugar, thyme, chili powder, cumin, and red pepper flakes in a mixing bowl.

4. Sprinkle the spice mixture inside the sea urchin shells. Return the sea urchin shells to the grill, and grill, covered with the grill lid, for 5 minutes. Pour ½ cup of the tomato broth into each shell and grill, covered, 5 more minutes or until the liquid begins to simmer. Remove from the grill, and top each with an okra pod, sesame seeds, and roasted peanuts.

To Drink: Oaked Chardonnay, rosé, Sangiovese, Barbera, Pinot Noir, amber beers, stouts
Serve with: Grilled seafood; grilled meats; poultry or spicy dishes; green salads; cornbread; quick bread

Tomato Granita with Horseradish and Oysters

When ugly tomatoes are overripe, jelly-like, and virtually unsliceable, their unparalleled natural sweetness comes through full force. Horseradish is a great foil for overripe tomatoes and provides astringent notes to balance the salinity of oysters in this dish. Freezing the tomato curbs the tomato's sweetness. This is important because the oysters also bring an inherent sweetness to the mix.

Serves 4

3 large very ripe tomatoes
½ cup finely grated fresh horseradish root
   (from 1 [3-inch] piece)
1 tablespoon Worcestershire sauce
½ lemon
2 teaspoons blended olive oil
½ teaspoon kosher salt

½ teaspoon coarsely ground black pepper
24 small to medium oysters on the half shell
Freshly ground black pepper (optional)
Basil flowers or small fresh basil leaves
   (optional)
Lemon wedges

1. Cut the tomatoes in half, and squeeze the juice and seeds into a bowl; discard the squeezed tomato halves. Sprinkle the horseradish over the tomato juice, and add the Worcestershire sauce. Grate the zest from the lemon to equal ½ teaspoon and squeeze the juice to equal 1½ tablespoons. Stir both the zest and the juice into the tomato mixture. Stir in the oil, salt, and pepper. Let stand for 20 minutes.

2. Stir the mixture again, and transfer to a glass, metal, or other freezer-proof 2-quart baking dish. Freeze 4 hours, scraping the mixture with a fork every hour.

3. Remove the tomato granita from the freezer, and scrape again. Spoon 1 tablespoon of granita onto each oyster. Garnish with freshly ground black pepper and basil flowers or leaves, if desired. Serve with lemon wedges.

To Drink: Sauvignon Blanc, sparkling wine, Champagne, Chardonnay, rosé, Gamay, Cabernet Sauvignon, amber beers, IPAs, hard ciders, Bloody Mary

Serve with: Green salads; crackers; tomato, spicy, olive, or pickled dishes

Baked Eggs in Tomato Sauce

Before my mother married my dad, she did everything to further her education, even though it meant living paycheck to paycheck. Sometimes meals were lavish and other times they were improvised from the best of what we had. At times she would laugh at her creations. One night all we had was tomato sauce and scrambled eggs and she cobbled together what seems like a classic Italian dish. Really, it is my Soul food because at its root, like most of Soul cuisine, it was born from making the best of what we had.

Serves 4 as an entrée

2 tablespoons blended olive oil

½ pound chicken gizzards (about 8 gizzards)

2 chicken necks (about 4 ounces)

3 teaspoons kosher salt

1 teaspoon coarsely ground black pepper

2 small yellow onions, diced (about 2 cups)

1 medium-size red bell pepper, diced (about 1 cup)

1 cup (8 ounces) chicken stock

1 cup (8 ounces) dry white wine

4 bay leaves

½ teaspoon red pepper flakes

1 ½ pounds plum tomatoes, cut into ½-inch pieces (about 4 cups)

3 tablespoons tomato paste

⅛ teaspoon freshly grated whole nutmeg

4 duck eggs or extra-large chicken eggs

1. Heat oil in a large ovenproof skillet over medium. Sprinkle the chicken gizzards and necks with ½ teaspoon each of the salt and black pepper. Arrange in the skillet in a single layer, and cook until browned on 1 side, 6 to 8 minutes.

2. Stir in the onions and bell pepper. Cook, stirring often, until the onions begin to brown, 10 to 12 minutes. Remove from the heat, and stir in the stock and wine.

3. Return the skillet to medium, and bring the mixture to a simmer. Add the bay leaves and red pepper flakes. Cook, stirring, until the liquid is reduced by about half, about 10 minutes. Cover, reduce heat to low, and simmer until the gizzards are tender, about 45 minutes.

4. Remove and set aside the gizzards and necks; keep warm. Add the tomatoes to the skillet; stir to combine. Cook, stirring often, until the tomatoes are softened, about 10 minutes. Stir in the tomato paste, and simmer 5 minutes. Stir in the nutmeg, and the remaining 2 ½ teaspoons salt and ½ teaspoon black pepper. Remove from the heat, and let stand 10 minutes. Remove and discard the bay leaves.

5. Preheat the oven to 375°F. Return skillet to medium, and bring to a simmer. Make 4 wells in the tomato mixture; crack 1 egg into each well. Bake in the preheated oven until the egg whites are set, about 10 minutes. Let stand 2 minutes before serving. Serve with the reserved chicken gizzards and necks.

To Drink: Grenache, American rosé, sparkling Shiraz, amber beers, hard ciders

Serve with: Braised greens; beans and field peas; avocado; buttermilk dressing; tomato, grits, or pork dishes

Baked Eggs in Tomato Sauce
(recipe opposite)

Fish Market Scallops
with Lemon Aioli
(page 129)

MELONS

European colonists and slaves brought melons to the Americas, and they became a key ingredient in Soul cuisine from the very start. In Africa, melons primarily were used as a source of hydration or as a portable canteen. Over time they were hybridized to produce sweet fruit. Every part of the melon was utilized. The fruit was sliced and eaten out of hand, while the seeds were either planted right away or saved for a future crop. Melon seeds were collected, dried, and then ground into a flour to be used as the base for fritters. The rinds were eaten pickled or candied, and even enlisted as soles for shoes. At the same time that the watermelon became a symbol of freedom for emancipated slaves who grew and sold melons to earn a living, it also became an enduring racist trope. Early in my career, I realized that avoiding this fruit so deeply rooted in African-American culture and embedded in Soul cuisine would be giving in to that negative stereotype. Instead, I embrace and subvert the contradictions by showcasing melons as both the main attraction on a plate and as an accent for countless other dishes.

Watermelon Lemonade

Watermelon: It's the most refreshing part of the summer. It's such a versatile fruit—even the often-overlooked rind can be pickled (page 198). Watermelon loves acidity to balance out its sweetness, and this recipe uses lemon to balance the natural sugars in the melon. Stir the lemonade well before serving to distribute the pulp since it settles to the bottom upon sitting. If you can't find yellow watermelon, the pink kind will do.

Serves 4

4 cups water	½ cup granulated sugar
1 ½ teaspoons lemon zest, plus 3 tablespoons juice (from 1 lemon)	4 basil sprigs
	4 thyme sprigs
5 mint sprigs	2 cups (16 ounces) sparkling water
1 small yellow watermelon	4 lime wedges

1. Bring 4 cups water, lemon zest, and 1 mint sprig to a boil in a saucepan over medium. Reduce the heat to medium-low.

2. Meanwhile, peel the watermelon and remove the rind. Cut the watermelon flesh into large chunks. (Reserve the rind for Pickled Rind (page 198). Add the watermelon chunks and sugar to the water, and cook for 5 minutes. Stir in the lemon juice, and remove from the heat. Let stand for 5 minutes. Remove and discard the mint sprig.

3. Process the watermelon mixture with an immersion blender or regular blender until smooth. Refrigerate 1 hour before serving.

4. Make 4 herb bouquets by tying 1 sprig of mint, basil, and thyme together with kitchen string.

5. To serve, pour ½ cup of watermelon lemonade in each of 4 (8-ounce) glasses. Fill each glass three-fourths full with ice. Add 1 herb bouquet to each glass, and top with about ½ cup sparkling water. Garnish with lime wedges.

Note: The amount of watermelon juice can vary from watermelon to watermelon. When making lemonade, you may have to adjust the amount of water added. Take your time, and note the viscosity of the mixture as it is pureed.

Serve with: This is a seasonal beverage and can be served with any seasonal item spring, summer, and early fall.

Watermelon Salad, Pickled Rind, Fromage Blanc, and Toasted Peanuts

Pickled rind is a great way to counter the sweetness of watermelon. It gives soft texture and a crunchy bite to salads. Any leftover pickled rind can be used for sandwiches as well as eaten alone as a snack.

Serves 4

1 cup Pickle Brine (page 354)
1 (4- to 5-pound) Sugar Baby watermelon, green skin and rind removed and reserved
2 tablespoons blended olive oil
½ cup (about 2 ounces) blanched unsalted peanuts

1 thyme sprig
½ teaspoon kosher salt
4 ounces fromage blanc cheese
1 cup edible flowers or mint leaves

1. Bring the Pickle Brine to a boil in a saucepan over medium heat.

2. Coarsely chop the reserved watermelon rind to equal 2 cups. Add the chopped watermelon rind to the brine. Reduce the heat to medium-low, and simmer for 15 minutes. Remove from the heat, cover, and let stand for 1 hour. Divide the pickled rind evenly between 2 (8-ounce) glass jars. Cover rind with pickling liquid. Screw on the lids, and refrigerate until chilled, about 1 hour.

3. Heat the oil in a skillet over medium-low. Add the peanuts.

4. Cook the peanuts, stirring constantly, until toasted, 3 to 5 minutes. Add the thyme and salt, and continue to cook until the peanuts are golden brown. Remove from the heat, and transfer the peanut mixture to paper towels to cool.

5. Cut the watermelon into 8 pieces. Place 2 pieces onto each of 4 plates. Top each serving with 1 tablespoon of fromage blanc. Thinly slice 20 to 25 (1-inch) pieces of pickled rind. (There will be some leftover.) Place 5 to 6 pieces of rind on top of the fromage blanc on each plate.

6. Remove the thyme sprigs from the peanuts, and sprinkle the leaves on top of the salad. Chop the peanuts. Garnish each serving with peanuts and edible flowers or mint.

To Drink: White Burgundy, Chardonnay, rosé, sparkling rosé, sparkling Shiraz, amber beers, light beers, gin cocktails, vodka cocktails
Serve with: Roasted, grilled, or smoked poultry dishes; roasted and pickled vegetables; rice or grits dishes

Cantaloupe Soup with Chorizo Relish and Black Pepper-and-Honey Whipped Goat Cheese

Melon puree may be used as a sauce for meats, frozen for sorbet, or as in this case, enjoyed as a soup. Soups are a simple way to introduce uncommon flavors of a new cuisine. A bowlful offers the comfort of a familiar dish and inventive taste combinations simultaneously.

Serves 4 as an appetizer

2 teaspoons blended olive oil

1 medium shallot, diced (about ¼ cup)

½ cup (4 ounces) unfiltered apple cider

1 tablespoon apple cider vinegar

1 teaspoon kosher salt

⅛ teaspoon red pepper flakes

1 (4-pound) cantaloupe, peeled and cut into chunks (about 8 cups)

1 (8-ounce) cucumber, peeled, seeded, and cut into chunks (about 1 cup)

¼ cup (2 ounces) extra-virgin olive oil

Black Pepper-and-Honey Whipped Goat Cheese (page 202)

Chorizo Relish (page 202)

1. Heat the oil in a saucepan over medium. Add the shallot, and cook, stirring often, until the shallot is tender, about 5 minutes.

2. Add the apple cider, apple cider vinegar, salt, and red pepper flakes, and simmer until the liquid is reduced by half, about 10 minutes. Add the cantaloupe, and cook until the cantaloupe begins to soften, about 5 minutes. Remove from the heat.

3. Process the cantaloupe mixture, cucumber, and olive oil in a blender until smooth, 30 seconds. Refrigerate until thoroughly chilled, about 4 hours.

4. Serve the soup with the Black Pepper-and-Honey Whipped Goat Cheese and Chorizo Relish.

Note: Cantaloupes vary in sweetness. Honey may or may not be needed in the goat cheese. Taste the soup before adding the honey to the goat cheese.

To Drink: White Burgundy, Chardonnay, rosé, sparkling rosé, sparkling Shiraz, amber beers, light beers, gin cocktails, vodka cocktails

Serve with: Smoked poultry dishes, grilled pork meats, green or watercress salads

black pepper-and-honey whipped goat cheese

4 ounces goat cheese, softened

2 tablespoons honey

½ teaspoon coarsely ground black pepper

Pinch of ground cinnamon

Whisk together the goat cheese, honey, black pepper, and cinnamon in a bowl until the goat cheese mixture is light and airy. Makes about ½ cup

chorizo relish

1 tablespoon blended olive oil

4 ounces dry-cured Spanish
  chorizo, diced

2 shallots, diced (about ⅓ cup)

½ cup (4 ounces) sherry vinegar

4 hard-cooked eggs, peeled and diced

1. Heat the oil, diced chorizo, and shallots in a saucepan over medium. Cook, stirring constantly, until the chorizo begins to brown and has released some oil, about 2 minutes.

2. Add the vinegar, and cook, stirring often, until the chorizo is tender, about 15 minutes. Remove from the heat, and let stand 1 hour.

3. Fold the eggs into the relish, and refrigerate at least 1 hour. (The relish can be made 1 day ahead.) Makes 1½ cups

Even after 20 years of cooking professionally, putting watermelon on a menu felt taboo. Sure, it had appeared in the mix on fruit plates, buffet platters, and fruit skewers, but I never put forth a creative effort to make watermelon the focus of a plate until 2012.

Highlighting an ingredient that has long been a racist symbol made me recoil. I also feared being overlooked as a skilled chef to be reckoned with. My insecurity was rooted in the past and fertilized by the fact that none of my peers in the kitchen looked like me so I had no sounding board for my anxieties. On the one hand, I didn't want to let my people down by giving credence to a negative stereotype on the menu, while on the other hand I was frustrated to feel so inhibited from sharing my creative expression using an ingredient I enjoyed eating. Eventually, I decided to let my art be my guide and not the impression of others.

Oysters and
Cucumber
Mignonette
(page 207)

Cucumber-Tomato
Salad (page 176)

Buttered
Couscous
(page 141)

Grilled Sardines
(page 141)

Cucumber Salad

My dad makes the best cucumber salad. He prepares it about a day before serving. This recipe can be served immediately or up to even five days later. While most places sell seedless or European cucumbers these days, and they're fantastic, but traditional heavy-skinned cucumbers work best here because they can absorb the liquid for longer periods of time.

Serves 4

2 cucumbers

1 shallot, thinly sliced

¼ cup fresh basil leaves, very thinly sliced

¼ cup (2 ounces) red wine vinegar

2 tablespoons extra-virgin olive oil

¾ teaspoon kosher salt

½ teaspoon coarsely ground black pepper

Peel ½-inch-wide strips every ¼ inch on the cucumbers. Cut the cucumbers into ⅛-inch-thick slices. Toss together all the ingredients in a large bowl. Let the salad stand for a minimum of 15 minutes before serving.

To Drink: White Burgundy, Champagne, Chardonnay, Pinot Gris, Pinot Noir, rosé, sparkling rosé, sparkling Shiraz, amber beers, light beers, gin cocktails, vodka cocktails

Serve with: Bean, potato, tomato, or toast and bread dishes

Oysters and Cucumber Mignonette

Both cucumbers and oysters pair well with salty ingredients. They also benefit from good amounts of vinegar to bring out their natural sweetness. Cucumbers are a refreshing accompaniment when consuming a dozen or so oysters. The water that is absorbed by the cucumber salad is like a beautiful burst of seawater with each bite.

Serves 2

¾ cup peeled, seeded, and finely diced cucumber (from 1 cucumber)

1 shallot, finely diced (about 2 tablespoons)

¼ cup (2 ounces) Champagne vinegar

1 tablespoon red wine vinegar

1 tablespoon extra-virgin olive oil

1 teaspoon coarsely ground black pepper

14 medium-size oysters on the half shell

1 tablespoon thinly sliced chives

1. Whisk together the cucumber, shallot, Champagne vinegar, red wine vinegar, olive oil, and black pepper in a medium bowl. Refrigerate until thoroughly chilled, about 45 minutes.

2. Top each oyster with cucumber mignonette, and sprinkle evenly with chives.

Note: Oysters vary in size and brininess.

To Drink: White Burgundy, Champagne, Chardonnay, Pinot Gris, Pinot Noir, rosé, sparkling rosé, sparkling Shiraz, amber beers, light beers, gin cocktails, vodka cocktails

Serve with: Bean, potato, tomato, or toast and bread dishes

Cucumber Soup with
Sun-Dried Tomato Relish
(page 210)

Grits Croutons
(page 156)

Shrimp Hot Chicken-Style
(page 211)

Cucumber Soup with Sun-Dried Tomato Relish and Shrimp Hot Chicken-Style with Fried Grits

Cucumber and tomato seasons run parallel. Admittedly, using sun-dried tomatoes in the peak of tomato season seems odd, but sun-dried tomatoes provide concentrated flavor that balances the slight bitterness of the cucumbers.

This soup provides a cooling effect to spicy dishes, which is why I like to serve it with spicy shrimp. The sauce for the shrimp requires temperature adjustments while cooking, so take your time.

Serves 4

SOUP:

4 cucumbers (about 2 ½ pounds), peeled and seeded

½ cup chopped fresh flat-leaf parsley

2 tablespoons chopped fresh mint leaves

1 teaspoon aged red wine vinegar

½ teaspoon kosher salt

½ teaspoon freshly ground black pepper

8 chives

1 cup crème fraîche

SUN-DRIED TOMATO RELISH:

2 tablespoons olive oil

1 small yellow onion, minced (about 1 cup)

4 garlic cloves, thinly sliced (1 tablespoon)

4 ounces dry-packed sun-dried tomatoes, rehydrated in hot water and chopped (about ¼ cup)

¼ cup dry sherry

2 tablespoons (1 ounce) sherry vinegar

½ teaspoon kosher salt

½ teaspoon coarsely ground black pepper

¼ cup chopped fresh flat-leaf parsley

2 teaspoons chopped fresh oregano

1. Prepare the Soup: Process the cucumbers, parsley, mint, vinegar, salt, pepper, and chives in a blender until smooth, stopping to scrape down the sides. Transfer to a medium bowl. Add the crème fraîche, and whisk to combine. (Do not process in the blender.) Cover and refrigerate until chilled, about 1 hour.

2. Prepare the Relish: Heat the oil in a saucepan over low. Add the onion and garlic. Cook, stirring, until the onions are translucent, 8 minutes. (Don't let the garlic brown.)

3. Add the sun-dried tomatoes, sherry, sherry vinegar, salt, and pepper, and cook until liquid is reduced by three-fourths and relish is thickened, 6 to 8 minutes.

4. Remove the pan from the heat. Fold in the chopped parsley and oregano. Let stand 20 minutes before serving. Refrigerate in an airtight container for up to 7 days.

5. To serve, garnish the soup with Sun-Dried Tomato Relish and serve with Shrimp Hot Chicken-Style, if desired (recipe follows).

To Drink: Vinho Verde, Sauvignon Blanc, late harvest Champagne, Chardonnay, rosé, amber beers, IPAs, hard ciders, Bloody Mary

Serve with: Green or pea salads; crackers; bean dishes

shrimp hot chicken-style

2 tablespoons plus 4 teaspoons blended
   olive oil

1 small yellow onion, diced (about 1 cup)

¼ cup (2 ounces) dry white wine

2 cups (16 ounces) heavy cream

¼ cup (2 ounces) hot sauce (such as Tabasco)

1 tablespoon cayenne pepper

2 teaspoons lemon zest

1 teaspoon kosher salt

1 teaspoon chili powder

1 teaspoon granulated garlic

1 teaspoon paprika

½ teaspoon coarsely ground black pepper

¼ teaspoon fennel seeds

20 unpeeled colossal raw shrimp (about
   1 ½ pounds), deveined

1 ounce (2 tablespoons) salted butter

¼ cup chopped fresh flat-leaf parsley

Grits Croutons (page 156)

1. Heat 2 tablespoons of the oil and the onion in a medium saucepan over medium-high. Cook, stirring, until the onion softens, about 2 minutes.

2. Add the white wine, and cook until reduced by half, 1 to 2 minutes. Add the cream, hot sauce, cayenne, zest, salt, chili powder, granulated garlic, paprika, black pepper, and fennel seeds. Peel the shrimp, and remove the heads; add the shrimp shells and heads to the pan. Bring to a simmer, and cook until reduced by half (about 2 ½ cups), 10 to 15 minutes. Remove from the heat; remove and discard shrimp heads and shells.

3. Transfer the mixture to a blender. Remove the center of the blender lid to allow steam to escape and to prevent overflowing. Process until smooth, about 30 seconds. (Mixture should equal about 2 cups.)

4. Heat the remaining 4 teaspoons oil in a large skillet over medium-high. Arrange the shrimp in the skillet in a single layer, being careful not to crowd the pan. Sear on 1 side for 2 minutes. Turn and cover with the sauce. Cover, remove from the heat, and let stand until shrimp is cooked through, about 4 minutes. Stir in the butter and parsley.

5. Place the Grits Croutons on a platter. Top with the shrimp and sauce. Serves 4

STONE FRUIT

Soft, ripe peaches, dripping with sweetness are the stuff of Southern culinary legend. Like many ingredients Southerners identify as our own, peaches and nectarines are not native. Originating in China, they were brought to the Americas by Spanish explorers and European settlers. Black cherries and a few varieties of plums did grow wild in the South, but the fruits were not grown commercially until after the Civil War. Until then, black cooks preserved foraged and fallen fruits in sweet-tart pickles, chutneys, jellies, and jams for themselves, and they were taught to make European-style cobblers and pies with the tree-ripened fruits from plantation gardens for their owners. Once commercial orchard production began, freed slaves were hired to prune, pick, and maintain orchards year-round. It didn't take long for states like Georgia, South Carolina, and Alabama to become the prolific peach-growing states they remain today. When it comes to stone fruit, I urge you to think beyond dessert. Like my ancestors, I use the fruit in savory dishes, sweet ones, or a blend of the two. I pickle the fruits in tart vinegar, temper their sweetness with salt, or change the flavor and texture altogether through the alchemy of cooking.

Peach Salad

Stone fruit really shines in dishes with berries. In this recipe, tart raspberry vinegar steps in as the "other" fruit and plays off the pleasant, bitter notes found in the darker peach flesh near the pit while tempering the sweetness of the fruit closer to the fuzzy skin. Two types of cheeses add a forgiving element to the salad, so it won't matter if the peaches are slightly underripe or even too ripe because the silky creaminess of the cheeses will marry the components beautifully. If you can't find watercress, substitute microgreens or arugula.

Serves 4 as an appetizer or 2 as an entrée

1 cup Pickle Brine (page 354)

8 frozen pearl onions

1 (4-ounce) log goat cheese, softened

1 cup crème fraîche, at room temperature

1 tablespoon chopped fresh flat-leaf parsley

¼ teaspoon coarsely ground black pepper

2 ripe peaches (about 10 ounces), each pitted and cut into 8 wedges

2 tablespoons raspberry vinegar

1 teaspoon honey

2 fresh basil leaves, sliced

1 tablespoon extra-virgin olive oil

1 bunch watercress

Summer Sausage Croutons (page 255)

1 teaspoon gray sea salt

1. Bring the Pickle Brine and pearl onions to a boil in a saucepan over medium. Reduce heat to low, and simmer 5 minutes. Remove from the heat. Let cool to room temperature, about 10 minutes.

2. Combine the goat cheese, crème fraîche, chopped parsley, and pepper in a small bowl.

3. Toss together the peaches, raspberry vinegar, honey, basil leaves, and the olive oil in a medium bowl.

4. Place 2 tablespoons of the herbed goat cheese mixture in the center of each plate, and top with 4 to 6 peach slices. Top evenly with watercress, pickled onions, and Summer Sausage Croutons. Drizzle any remaining raspberry vinegar mixture over the salads, and sprinkle with gray sea salt.

Note: Serve on toast as appetizer or add cornbread croutons for a heartier salad.

To Drink: White Burgundy, Chardonnay, Merlot, Pinot Noir, red blends, rosé, sparkling rosé, sparkling Shiraz, full hoppy beers, bourbon cocktails

Serve with: Grilled and smoked meats; grilled, smoked, and fried fish; roasted, grilled, and smoked poultry dishes; roasted and pickled vegetables; rice or grits dishes

Grilled Peach Toast with Pimiento Cheese

Tradition is an aesthetic in modern cooking. My ancestral tree has its roots in West Africa, where the indigenous cuisine's pairing of savory items with sweet is as ancient as the continent itself. From simple dishes of toast and honey or sweet potatoes with bitter greens, sweet and savory have long been the hallmark of traditional coastal African cooking.

Great pimiento cheese is all about spice. Red peppers and hot sauce are essential to cutting through the richness of the cream cheese and Cheddar. You need that spicy zing to tame the fat. Mustard also steps in to balance the rich flavors.

Serves 4 as an appetizer or 2 as an entrée

2 firm-ripe peaches, halved and pitted

2 tablespoons plus 1 teaspoon blended oil

1 medium-size ripe avocado

4 (½-inch-thick) slices multigrain boule-style bread

Pimiento Cheese (page 220)

2 tablespoons extra-virgin olive oil

¼ cup thinly sliced red radishes (about 3 ounces)

1 bunch watercress

1 teaspoon gray sea salt

½ teaspoon coarsely ground black pepper

1. Preheat a grill to medium-high (450°F).

2. Brush the peach halves with 1 tablespoon of the blended oil, and place on the grill grates, cut sides down. Grill, uncovered, until grill marks appear and the juices begin to release, about 3 minutes. Remove from the grill, and slice. Set aside.

3. Cut the avocado in half lengthwise, pit, and brush cut sides with 1 teaspoon of the blended oil. Place halves, cut sides down, on the grill grates. Grill, uncovered, just until the avocado is charred and begins to soften, about 5 minutes. Remove from the grill.

4. Brush the bread slices with the remaining 1 tablespoon oil, and place on the grill grates. Grill until the bread is toasted, about 2 minutes per side. Remove from the grill.

5. Spread Pimiento Cheese onto 1 side of each piece of toast. Cut each piece into 4 equal rectangles, keeping the pieces together.

6. Scoop the avocado from the peel into a medium bowl and mash with 1 tablespoon of the extra-virgin olive oil until it is chunky and spreadable. Spoon onto the toast, and top with sliced peaches.

7. Top the toast slices with radish slices and watercress leaves. Drizzle the remaining 1 tablespoon extra-virgin olive oil over the toast slices, and sprinkle with gray sea salt and black pepper.

Note: If watercress is unavailable, arugula or curly mustard greens can be substituted.

To Drink: White Burgundy, Chardonnay, Merlot, Pinot Noir, red blends, rosé, sparkling rosé, sparkling Shiraz, full hoppy beers, bourbon cocktails

Serve with: Lamb sausage; red beans with shrimp; grilled sardines; grilled and smoked meats; grilled, smoked, and fried fish; roasted, grilled, and smoky poultry dishes; roasted and pickled vegetables; rice or grits dishes

pimiento cheese

4 bacon slices

1 tablespoon blended olive oil

2 small red bell peppers, stems removed, finely diced (about 1 ¼ cups)

2 teaspoons adobo sauce from canned chipotle peppers

¼ cup mayonnaise

1 tablespoon apple cider vinegar

2 teaspoons hot sauce

½ teaspoon dry mustard

½ teaspoon granulated garlic

¼ teaspoon coarsely ground black pepper

4 ounces white Cheddar cheese, shredded (about 1 cup)

4 ounces sharp Cheddar cheese, shredded (about 1 cup)

4 ounces cream cheese, softened

2 tablespoons thinly sliced chives

1. Cook bacon in a heavy-bottomed skillet over medium-high 5 to 6 minutes or until crisp. Remove bacon from skillet and drain on paper towels; chop. Reserve 1 tablespoon bacon drippings, and set aside. Wipe the skillet clean.

2. Return the skillet to medium. Add the blended oil and the red bell peppers. Cook until tender, about 2 minutes. Stir in the bacon drippings. Add the adobo sauce, and cook 2 minutes. Remove from the heat. Stir in the bacon, mayonnaise, vinegar, hot sauce, dry mustard, granulated garlic, and black pepper.

3. Combine the Cheddar cheeses, cream cheese, and bell pepper mixture in a large bowl. Stir in the chives, and serve at room temperature. Makes about 3 cups

At our church picnics there was rarely judgment about the crispness of the cornmeal coating on the fish or the creaminess of the potato salad (after all, hot sauce is the fixer of all things mediocre). It was always peach cobbler that fueled intense debate among parishioners.

The first judgment was about the quality of the crust. There had better be two layers. If there was no bottom crust, unapologetic shoulder shrugging commenced with fierce comments like "That's white folks' cobbler," which meant the cook had bucked tradition and gone fancy. Of course, the crust had better be flaky. Those church ladies would lift it and peek underneath to see what fat was used in the dough. If butter, instead of shortening or lard, was suspected, rest assured more scolding rang out.

The second judgment was about the quality of the fruit. Fresh, canned, or frozen peaches were all acceptable as long as the flock couldn't tell the difference. Comments such as "She didn't even drain the juice," "This tastes like a freezer," or "She spent all day in the kitchen cuttin' these when she could've made the same thing with frozen ones"...all this talk happened while the others nodded in reproach.

I laughed at these judgments and criticisms. Not one of those critics could produce a cobbler any better. If they dared, it would be picked apart just the same. The critics' contributions were those other desserts, sitting off to the side as lonely as lonely could be on the picnic table, not even buzzed by a fly. The real judgment was the fact that the peach cobbler was always gone before anything else.

Breakfast Sausage with Ginger Peach
Relish on Erika Council's Black
Pepper-Thyme Cornmeal Biscuits
(page 224)

Breakfast Sausage with Ginger Peach Relish on Erika Council's Black Pepper–Thyme Cornmeal Biscuits

Sage is a strong herb often used in sausage making or with poultry. Though pork has enough fat to tame strong flavors, cheese provides the same effect. Breadcrumbs serve the dual purpose of binding the sausage and developing texture.

Biscuits and cornbread are staples of the Southern table. Erika Council's are a love child of both. They have the crunchy, nutty-sweet flavor of yellow cornmeal floating in each light-and-fluffy biscuit layer.

Serves 12

1 pound ground pork

4 ounces cooked ham, finely chopped

2 ounces Cheddar cheese, shredded (about ½ cup)

⅓ cup soft, fresh breadcrumbs

2 teaspoons sorghum syrup

1 ½ teaspoons minced fresh sage

1 teaspoon kosher salt

½ teaspoon coarsely ground black pepper

¼ teaspoon red pepper flakes

¼ teaspoon ground coriander

1 large egg, beaten

Erika Council's Black Pepper–Thyme Cornmeal Biscuits (recipe follows)

Ginger Peach Relish (recipe follows)

1. Stir together the pork and the next 10 ingredients in a large bowl; let stand 15 minutes. Scoop the mixture by ¼-cupfuls onto a wax paper-lined baking sheet, and shape into 12 (½-inch-thick) patties.

2. Heat a cast-iron skillet over medium-high. Brown the patties in the pan in batches, until golden brown on 1 side, 3 to 4 minutes. Turn, cover, and continue to cook until the sausage is just done, about 4 minutes. Remove from the pan.

3. Split the biscuits. Top the bottom half of the biscuits with a sausage patty and some Ginger Peach Relish. Cover with top halves.

To Drink: White Burgundy, Chardonnay, Merlot, Pinot Noir, red blends, rosé, sparkling rosé, sparkling Shiraz, full hoppy beers, bourbon cocktails, coffee

Serve with: Roasted and pickled vegetables; rice, grits, or egg dishes

erika council's black pepper–thyme cornmeal biscuits

1 ½ cups (about 6 ⅜ ounces) all-purpose flour, plus more for dusting

1 cup (about 4 ½ ounces) coarse yellow cornmeal

1 tablespoon baking powder

½ teaspoon baking soda

1 teaspoon kosher salt

1 teaspoon freshly ground black pepper

2 tablespoons cold vegetable shortening, cut into ½-inch chunks

4 ounces (½ cup) unsalted butter, chilled, cut into ⅛-inch slices

1 ¼ cups (10 ounces) buttermilk, chilled

2 teaspoons chopped fresh thyme

1 ounce (2 tablespoons) unsalted butter, melted

1. Whisk together the flour, cornmeal, baking powder, baking soda, salt, and pepper in a large bowl. Work the shortening into the flour mixture by breaking up the chunks with your fingertips until only small pea-size pieces remain. Add in a few slices of the chilled butter and coat in the flour. Press the pieces between well-floured fingertips into flat (nickel-size) pieces. Repeat until all the chilled butter is incorporated.

2. Freeze the flour mixture (in the bowl) until chilled, 15 minutes. Preheat the oven to 450°F. Gently stir the buttermilk into the flour with a fork. Add the thyme. Stir until the dough forms a ball and no dry bits of flour remain. (The dough will be sticky and shaggy.) Turn the dough out onto a floured surface. With floured hands, pat it to a ¼-inch-thick 10-inch rectangle. Add more flour if needed to prevent sticking.

3. Fold the dough into thirds using a bench scraper or metal spatula. Lift the short end of the dough and fold in thirds again. Rotate the dough 90°, dusting the work surface underneath with flour. Roll and fold again into a 10-inch square about ½ inch thick.

4. Cut out 12 biscuits using a 2-inch round floured cutter. Place 1 inch apart on an ungreased baking sheet. Brush biscuit tops with melted butter. Bake in the preheated oven until the tops are golden brown, about 15 minutes. Makes 12 biscuits

ginger peach relish

2 teaspoons blended olive oil

1 shallot, sliced into small rings

2 tablespoons peeled and minced ginger

1 pound fresh peaches (about 3 medium peaches), finely chopped

½ cup granulated sugar

½ cup (4 ounces) apple cider vinegar

¼ cup honey

1 jalapeño chile, stemmed, seeded, and minced

Heat the oil in a saucepan over medium-high. Add the shallot and ginger. Reduce the heat to medium. Cook, stirring often, until softened, about 3 minutes. Add the peaches and remaining ingredients. Cook until liquid is reduced and syrupy, about 10 minutes. Remove from the heat, and let stand for 20 minutes. Makes 1 cup

Peach Salsa, Chicken Liver Pâté, and Apple Aspic on Zucchini Bread

Many of us have heard stories of parents or grandparents wringing the neck of a chicken in the yard. Once a part of everyday life, it is now a bigger part of Southern folklore. It sounds almost Southern Gothic, walking out back, grabbing a chicken, and swinging it around in anticipation of Sunday supper. It is always the breast of the chicken that is showcased on the supper table—crispy skin, golden-brown, and glistening with a mouthwatering aroma. Traditionally, the innards were never discarded.

The most remarkable part of chicken cookery for me is how these bits were utilized—livers preserved or fried, along with gizzards, hearts, and other parts. Letting the livers rest and processing them with additional stock makes for a smoother, less grainy pâté.

Molasses is essential to zucchini bread. It provides a smoky, caramelized flavor to the loaf. The moisture in the zucchini creates steam as the batter cooks, creating a soft texture and crusty exterior to the bread. Be sure to just fold the ingredients together to keep the batter airy and light.

Serves 8

4 ripe peaches (about 1 ½ pounds), peeled and finely chopped

2 tablespoons apple cider vinegar

1 small jalapeño chile, stemmed, seeded, and minced (about 2 tablespoons)

2 tablespoons finely chopped shallot (from 1 small shallot)

2 tablespoons minced fresh ginger

¼ cup honey

1 tablespoon blended olive oil

¼ teaspoon flaky sea salt (such as Maldon)

Sliced Zucchini Bread (page 228), toasted

Chicken Liver Pâté with Apple Aspic (page 229)

1. Combine first 8 ingredients in a large bowl, and stir well. Refrigerate until thoroughly chilled, about 2 hours.

2. To serve, spread the Zucchini Bread toasts with the pâté and arrange on a serving platter. Top each toast with the Peach Salsa.

Note: Ginger Peach Relish (page 225) can be used for this dish as well.

To Drink: White Burgundy, Chardonnay, Merlot, Pinot Noir, red blends, rosé, sparkling rosé, sparkling Shiraz, full hoppy beers, bourbon cocktails

Serve with: Grilled and smoked meats; grilled, smoked, and fried fish; roasted, grilled, and smoked poultry dishes; roasted and pickled vegetables; rice or grits dishes

zucchini bread

5 large eggs

2 ½ cups granulated sugar

1 ¼ cups (10 ounces) vegetable oil

¼ cup molasses

1 teaspoon vanilla bean paste

3 ¾ cups (about 16 ounces) all-purpose flour

2 teaspoons baking powder

¾ teaspoon baking soda

½ teaspoon kosher salt

¼ teaspoon ground cinnamon

2 ½ cups shredded zucchini (about 2 [12-ounce] zucchini)

1. Preheat oven to 350°F. Whisk together the eggs, sugar, oil, molasses, and vanilla bean paste in a large bowl. Sift together the flour, baking powder, baking soda, salt, and cinnamon in a separate bowl.

2. Fold the flour mixture into the egg mixture and stir just until most of the flour mixture is moistened. Fold in the zucchini just until incorporated.

3. Lightly grease 2 (8- x 4-inch) loaf pans. Pour the batter evenly into each pan. Place the pans in the preheated oven, and bake until a wooden pick inserted in the center comes out clean, about 1 hour.

4. Place pans on a wire rack and cool 20 minutes. Turn out the bread from the pans, and cool completely before slicing and serving, about 2 hours. Makes 2 (8- x 4-inch) loaves

chicken liver pâté with apple aspic

CHICKEN LIVER PÂTÉ:

2 tablespoons blended olive oil

¼ cup finely chopped shallots (from 2 small shallots)

2 garlic cloves, thinly sliced

2 thyme sprigs

¼ cup (2 ounces) bourbon

2 cups plus 6 tablespoons Chicken Stock (page 350)

1 pound chicken livers

2 ounces (¼ cup) unsalted butter, softened

1 teaspoon ground white pepper

½ teaspoon kosher salt

APPLE ASPIC:

½ cup (4 ounces) apple cider

1 (¼-ounce) envelope unflavored gelatin

1 tablespoon (½ ounce) bourbon

1. Prepare the Chicken Liver Pâté: Heat the oil in a saucepan over medium. Add the shallots and garlic, and cook, stirring often, until tender, 5 minutes. Add the thyme, bourbon, and 2 cups of the Chicken Stock, and bring to a simmer. Simmer until the liquid is reduced slightly, about 10 minutes.

2. Add the chicken livers, and return to a gentle simmer. Remove from the heat. Cover and let stand until the livers are cooked through, about 10 minutes. Remove the livers from the pan, and discard the poaching liquid. Cool the livers on a wire rack for 20 minutes. Transfer the livers to a rimmed baking sheet lined with paper towels, and chill 2 hours.

3. Process the chicken livers and butter in a food processor until almost smooth, about 2 minutes. Add the white pepper, kosher salt, and remaining 6 tablespoons stock, and process until smooth, about 1 minute.

4. Spoon the chicken liver puree into a 24-ounce round baking dish, leaving at least ¼ inch space for the Apple Aspic at the top. Refrigerate until set, about 2 hours.

5. Prepare the Apple Aspic: Place ¼ cup of the apple cider in a small bowl, and sprinkle gelatin over the top. Set aside. Bring the bourbon and remaining ¼ cup apple cider to a simmer in a small saucepan over medium-high. Remove from the heat, and carefully pour over gelatin mixture. Stir until the gelatin dissolves completely. Let cool for at least 30 minutes.

6. Pour the aspic over the top of the pâté, and refrigerate until set, about 30 minutes. Serves 8

Pickled Plum and Mustard
Greens Salad (page 233)

Pineapple-Glazed Spareribs
(page 232)

Pineapple-Glazed Spareribs with Pickled Plum and Mustard Greens Salad

Plums are a catalyst fruit when served with savory dishes. They bridge umami flavors as we have here: smoke and ginger. The fruit's tartness and texture are a vehicle for the other flavors. Pairing fruits and fatty meats like these sticky spareribs and the ham hock meat in the salad is a great way to showcase the distinctive flavors of the proteins while preventing the taste buds from getting bored. The plum pickling liquid's acidity and spices pair beautifully with the meat. Whole-grain mustard is a classic with ham and emulsifies the vinegar and oil.

Serves 4

1 rack pork spareribs

1 tablespoon plus 1 teaspoon blended olive oil

½ cup Basic Dry Rub (page 351)

1 pound pecan wood chips, soaked in water 30 minutes

½ pineapple, cut into large pieces

½ cup packed light brown sugar

½ cup (4 ounces) bourbon

¼ cup pineapple juice

¼ cup (2 ounces) fresh orange juice (from 1 orange)

1 jalapeño chile, stemmed, seeded, and finely minced

1 teaspoon ground ginger

Pickled Plum and Mustard Greens Salad (recipe follows)

1. Light charcoal in a charcoal chimney starter. When charcoal is covered with gray ash, pour into the bottom grate of the grill, and then push to 1 side of the grill. Bring internal temperature to very low (about 250°F). (If using a gas grill, preheat 1 side of the grill to 210° to 250°F.)

2. Place the ribs, meat side up, on a cutting board. Score the ribs in a crosshatch pattern using a knife. Rub the ribs all over with 1 tablespoon of the oil, and coat with the dry rub. Let stand 15 minutes.

3. Add the wood chips to the charcoal. Coat the top grill grate with oil; place on grill. Place the ribs, meat side up, on the oiled grill grate over the unlit side. Grill, covered with the grill lid, until ribs begin to fall apart when lifted with tongs, about 3 hours, turning ribs every 30 minutes.

4. Meanwhile, heat remaining 1 teaspoon of the oil in a heavy-bottomed stockpot over medium. Add the pineapple, and cook, stirring often, until golden brown, 4 to 5 minutes. Add the brown sugar, bourbon, pineapple juice, orange juice, jalapeño, and ginger. Bring to a simmer, and cook until reduced by half, about 15 minutes. Remove from the heat, and let stand 15 minutes.

5. Brush the ribs with the ginger glaze. Cover and grill 5 minutes. Remove from the grill, and let the ribs stand 15 minutes before slicing. Serve with Pickled Plum and Mustard Greens Salad.

Note: If young mustard greens are not available, arugula or rocket is a perfect substitute. Mustard greens should not be more than 4 inches tall.

To Drink: White Burgundy, Chardonnay, Merlot, Pinot Noir, red blends, rosé, sparkling rosé, sparkling Shiraz, full hoppy beers, bourbon cocktails, IPAs, stouts

Serve with: Roasted and pickled vegetables; rice dishes; grits dishes; Smoked Fingerling Sweet Potatoes (page 332)

pickled plum and mustard greens salad

2 tablespoons pickled plum liquid (from Pickled Plums, recipe follows)

2 tablespoons blended olive oil

½ teaspoon coarse-grain mustard

½ teaspoon granulated sugar

¼ teaspoon kosher salt

½ pound young mustard greens, washed and trimmed

4 Pickled Plums (recipe follows), pitted and cut into ¼-inch pieces

½ cup packed fresh cilantro leaves

3 tablespoons roasted peanuts, coarsely chopped

Whisk together pickling liquid, oil, mustard, sugar, and salt in a large bowl. Add the greens, and toss to coat. Transfer to a serving dish. Top evenly with the plums, cilantro, and peanuts. Serves 4

pickled plums

2 cups (16 ounces) water

1 cup (8 ounces) ume plum vinegar

1 cup (8 ounces) apple cider vinegar

1 cup granulated sugar

1 tablespoon chopped fresh ginger

1 teaspoon black peppercorns

¼ teaspoon red pepper flakes

½ teaspoon kosher salt

2 bay leaves

2 star anise pods

1 cinnamon stick

1 ½ pounds fresh plums

1. Bring 2 cups water, both vinegars, sugar, ginger, peppercorns, red pepper flakes, salt, bay leaves, star anise, and cinnamon stick to a simmer in a heavy-bottomed stockpot over medium. Simmer until the sugar and salt are completely dissolved, about 5 minutes.

2. Add the plums. Cover and cook for 8 minutes. Remove from the heat, and let stand for 15 minutes.

3. Place the plums and the pickling liquid in a clean 4-quart glass container. Refrigerate for 4 hours before serving. Makes 4 quarts

Pickled Plum Salad with Braised Ham Hock, Onions, and Mint

In an attempt to pay homage to the ham hock as the unsung hero of greens, I decided to make it an intricate part of a dish rather than a to-be-discarded horseshoe. So I came up with ham hock and eggs, ham hock ramen, and ham hock terrine, and my favorite: ham hock and mint. The salt and herb tame the smoke. Pickled onions give zest and life. Plums lend a creamy mouthfeel.

Beer is one of the best liquids for braising ham hocks. It breaks down the connective tissue and infuses the meat with flavor. Amber beer brings the flavors of cumin and garlic to the forefront. It reminds me of braising sausages and hot dogs in beer with onion and aromatics. The same principle applies to both, although ham hock has a different flavor and texture.

Serves 4

2 tablespoons Pickled Plums pickling liquid (page 233)

1 tablespoon blended olive oil

½ teaspoon coarse-grain mustard

¼ teaspoon kosher salt

4 Pickled Plums (page 233), pitted and cut into ¼-inch pieces

4 wedges braised and chilled onions (from the Braised Ham Hock recipe, page 237)

1 ham hock, meat pulled (from the Braised Ham Hock recipe, page 237) (about ½ cup)

2 tablespoons roasted peanuts, coarsely chopped

2 tablespoons mint leaves

1. Whisk together the pickling liquid, oil, mustard, and salt in a medium bowl.

2. Toss the Pickled Plums with the vinaigrette. Arrange the plums on a serving platter with the onions and ham hock meat. Sprinkle with peanuts and mint.

Note: Different meats can be used; sausages can be braised and used in place of the ham hock. Reserve the ham hock stock for braising greens or cooking field peas.

To Drink: White Burgundy, Chardonnay, Merlot, Pinot Noir, red blends, rosé, sparkling rosé, sparkling Shiraz, full hoppy beers, bourbon cocktails, IPAs, stouts

Serve with: Roasted and pickled vegetables; rice, grits, or smoked meat dishes

braised ham hock

¼ cup (2 ounces) blended olive oil

4 (3-ounce) smoked ham hocks

2 carrots, peeled and diced

8 garlic cloves

6 cups (48 ounces) chicken stock

4 cups (32 ounces) water

1 (12-ounce) bottle amber beer

4 bay leaves

4 thyme sprigs

1 teaspoon cumin seeds

1 large yellow onion, cut into 8 wedges

2 teaspoons kosher salt

1 teaspoon black peppercorns

1. Heat 2 tablespoons of the oil in a stockpot over medium. Add the ham hocks, carrots, and garlic. Cook, stirring often, until the hocks are browned on all sides, 10 minutes. Add the chicken stock, 4 cups water, and beer. Stir in the bay leaves, thyme, and cumin.

2. Bring to a boil. Cover, reduce the heat to low, and simmer until the meat easily pulls away from the bone, about 2 hours. Remove from the heat, and let stand for 15 minutes. Remove the hocks from the broth, and let hocks cool for 10 minutes. Reserve the broth.

3. Heat the remaining 2 tablespoons oil in a heavy-bottomed skillet over medium. Add the onions, kosher salt, and peppercorns, and cook, stirring occasionally, until the onion begins to brown. Add 3 to 4 cups of ham hock broth (just enough to cover onions). Cover and cook until slightly firm and not mushy, about 10 minutes.

4. Remove the onions from the skillet, and place on a rimmed baking pan; cool completely, about 10 minutes. Refrigerate until thoroughly chilled. (Reserve the cooled onion wedges for the Pickled Plum Salad [page 234]).

5. Remove the ham hock meat from the bones, discarding the skin, fat, and bones. Place the meat in a bowl, and add ¼ cup of ham hock broth. Reserve the remaining ham hock broth for another use. Makes about 1½ cups picked meat

Smoked Duck Breasts with Brandied Cherries, Pound Cake, and Whipped Cream

Serving pickled and salted items with bitter vegetables or sweet fats has always been the hallmark of Soul food. These pairings excel at what Thanksgiving dinner is—the essential balance of flavors. When planning meals—or attempting to push a cuisine forward—modern dishes do not need to be limited to particular courses. Contemporary cuisine lets you have your cake and eat it, too, as long as you have a central theme to bind them together.

If there is any dish that requires technique, it is pound cake. The eggs must be whipped one at a time to build the protein structure of the cake. The whipping of each egg emulsifies the sugar and flour while also adding air to the batter. The combination makes for an airy pound cake—not a dense one. It also ensures that the crust cooks evenly, forming a spectacular border to house the lemony cake.

Serves 4

8 cups Sweet Tea Brine (page 355)
4 (6 ½-ounce) duck breasts, skin scored
⅛ inch deep
2 pounds pecan wood chips, soaked in water
30 minutes
1 tablespoon blended olive oil

2 tablespoons Curried Coffee Rub
(page 351)
Smoked Fingerling Sweet Potatoes
(page 332)
Brandied Cherries (page 240)
Pound Cake with Whipped Cream (page 241)

1. Combine the brine and duck in an airtight container. Refrigerate 8 hours or overnight.

2. Light charcoal in a charcoal chimney starter. When charcoal is covered with gray ash, pour into the bottom grate of the grill, and then push to 1 side of the grill. Bring temperature to low (about 275° to 300°F). (If using a gas grill, preheat 1 side of grill to 210° to 250°F.) Place the wood chips on the hot coals, and close the lid.

3. Meanwhile, remove the duck breasts from the brine, and pat dry with paper towels. Rub the duck breasts with the oil and the coffee rub. Let stand for 15 minutes.

4. When wood begins to smoke, place duck breasts, skin sides down, on the grill grates over the unlit side. Grill, covered with the grilled lid, until a meat thermometer inserted in the thickest portion registers 140°F, about 25 minutes, turning halfway through.

5. Remove the duck breasts from the grill, and let rest for 15 minutes before slicing.

6. Serve with the Smoked Fingerling Sweet Potatoes, Brandied Cherries, and Pound Cake with Whipped Cream.

Note: Duck can be pan roasted instead of smoked and will achieve the same caramelized skin.
To Drink: White Burgundy, Chardonnay, Merlot, Pinot Noir, red blends, rosé, sparkling rosé, sparkling Shiraz, full hoppy beers, bourbon cocktails, IPAs, stouts
Serve with: Bitter greens; green salads; creamed dishes

Pound Cake and
Whipped Cream
(page 241)

Brandied Cherries
(page 240)

brandied cherries

½ cup (4 ounces) bottled cherry juice
½ cup raw sugar
½ cup (4 ounces) brandy
½ cup (4 ounces) dark rum
1 tablespoon cocoa nibs

8 coffee beans
8 dried culinary lavender flowers
1 pound fresh sweet cherries, pitted
1 thyme sprig

1. Bring the cherry juice, sugar, brandy, rum, cocoa nibs, coffee beans, and lavender to a simmer in a heavy-bottomed stockpot over medium, and cook until syrupy, about 15 minutes. Remove from the heat.

2. Add the cherries, stirring to completely cover in the syrup. Add the thyme, and let stand 25 minutes. Transfer the cherries with the syrup to a clean glass jar, and let cool to room temperature, about 1 hour. Refrigerate 2 hours. Store in the refrigerator for up to 1 week. Makes 1 (2-quart) jar

Note: Don't be afraid to smoke the cherries alongside the duck breasts prior to making the brandied cherries.

pound cake and whipped cream

10 ounces (1 ¼ cups) unsalted butter, softened

2 ½ cups plus 1 tablespoon granulated sugar

6 large eggs

1 large egg yolk

½ cup (4 ounces) whole buttermilk

1 teaspoon bourbon vanilla extract

1 teaspoon lemon zest (from 1 lemon)

3 cups (about 12 ¾ ounces) all-purpose flour

4 teaspoons plain yellow cornmeal

1 cup (8 ounces) heavy cream

1 tablespoon bourbon vanilla bean paste

Brandied Cherries (recipe opposite)

1. Preheat the oven to 325°F. Beat the butter with an electric mixer on medium speed until creamy, about 1 minute. Gradually add 2 ½ cups of the sugar, and beat until fluffy, about 3 minutes. Add the eggs and the egg yolk, 1 at a time, beating on low after each addition.

2. Stir together the buttermilk, vanilla extract, and lemon zest. Add the flour to the butter mixture alternately with the buttermilk mixture in 3 additions, beating on low after each addition, and ending with the buttermilk mixture.

3. Lightly grease a Pullman-style loaf pan or 2 (8- x 4-inch) loaf pans. Sprinkle cornmeal in the pan, and turn to coat the inside of the pan completely. Discard any excess cornmeal.

4. Pour the batter into the prepared pan. Tap the pan on counter to remove any air bubbles. Bake in the preheated oven until a wooden pick inserted in center comes out clean, about 1 hour and 20 minutes. Cool in pan 15 minutes; run a knife around edges of pan, and turn out onto a wire rack. Cool completely, about 2 hours.

5. Freeze a large metal bowl for 20 minutes. Remove from freezer, and add the heavy cream, vanilla bean paste, and remaining 1 tablespoon sugar to the bowl. Beat until stiff peaks form. Slice the cake and serve with whipped cream and Brandied Cherries. Makes 1 Pullman loaf or 2 (8- x 4-inch) loaves

Note: The pound cake slices can be toasted on the grill as well.

EGGS & POULTRY

Eggs can be the simplest of fortifying meals or, used in combination with other ingredients, form the framework for countless recipes. Hard-boiled eggs are an easy and nutritious portable protein source that could be eaten in the fields or while traveling. Scrambled, eggs are a delicious medium for using up extra bits and scraps from cooking, such as scallions, cheese, vegetables, and meats. From quail and squab to duck and chicken, Soul cuisine embraces eggs in all forms. Beyond scrambled, fried, baked, or poached, Soul cooks turn to eggs to enrich cornbread, spoon bread, and moist batter cakes. This most basic of ingredients is perhaps the most essential tool in a cook's arsenal, and it is by far the one ingredient I most revere. Cooking them properly requires patience, skill, and a real understanding of how they react with heat and other ingredients. I showcase eggs of all kinds in all forms, especially in contrast with cooked chicken as in deviled egg spread smeared on toast points topped with chicken hearts or fried chicken on a sweet potato waffle that gets body and crunch from the richness eggs provide.

Cheese Eggs and
Sage Sausage
on a Biscuit
(page 248)

Silky Soft Eggs and Sage Sausage on a Biscuit

If you're into BBQ, you've heard the phrase "low and slow." It's a technique that also applies to scrambled eggs. Scramble over high heat and the lean egg white cooks before the richer yolk is done. The eggs get tough because the white seizes under high temperature. If your pan gets too hot while cooking, remove it from the heat, place it on a rack and continue to scramble the eggs. The air beneath will cool the pan faster than just turning off the heat.

Eggs are quite honestly my most favorite food to eat. Soft scrambled eggs with or without cheese demand good-quality butter, sea salt, and patience to become perfectly light and silky. Patience is a must if the eggs are to set without drying out or browning. If your pan is too hot or you are too vigorous in scrambling, the curds of cooked egg will get tough and dry. Even if you like to eat your eggs well done, slow, steady stirring is the proper method for scrambling them.

Serves 2

4 large eggs, lightly beaten	Pinch of sea salt
1 tablespoon ice-cold water	4 chives, thinly sliced
¼ teaspoon kosher salt	2 Erika Council's Black Pepper-Thyme
2 ounces (¼ cup) unsalted butter	Cornmeal Biscuits (page 225)
Freshly ground white pepper	Sage Sausage (recipe follows)

1. Whisk together the eggs, 1 tablespoon ice water, and salt in a medium bowl until foamy.

2. Melt 2 tablespoons of the butter in an 8-inch nonstick skillet over medium. Cook until the butter is foamy and clear, about 15 seconds. Add the egg mixture, and shake the skillet gently to ensure the butter remains beneath the eggs. Cook until the eggs are set on the bottom. (Do not let them brown.)

3. Gently lift the eggs with a spatula, allowing the uncooked egg to flow underneath. Cook until almost completely set, 3 to 4 minutes. Reduce the heat to low. Top the eggs with the remaining 2 tablespoons butter, and sprinkle with freshly ground white pepper and sea salt.

4. Remove the skillet from heat, and transfer the eggs to a plate. Sprinkle with the chives.

5. To serve, split the biscuits. Top the bottom half of the biscuit with 1 sausage patty. Top evenly with the eggs and replace the biscuit top. Serve immediately.

Note: To make Cheese Eggs, add 1 ½ tablespoons of shredded aged Cheddar cheese to the eggs in Step 3, just before the eggs are almost set.

To Drink: Blanc de blancs Champagne, blanc de noirs Champagne, Chardonnay, dry Riesling, rosé, sparkling rosé, Sauvignon Blanc, amber beers, dark beers, hard ciders, IPAs

Serve with: Grits dishes; other breakfast items; salads

sage sausage

3 fresh sage leaves

2 thyme sprigs, leaves removed

1 pound ground pork

3 tablespoons lard

1 ½ teaspoons kosher salt

½ teaspoon red pepper flakes

½ teaspoon freshly ground black pepper

2 garlic cloves, minced

1. Finely chop the sage and thyme leaves. Combine the pork, lard, salt, red pepper, black pepper, garlic, sage, and thyme in a medium bowl, and stir until combined. Cover and refrigerate until chilled, about 30 minutes.

2. Shape the pork mixture into about 16 (2 ½-inch) patties.

3. Heat a skillet over medium. Cook the sausage patties, in batches, until lightly browned on the bottom, 3 to 4 minutes. Turn and cook until cooked through, 2 to 3 minutes. (Extra cooked patties will keep in the refrigerator up to 1 week or may be frozen up to 3 months.) Makes 16 patties

Deviled Egg
Spread Toasts
with Chicken
Hearts
(page 252)

Angel Eggs

Angel Eggs are a version of Deviled Eggs. Greek yogurt in place of mayonnaise results in a slightly tangier, lighter rendition. Angel Egg filling is versatile as a sauce that pairs well with dishes such as lamb and vegetables. You can chop the egg whites to add to any leftover chicken or smoked turkey to make a delicious chicken or turkey salad.

Serves 8

4 cups (32 ounces) water

2 tablespoons plus ½ teaspoon kosher salt

1 celery stalk, peeled and halved crosswise

1 tablespoon white vinegar

4 large eggs

¼ cup plain Greek yogurt

2 teaspoons Dijon mustard

1 teaspoon aged red wine vinegar

1 teaspoon hot sauce

6 chives, thinly sliced

¼ teaspoon coarsely ground black
   pepper

Paprika (optional)

Fresh micro herbs (optional)

1. Fill a large bowl with ice and water.

2. Bring 4 cups of water and 2 tablespoons of the salt to a boil in a deep stockpot over medium heat. Add the celery, and cook 2 minutes. Transfer the celery to the ice bath using a slotted spoon.

3. Add the white vinegar to the stockpot, and return to a boil.

4. Carefully place the eggs in a single layer in the pot, and cook 10 minutes. Transfer the eggs to the ice bath using a slotted spoon. Let stand until cool, about 20 minutes. Drain.

5. Tap the eggs on the counter until cracks form; peel. Slice the eggs in half lengthwise, and carefully remove the yolks. Mash together the yolks, yogurt, mustard, vinegar, and hot sauce with a fork until smooth. Dice the celery, and fold into the egg yolk mixture. Fold in the chives, black pepper, and remaining ½ teaspoon salt.

6. Spoon the egg yolk mixture into the egg white halves. Garnish with paprika and micro herbs, if desired.

Deviled Egg Spread Toasts with Chicken Hearts

Doubling down on proteins in recipes shows sophistication and speaks to a hallmark of Soul cuisine—utilizing the entire animal. Chicken hearts are an underutilized part of the chicken. They provide an earthiness to dishes that allows fattier, delectable morsels of food to stand tall. You can find this same quality in mushrooms, but I think hearts are a fun way to explore new techniques.

Serves 4

3 tablespoons blended olive oil
1 pound chicken hearts
½ cup Seasoned Flour (page 352)
1 small white onion, thinly sliced
  (about 1½ cups)
2 garlic cloves, minced
4 cups (32 ounces) chicken stock
1 cup (8 ounces) dry white wine
4 bay leaves
1 rosemary sprig
Pinch of red pepper flakes

1 ounce (2 tablespoons) salted butter,
  softened
4 (1½-ounce) sourdough bread slices, toasted
¾ cup Deviled Egg Spread, plus chopped
  egg whites (from Deviled Egg Spread
  recipe, page 143)
¼ cup thinly sliced radish (from 2 radishes)
16 thin jalapeño chile slices (from 1 small
  jalapeño)
¼ teaspoon freshly ground black pepper
Pinch of gray sea salt

1. Heat the oil in a deep skillet over medium-high.

2. Dredge the chicken hearts in the Seasoned Flour, and shake off excess. Brown the chicken hearts in the hot oil on all sides, about 10 minutes.

3. Remove the hearts from the skillet, and set aside. Add the onion to the skillet, and cook until browned and softened, about 4 to 5 minutes. Add the garlic, and cook 30 seconds. Return the hearts to the skillet.

4. Add the chicken stock and next 4 ingredients to the skillet; bring to a simmer. Cover, reduce heat to medium-low, and simmer until the hearts are tender, about 30 minutes.

5. Remove and discard the bay leaves and rosemary sprig. Let stand for 15 minutes. Remove the hearts from the skillet, and finely chop. Discard the braising liquid.

6. Spread ½ tablespoon butter onto 1 side of each toasted bread slice. Cook, buttered sides down, in a skillet over medium until toasted, about 2 minutes. Cut each slice in half diagonally. Spread 1½ tablespoons of the Deviled Egg Spread onto each toasted bread slice.

7. Spoon chicken hearts evenly onto each toast piece. Top with the chopped egg whites, radishes, and jalapeño slices. Sprinkle with the black pepper and gray sea salt.

To Drink: Blanc de blancs Champagne, blanc de noirs Champagne, Chardonnay, dry Riesling, rosé, sparkling rosé, Sauvignon Blanc, amber beers, dark beers, hard ciders, IPAs
Serve with: Grits, tomato, or rice dishes; green salads, soups

I have an affinity for eggs. They are an intrinsic part of any cuisine. Every culture has versions of fried, scrambled, hard-boiled, and even deviled eggs. They are a perfect food, packing nutrition and unique properties that make them a cornerstone of cooking. They are utilized not only as a leavening agent in baking but as an aerator that provides structure for foams and soufflés. Eggs bind and emulsify incompatible liquids to create silky dressings and are the perfect tool for thickening sauces and custards. They are so important to cooking yet so sorely underappreciated because of their ubiquitousness. It's critical to understand that without eggs countless dishes just wouldn't work. Sure, we have an arsenal of egg substitutes—xanthan gum, guar gum, etc.—but traditionally without eggs, things just didn't come together. What would Southern cuisine be without deviled eggs? Fried green tomatoes wouldn't have that welcome crunch without eggs to bind the coating. How can you ignore the richness and texture eggs give cakes? The same goes for poultry. Where would we be without the array of birds—quail, chicken, duck, and ostrich—and the wonderful varieties of eggs they produce? More than any ingredient in my toolbox, eggs are the one that I would be lost without in the kitchen.

Stone-Ground
Grits Soufflés
(page 157)

Pickled
Mushrooms
(page 350)

Egg-in-the-Hole with Summer Sausage Croutons

I like serving Egg-in-the-Hole as a way of getting skeptical people comfortable with over-easy eggs. The crunchy toast embraces the wonderful runny yolk.

Bacon and sausage are standards served with eggs. I like using summer sausage in this recipe because it is the best of both worlds. The sausage has wonderful spice, and when sliced thin and fried, it gets the crispy texture of bacon.

Serves 4 as an entrée

6 tablespoons plus 1 teaspoon (about 3 ounces) blended olive oil

4 ounces hard summer sausage, thinly sliced

4 multigrain or spelt bread slices

4 duck eggs or extra-large chicken eggs

1 teaspoon kosher salt

½ teaspoon coarsely ground black pepper

Stone-Ground Grits Soufflés (page 157)

Pickled Mushrooms (page 350)

1. Preheat the oven to 375°F. Grease a rimmed baking sheet with 1 tablespoon of the oil. Arrange the sausage slices on the prepared baking sheet in a single layer, and bake in the preheated oven 10 minutes. Turn the sausage, and bake until crispy, 4 to 5 minutes. Drain on paper towels; reserving drippings from baking sheet.

2. Cut out the centers from the bread slices using a 2 ½-inch round cutter. Set aside.

3. Heat the reserved sausage drippings and 2 tablespoons of the oil in a sauté pan or skillet over medium.

4. Place 1 bread slice in pan, and break an egg into the center. Cook until the bottom of the egg white is set, occasionally spooning the oil mixture over the yolk. Carefully turn, and cook until the egg is set. Transfer to a plate. Repeat the process with 3 tablespoons of the oil and remaining 3 bread slices and 3 eggs.

5. Add remaining 1 teaspoon of the oil to pan, and add the centers of bread. Cook until toasted on both sides.

6. Sprinkle the toast slices evenly with salt and pepper. Serve the toast slices and the toasted bread centers with the Stone-Ground Grits Soufflés. Top the eggs with Pickled Mushrooms and summer sausage croutons.

Note: This dish can be served all day long. Don't limit it to breakfast. Cremini mushrooms, cut in half, can also be substituted for the shimeji mushrooms.

To Drink: White Burgundy, blanc de blancs Champagne, NV Grand Cru Champagne, Gamay, Grenache, rosé, vintage sparkling rosé, unoaked Sauvignon Blanc, sherry, amber beers, light beers, hard ciders

Serve with: Braised greens; fish or smoked dishes; green salads; slaws

Fried Chicken and Sweet Potato Waffles

This recipe is as American as apple pie. Yet most every culture has a version of it.
I prefer to brine all birds before cooking for best flavor and texture.

Serves 4

4 cups (32 ounces) water

1 cup (8 ounces) whole buttermilk

6 tablespoons kosher salt

2 tablespoons hot sauce

2 tablespoons granulated sugar

2 tablespoons granulated garlic

2 teaspoons onion powder

1 ½ teaspoons red pepper flakes

1 (4-pound) whole chicken, cut into 8 pieces

5 cups (40 ounces) vegetable oil

Seasoned Flour (page 352)

Sweet Potato Waffles (recipe follows)

Maple syrup

1. Stir together 4 cups water, buttermilk, and next 6 ingredients in a large bowl; add the chicken pieces to the brine. Refrigerate for at least 12 hours and up to 28 hours.

2. Heat the oil in a deep cast-iron skillet over medium. Remove chicken from the brine, and let any excess liquid drip off; discard the brine.

3. Dredge chicken in Seasoned Flour to coat; add to the hot oil, 1 piece at a time. Cook, turning every few minutes, until golden and a meat thermometer registers 165°F. Drain on paper towels. Serve chicken on Sweet Potato Waffles with maple syrup.

sweet potato waffles

1 medium-size sweet potato

¼ teaspoon blended olive oil

2 cups (about 8 ½ ounces) all-purpose flour

2 tablespoon granulated sugar

2 teaspoons baking powder

1 teaspoon kosher salt

1 cup (8 ounces) whole milk

½ cup (4 ounces) whole buttermilk

3 ounces (about ⅓ cup) butter, melted

1 teaspoon vanilla extract

½ teaspoon maple extract

2 large eggs

1. Preheat the oven to 375°F. Rub the potato with the oil. Bake in the preheated oven until tender, about 40 minutes. Remove from the oven, and cool for 20 minutes.

2. Preheat a Belgian waffle iron according to manufacturer's instructions. Stir together the dry ingredients in a bowl. Stir together the wet ingredients in a separate bowl.

3. Peel and mash the sweet potato, and stir into the milk mixture. Stir milk mixture into the flour mixture. Pour about ½ cup of batter onto hot waffle iron, and cook according to manufacturer's instructions until golden brown. Makes 4 (8-inch) round waffles

To Drink: Blanc de blancs Champagne, blanc de noirs Champagne, Chardonnay, dry Riesling, rosé, sparkling rosé, Sauvignon Blanc, amber beers, dark beers, hard ciders, IPAs

Serve with: Egg dishes, green salads, braised vegetables

⋖ BREAKFAST FOR DINNER ⋗

*For generations, people have gathered to eat breakfast again
for a late-night dinner after working up an appetite enjoying
an evening of blues or jazz. Grits from the morning and fried
chicken from lunch would be served in a new way. Utilizing what
you have instead of wasting food is part of the inventiveness of
Soul cuisine. Communion over a plate of chicken and waffles or
eggs and fried grits satisfies hunger and the desire to replay the
night's events with friends before parting ways.*

Fried Chicken and Sweet Potato Waffles
(page 256)

Baked Eggs in Tomato Sauce (page 192)

Grits Croutons (page 156)

Blueberry Sweet Tea (page 92)

Strawberry-Rum Coolers (page 84)

ON THE RADIO

"On Your Face" — *Earth, Wind & Fire*
"Liberation" — *OutKast*
"Here But I'm Gone" — *Curtis Mayfield and Lauryn Hill*
"Beasts of No Nation" — *Fela Kuti*

Grits Croutons
(page 156)

Baked Eggs in
Tomato Sauce
(page 192)

Blueberry Sweet Tea
(page 92)

Fried Chicken and
Sweet Potato Waffles
(page 256)

PORK & BEEF

South Carolina had a robust cattle industry in the early 1700s that supplied the British colonies of the Caribbean with salted beef in return for sugar, as well as the slaves and cash that fueled the Lowcountry's rice economy. Slaves braised fresh beef in stock or tomato broth. Meat that could not be eaten immediately after slaughter was smoked, cured, pickled, or otherwise preserved. Once the Spanish introduced pigs to the Americas, pork took the South by storm. It quickly became the centerpiece of the region's cuisine due in part to the low cost of raising the animals and their role as cleaners of the field and farm. Slaves turned to their native methods—slowly cooking the meat with vinegar and spices—and the result became one of the most iconic dishes of Soul and Southern food: barbecue. Organ meats were never overlooked. Beef tripe and pork chitlins were staples that exemplified the ways creative cooks used every part of an animal out of sheer necessity. The resulting dishes have become enduring Soul food staples that I continue to tinker with in the kitchen. Fried like calamari and served with Asian-style hot fried rice, chitlins can go mainstream. Braised, oxtails become the sublime surprise cloaked in the flaky crust of potpie.

Pork Jowl with Brussels Sprouts Slaw

Pork jowl is one of the most delicious parts of the pig. It's basically bacon from the cheek, and it's a lot cheaper. It has the fattiness of pork belly yet a texture similar to pork tenderloin. It requires very little work to make it delicious and is forgiving for the novice cook.

Serves 4

SLAW:
½ cup mayonnaise
2 tablespoons apple cider vinegar
1 tablespoon honey
1 large carrot
4 cups thinly sliced Brussels sprouts (about
   16 large sprouts)
1 teaspoon kosher salt

1 tablespoon thinly sliced fresh mint
½ teaspoon freshly ground black pepper
Pinch of red pepper flakes

PORK JOWL:
1 teaspoon blended olive oil
8 ounces pork jowl, cut into ¼-inch strips
½ teaspoon freshly ground black pepper

1. Prepare the Slaw: Stir together the mayonnaise, vinegar, and honey in a small bowl; set aside.

2. Peel the carrot, and shave into thin strips using a vegetable peeler to equal about 1½ cups. Toss together the carrot, Brussels sprouts, and salt in a medium bowl. Let stand 20 minutes.

3. Drizzle the Brussels sprouts mixture with the mayonnaise mixture. Add the mint, ground black pepper, and red pepper; toss to combine. Refrigerate 2 hours.

4. Prepare the Pork Jowl: Heat the oil in a skillet over medium. Sprinkle jowl slices evenly with the black pepper. Cook, stirring occasionally, until golden brown, 8 to 11 minutes. Drain on a plate lined with paper towels. To serve, top the slaw with the pork jowl slices.

Note: Pork jowl can be sold with or without skin. If the jowl isn't skinless and is chewy, then remove the skin before serving.

To Drink: Blanc de blancs Champagne, blanc de noirs Champagne, Chardonnay, dry Riesling, rosé, sparkling rosé, Sauvignon Blanc, amber beers, dark beers, hard ciders, IPAs

Serve with: Grits, bread, egg, bean, or rice dishes

Candied Bacon with Turnip Hash

Bacon adds a welcome savoriness to a variety of dishes, including turnips. Since they don't show up routinely on many dinner tables, adding bacon to turnips is a delicious way to showcase this vegetable that many people tend to overlook.

Serves 4

8 thick-cut bacon slices

1 teaspoon granulated sugar

½ teaspoon freshly ground black pepper

1 tablespoon chopped fresh rosemary (from 2 sprigs)

4 medium turnips

1 white potato

3 tablespoons kosher salt

2 tablespoons blended olive oil

1 yellow onion, finely diced

1 teaspoon fresh thyme leaves (from 2 sprigs)

½ bunch fresh flat-leaf parsley, coarsely chopped

¼ cup sour cream

1. Preheat the oven to 350°F. Place a wire rack on a rimmed baking sheet. Arrange the bacon on the rack in a single layer. Stir together the sugar and pepper, and sprinkle the bacon with the sugar mixture. Bake in the preheated oven 8 minutes. Sprinkle the bacon with the rosemary. Return to the oven, and bake until the bacon is crispy, 15 to 20 minutes. Reserve 1 tablespoon of the drippings.

2. Combine the turnips, potato, and water to cover in a large pot. Add 2 ½ tablespoons of the salt. Bring to a boil over high. Reduce the heat to medium-low and simmer until vegetables are slightly tender and a knife can be inserted in the center with some resistance, 15 to 20 minutes. Drain and let stand until cool enough to handle. Remove the peels with a paper towel. Cut the turnips and potato into medium-size pieces.

3. Heat the oil in a skillet over medium. Add the onion, and cook, stirring often, about 3 minutes. Add the turnips and potato, and cook, stirring often, until golden brown on all sides, 10 to 15 minutes.

4. Add the reserved bacon drippings and thyme. Reduce the heat to very low, and cook, stirring occasionally, for 1 minute. Sprinkle with the remaining ½ tablespoon salt, and remove from heat. Stir in the parsley.

5. Divide the hash evenly among 4 plates, and place 2 bacon slices on each plate. Top each serving with 1 tablespoon sour cream.

To Drink: Blanc de blancs Champagne, blanc de noirs Champagne, Chardonnay, dry Riesling, rosé, sparkling rosé, Sauvignon Blanc, amber beers, dark beers, hard ciders, IPAs

Serve with: Bread, egg, rice, or other pork dishes; green salads

Crispy Chitlins with Hot Fried Rice

If your first reaction to this recipe is to turn up your nose, then you should also stop eating sausages, headcheese, or any other offal. What would a good hot dog or Italian sausage be without the snap that the casing provides? Here, that casing is celebrated as the textural main attraction. It's an important Soul food ingredient that has a steadfast place in contemporary cuisine.

Any way or any time of day you serve it, I'm a rice lover. It's so versatile. Serving chitlins with stir-fried rice is hardly the norm (but the norm is rarely what I do!), but it works so well with the hot fried chitlins. The radish, rutabaga, and carrot make this stir-fry more Soul or South than Far East.

Serves 4

1 teaspoon blended olive oil

1 white onion, halved

1 pound pork chitlins, rinsed with cold water 4 times until fully cleaned

4 cups (32 ounces) chicken stock

2 teaspoons kosher salt

1 teaspoon black peppercorns

¼ teaspoon red pepper flakes

4 bay leaves

1 thyme sprig

4 cups (32 ounces) vegetable oil

2 cups (16 ounces) water

1 cup (8 ounces) whole buttermilk

1 large egg

4 cups Seasoned Flour (page 352)

1 ½ teaspoons fine sea salt

Hot Fried Rice (page 270)

1. Heat the olive oil in a deep stockpot over medium. Add the onion, and cook 1 minute. Add the chitlins, stock, kosher salt, peppercorns, red pepper flakes, bay leaves, and thyme sprig. Bring to a boil; reduce the heat to medium-low, and simmer until the chitlins are tender, about 2 hours.

2. Remove the stockpot from the heat, and let stand 30 minutes. Remove the chitlins, and cool completely, about 1 hour. Discard the cooking liquid and other solids.

3. Cut the chitlins in half lengthwise, and cut into ½-inch square pieces.

4. Heat the vegetable oil in a deep skillet over medium-high to 375°F.

5. Whisk together 2 cups water, buttermilk, and egg in a large bowl. Place the Seasoned Flour in a shallow dish. Dip the chitlins in the buttermilk mixture, allowing excess to drip off, and then dredge in the flour. Fry in the hot oil, in batches, until crispy, 2 to 4 minutes.

6. Drain on a plate lined with paper towels, and sprinkle with the sea salt. Serve over the Hot Fried Rice. Makes 1 pound chitlins

Note: Many companies sell precleaned chitlins. I find that frozen tends to be the cleanest.

To Drink: Blanc de blancs Champagne, blanc de noirs Champagne, Chardonnay, dry Riesling, rosé, sparkling rosé, Sauvignon Blanc, amber beers, dark beers, hard ciders, IPAs

Serve with: Bread, egg, rice, or other pork dishes; green salads

hot fried rice

2 red radishes
4 cups (32 ounces) water
2 cups uncooked white rice
1 teaspoon kosher salt
¼ cup (2 ounces) blended olive oil
1 medium carrot, peeled and cut into medium-size pieces (about ⅓ cup)
1 small rutabaga, peeled and cut into medium-size pieces (about ½ cup)
½ cup (4 ounces) chicken stock
1 ½ tablespoons sweet soy sauce
1 tablespoon reduced-sodium soy sauce
4 mustard green leaves, cut into long, thin strips
1 ¼ teaspoons red pepper flakes
1 bunch scallions, thinly sliced
¼ bunch fresh flat-leaf parsley, chopped
1 lime, cut into 8 wedges

1. Thinly slice the radishes and place in a bowl of cold water. Set aside.

2. Bring 4 cups water, rice, and salt to a boil in a saucepan. Cover, reduce heat, and simmer until water is absorbed and rice is tender, about 20 minutes. Remove from the heat, and let stand 10 minutes.

3. Heat 2 tablespoons of the oil in a skillet over medium. Add the carrot and rutabaga, and cook, stirring often, until golden brown, about 2 minutes. Add the chicken stock and cover. Cook until the liquid is completely evaporated, 3 to 5 minutes. Add the remaining 2 tablespoons oil, and stir to combine. Stir in the cooked rice. Cook, stirring and scraping to loosen the browned bits from the bottom of skillet, until the rice is caramelized, about 4 minutes.

4. Add both soy sauces, and cook, stirring often, 3 to 5 minutes. Stir in the mustard greens and red pepper flakes, and remove from heat.

5. Divide the fried rice evenly among 4 bowls, and top with the Crispy Chitlins. Garnish with the scallions, parsley, radish slices, and lime wedges. Makes about 7 ½ cups

Pork Chops with Apple
Butter and Spiced Pumpkin
Seeds (page 274)
Turnip Hash (page 267)

Pork Chops with Apple Butter and Spiced Pumpkin Seeds

There is a must when it comes to cooking pork chops: They must have a bone in them! Cooking boneless pork chops means you are missing out on one of the most essential flavor components. Not only does the bone release a meaty essence, it helps the meat retain moisture while it cooks.

Apples and pork are a classic autumn pairing. The caramelized flavors of apple butter and warm spices of the pumpkin seeds highlight the rich, meaty goodness of the chops.

Serves 4

4 (10-ounce) bone-in pork chops
  (about ½ inch thick)
4 cups (32 ounces) Sweet Tea Brine
  (page 355)
2 tablespoons blended olive oil
1 teaspoon kosher salt

1 teaspoon coarsely ground black pepper
½ cup (4 ounces) bourbon
2 ounces (¼ cup) unsalted butter
Apple Butter and Spiced Pumpkin Seeds
  (recipe follows)

1. Combine the pork and Sweet Tea Brine in a 13- x 9-inch baking dish. Cover and refrigerate 8 hours or overnight.

2. Remove the pork chops from the brine; discard brine. Let pork chops come to room temperature, about 30 minutes. Rub the pork chops with the oil, and sprinkle evenly with the salt and pepper.

3. Bring the bourbon to a simmer in a saucepan over medium. Cook until reduced by half, about 8 minutes. Remove from heat, and whisk in the butter. Set aside.

4. Preheat a grill or smoker to medium-high (450°F) according to manufacturer's instructions. Grill the pork chops, uncovered, until golden brown and slightly crispy on the bottom, about 6 minutes, basting occasionally with the bourbon butter. Turn the pork chops, and cook until the meat begins to draw close to the bone, about 4 minutes.

5. Transfer to a wire rack; let stand 15 minutes, basting occasionally with any remaining bourbon butter. Serve with the Apple Butter and Spiced Pumpkin Seeds.

Note: This recipe can be used with all types of pork chops, including Porterhouse pork chops.
To Drink: Pinot Noir, red blends, rosé, red Zinfandel, amber beers, dark beers, hard cider, IPAs, stouts
Serve with: Collard green dishes

apple butter and spiced pumpkin seeds

APPLE BUTTER:

4 ounces (½ cup) unsalted butter, melted

8 red apples, cored

¼ cup packed light brown sugar

1 teaspoon ground cinnamon

½ teaspoon ground cloves

½ teaspoon ground allspice

½ teaspoon kosher salt

Pinch of freshly ground black pepper

SPICED PUMPKIN SEEDS:

2 tablespoons blended olive oil

1 cup pumpkin seeds

½ teaspoon gray sea salt

½ teaspoon curry powder

¼ teaspoon freshly ground black pepper

1. Prepare the Apple Butter: Preheat the oven to 350°F. Combine the melted butter and apples in a 13- x 9-inch baking dish, turning to coat the apples in the butter. Bake in the preheated oven until the apples are very tender and the skins pop, 50 minutes to 1 hour.

2. Sprinkle the apples with the brown sugar, cinnamon, cloves, allspice, kosher salt, and pepper. Return to oven, and bake until the sugar melts, about 5 minutes.

3. Remove from the oven, and let stand for 15 minutes. Transfer the apple mixture to a blender, and process until smooth. Let stand 30 minutes at room temperature or refrigerate overnight.

4. Prepare the Spiced Pumpkin Seeds: Heat the oil in a skillet over medium. Add the pumpkin seeds, and cook, stirring occasionally, until golden brown, about 2 minutes. Remove from the heat. Stir in the sea salt, curry powder, and pepper. Drain on a plate lined with paper towels. Makes 1 cup each apple butter and pumpkin seeds

Okra Seed Porridge with Pork Jowl and Pan-Roasted Okra

In late summer, okra bolts and the pods become too woody and tough to eat. The seeds, however, are the ideal size to use like couscous. It's a delicious way to support local farmers and to use late-harvest okra you might otherwise discard.

Serves 1

16 extra-large fresh okra pods

4 medium-size fresh okra pods

2 tablespoons plus 1 teaspoon kosher salt

1 tablespoon blended olive oil

¼ cup chopped pork jowl (about 2 ounces)

¼ cup minced shallot (from 1 large shallot)

2 garlic cloves, thinly sliced

¼ cup (2 ounces) dry white wine

1 thyme sprig

½ cup (4 ounces) heavy cream

¼ teaspoon ground white pepper

1 ounce smoked Cheddar cheese, shredded (about ¼ cup)

2 teaspoons chopped fresh flat-leaf parsley

⅛ teaspoon freshly grated nutmeg

¼ teaspoon Vadouvan curry powder or regular curry powder

Pan-Roasted Okra (recipe follows)

1. Cut the okra in half lengthwise. Remove the seeds and discard the pods. Combine a handful of ice and water in a medium bowl.

2. Fill a saucepan with water and 2 tablespoons of the salt. Bring to a boil in a saucepan over medium-high. Add the okra seeds, and cook 2 minutes. Drain in a fine wire-mesh strainer, and place the strainer in the ice bath to stop the cooking process. Drain and set aside.

3. Wipe the saucepan dry with paper towels. Add the oil, and heat over medium. Add the jowl and cook until browned. Add the shallot and garlic, and sauté until just softened, about 2 minutes. Add the wine and thyme. Cook until the liquid is reduced by half. Stir in heavy cream, white pepper, and remaining 1 teaspoon salt. Cook until the liquid is reduced by half, about 5 minutes.

4. Reduce the heat to low. Stir in the reserved okra seeds and cheese. Cook, stirring constantly, until the cheese melts. Stir in the parsley, and transfer to a serving dish. Sprinkle with the nutmeg and curry powder, and top with the Pan-Roasted Okra.

pan-roasted okra

5 small to medium-size fresh okra

1 teaspoon blended oil

½ teaspoon kosher salt

¼ teaspoon freshly ground black pepper

1. Halve 4 of the okra lengthwise. Slice remaining okra crosswise; set aside.

2. Heat the oil in a saucepan over medium-high. Add the okra, salt, and pepper. Cook, stirring constantly, until golden brown, 2 minutes. Drain on a plate lined with paper towels. Makes 1 serving

Okra, Andouille, and Crab Fritters

I don't know a single chef who doesn't like snack food. Our lives are pretty hectic, and having a quick snack between service is our time to replenish and relax (if that is even possible). Our midday snacks often translate into appetizers at home or even become part of the menu. This one is a favorite.

Serves 4

½ cup (about 2 ⅛ ounces) all-purpose flour

½ cup (about 2 ⅛ ounces) plain yellow cornmeal

1 teaspoon kosher salt

1 teaspoon baking soda

Pinch of cayenne pepper

½ cup (4 ounces) whole milk

2 large eggs

½ cup (3 ounces) fresh lump crabmeat, drained

½ cup sliced fresh okra (about 2 ounces)

¼ cup chopped andouille sausage (about 3 ounces)

2 tablespoons thinly sliced scallions

1 ounce (2 tablespoons) unsalted butter, melted

4 cups (32 ounces) vegetable oil

Pinch of flaky sea salt

1. Whisk together the flour, cornmeal, salt, baking soda, and cayenne pepper in a medium bowl. Whisk together the milk and eggs in a small bowl, and add to the flour mixture, stirring to combine. Pick the crabmeat, removing any bits of shell. Fold the crabmeat, okra, sausage, scallions, and melted butter into the mixture.

2. Heat the oil to 350°F in a stockpot over medium. Drop batter by tablespoonfuls into the hot oil, being careful to not overcrowd the pot. Fry, in batches, until golden brown on 1 side, about 3 minutes. Turn and fry until golden brown, 2 to 3 minutes. Drain on a plate lined with paper towels. Season with sea salt flakes. Serve hot.

To Drink: Vinho Verde, Sauvignon Blanc, late harvest Champagne, Chardonnay, rosé, amber beers, IPAs, hard ciders, Bloody Mary

Serve with: Onion, greens, potato, or tomato dishes; green or tomato salads

Oxtail Potpies

I was an elementary school kid visiting my friend Patrick Bayard's house the first time I had oxtails. I didn't know what I was eating...just that it was meltingly tender, spicy, colorful, and served with rice—saffron rice. I remember the rice was so vivid I didn't want the oxtails to cover it up...only I wanted more oxtails! Little did I know at the time that dish would be the standard by which all oxtail dishes in my life would be measured. Thirty-five years later, I still recall the day I tasted it.

Tender chunks of generously spiced oxtail meat is like the perfect mealtime gift encased in Erika Council's Piecrust (page 352), which serves the same purpose as that saffron rice did so long ago. It absorbs the meaty juices and provides a welcome textural counterpoint to the meat and vegetables.

Serves 6

1 cup (about 4 ¼ ounces) all-purpose flour

1 teaspoon coarsely ground black pepper

½ teaspoon ground cumin

½ teaspoon curry powder

½ teaspoon onion powder

½ teaspoon garlic powder

1 tablespoon plus 2 teaspoons kosher salt

5 pounds oxtails, trimmed, patted dry, and cut into 1-inch pieces

½ cup (4 ounces) blended olive oil

2 yellow onions, cut into 1 ½-inch pieces

2 medium carrots, cut into 1 ½-inch pieces

10 garlic cloves

6 bay leaves

3 thyme sprigs

2 cups red table wine (any variety except Zinfandel)

1 cup port

4 cups (32 ounces) unsalted beef broth

6 cups plus 1 tablespoon water

1 rutabaga, peeled and cut into ½-inch cubes (about 8 ounces)

6 fingerling potatoes, cut into ½-inch rounds (about 8 ounces)

¼ cup sour cream

1 tablespoon chopped fresh flat-leaf parsley

Erika Council's Piecrust (page 352) or 1 (14.1-ounce) package refrigerated piecrusts

1 large egg

2 teaspoons flaky sea salt (such as Maldon)

½ teaspoon fresh thyme leaves

1. Preheat the oven to 350°F. Stir together the flour, black pepper, cumin, curry powder, onion powder, garlic powder, and 2 teaspoons of the kosher salt in a large bowl. Add the oxtail pieces, and toss to coat.

2. Heat ¼ cup of the oil in a large Dutch oven over medium. Add the oxtails. Brown on all sides, 8 to 10 minutes. Transfer to a plate, reserving the drippings in the Dutch oven.

3. Add the remaining ¼ cup oil to the drippings in the Dutch oven. Add the onions, carrots, and garlic, and cook, stirring often, until caramelized, 8 to 10 minutes. Return the oxtails to the Dutch oven, and add the bay leaves and thyme sprigs. Pour in the red wine and port. Cook, stirring occasionally, until the liquid is reduced by half, 6 to

continued

8 minutes. Add the beef broth, and bring to a simmer. Cover and place in the preheated oven. Bake until the oxtails are tender when pierced with a fork, 3 hours to 3 hours and 30 minutes.

4. Remove from the oven, and let stand 1 hour. Remove the oxtails and carrots from the Dutch oven. Separate the meat from the bones, reserving the bones. Place the meat and carrots in a large heatproof bowl.

5. Return the oxtail bones to the Dutch oven. Bring to a simmer over medium, and cook until the liquid is reduced by half. Pour the mixture through a fine wire-mesh strainer over the oxtails. Discard solids.

6. Bring 6 cups of the water and the remaining 1 tablespoon kosher salt to a boil in a stockpot over medium. Add the rutabaga, and cook 5 minutes. Transfer the rutabaga pieces to a bowl of ice and water using a slotted spoon. Add the potatoes to the boiling water, and cook 5 minutes. Transfer the potatoes to the bowl of ice and water using a slotted spoon. Let stand until cool. Drain.

7. Divide the oxtail mixture evenly among 6 large ramekins (or an 8-inch square baking dish), filling each two-thirds full. Top evenly with the rutabaga mixture, sour cream, and parsley, and stir each to combine.

8. Cut the piecrust into 6 circles to fit tops of ramekins, and place 1 piecrust round on each ramekin, pressing the edges to seal. Discard any excess piecrust.

9. Whisk together the egg and the remaining 1 tablespoon water in a small bowl. Brush the piecrust dough evenly with the egg wash, and sprinkle evenly with the sea salt and thyme. Cover and refrigerate. Chill at least 1 hour or overnight.

10. Preheat the oven to 350°F. Place the ramekins on a baking sheet, and bake in the preheated oven until the filling is hot and the crust is golden brown, about 45 minutes. Let stand 15 minutes before serving.

Note: The potpie can be made in an 8-inch square baking dish following the same method. Oxtails should be cut the same length for consistent cooking. The filling for the potpies is best cooked a day ahead.

To Drink: Barolo, red Bordeaux, Cabernet or Cabernet/Merlot blend, Rioja Reserva, Chianti Classico, Northen Rhône red, IPAs, stouts, hard ciders

Serve with: Onion, greens, potato, rice, or bean dishes; roasted vegetables; herbaceous salads

It pains me to see food go to waste. We have regular discussions about it in my kitchen. As far as I'm concerned, throwing away food is more about the uninspired cook than a purposefully wasteful one. Inspired cooks tend to find ways to utilize all of the ingredients at their disposal—beef bones become rich stock and pork skin gets fried and turned into a perfect snack. Throwing away food disregards the ranchers, farmers, and artisans who produce it. I revere the ingredients that I am fortunate to have at my disposal, and transform them with passion and creativity into delicious meals for my family, friends, and patrons. I urge you to do the same. Think of leftovers, bits, and pieces as an opportunity to get creative and test your skills in the kitchen.

BEANS & RICE

Fresh and dried beans as well as peanuts have been a versatile source of protein in Soul cuisine since the very beginning. As in the simple dishes of other bean eaters around the world, legumes were cooked with the day's ration of rice, aromatics, and spices in long-simmered dishes that have stood the test of time, such as red beans and rice or rice and peas. Peanuts were eaten, boiled or roasted, straight from the shell, stewed, or pureed. While wild rice is native to the Americas, cultivated rice—the short- and long-grain varieties indigenous to Asia and West Africa—came to this country with European settlers, but only became a thriving industry on the backs of slaves. For centuries, Native Americans harvested wild rice where it grew along riverbanks and marshlands, and slaves adopted the practice. Black cooks used both types of rice in stews, as porridge cereal, and in desserts. Rice is one of my favorite comfort foods. The simple joy I get from enjoying a bowl of cooked white rice speckled with black pepper and topped with a pool of melting butter is primal.

Rice with Butter and Honey

My mother served rice for breakfast, lunch, and dinner. Breakfast rice was prepared more like cereal. My mother didn't like for me to have refined sugar, but honey was acceptable. The best part of this is the rice starch and butter that seep to the bottom of the bowl is laced with the honey. I never had to wait for a cold pat of butter to melt in hot cereal. Mom kept the butter on the table.

Serves 4

1 ½ cups (12 ounces) water

1 cup uncooked long-grain white rice

1 teaspoon kosher salt

2 teaspoons salted butter

¼ teaspoon freshly ground black pepper

½ teaspoon honey

1. Bring 1½ cups water, rice, and salt to a boil in a saucepan.

2. Cover, reduce heat to medium-low, and simmer for 15 to 18 minutes. Remove from the heat, and let stand until all of the water is absorbed, about 5 minutes.

3. Transfer the rice to a serving bowl. Top with the butter, pepper, and honey.

Rice with Butter and Black Pepper

The laughter at the table while eating with my family is immensely satisfying. My family folklore includes a story that once while eating rice at the table, I laughed so hard it came out of my nose. (It was my aunt's fault. She had a wry sense of humor and would patronize silly kids with knock-knock jokes and other childish fodder.)

Rice was a mainstay of our family meals. Whether it was rice served at home with oxtails or the fried rice we ordered in Chinatown, each grain had to be perfect, not dry, not clumpy, and never overcooked.

Serves 4

1 ½ cups water

1 cup uncooked long-grain white rice

1 teaspoon kosher salt

2 teaspoons salted butter or 1 teaspoon bacon
   drippings

¼ teaspoon cracked black pepper

1 small scallion, thinly sliced (about
   2 tablespoons)

1. Bring 1 ½ cups water, rice, and salt to a boil in a saucepan.

2. Cover, reduce heat to medium-low, and simmer for 15 to 18 minutes. Remove from the heat, and let stand until all of the water is absorbed, about 5 minutes.

3. Transfer the rice to a serving bowl. Top with the butter or bacon drippings, pepper, and scallions.

To Drink: Vinho Verde, pale ale, saki
Serve with: Grilled seafood; grilled meats; poultry, spicy, or braised dishes

Rice Porridge

Porridges have always been a part of my lexicon of dishes because they convey the honest intent of each ingredient. Using lemon zest in this recipe accentuates the natural flavor of rice so that it doesn't get lost in the spices and rich flavors.

Serves 10

1 ½ cups (12 ounces) water

1 cup uncooked long-grain white rice

1 teaspoon kosher salt

4 cups (32 ounces) chicken stock

½ cup (4 ounces) heavy cream

¼ teaspoon ground cumin

¼ teaspoon curry powder

⅛ teaspoon red pepper flakes

½ teaspoon honey

2 teaspoons salted butter

¼ teaspoon freshly ground black pepper

1 tablespoon lemon zest (from 1 lemon)

2 tablespoons sliced scallion (about 1 scallion)

1. Bring 1½ cups water, rice, and salt to a boil in a saucepan.

2. Cover, reduce heat to medium-low, and simmer for 15 to 18 minutes. Remove from heat, and let stand until all of the water is absorbed, about 5 minutes.

3. Bring the chicken stock, heavy cream, cumin, curry powder, red pepper flakes, and honey to a simmer in a stockpot over medium-high.

4. Add the cooked rice to the chicken stock mixture; reduce the heat to medium, and simmer until creamy, 8 to 10 minutes. Stir in the butter.

5. Transfer the rice porridge to a serving bowl, and sprinkle with the pepper, lemon zest, and scallions.

Note: High-quality butter is always key for rice dishes. Margarine should never be used.

To Drink: Bordeaux, Cabernet Sauvignon, Chianti Classico, honey wine, Northern Rhône red, red blend, Rioja Reserva, amber beers, light beers, hard ciders, coffee beverages, IPAs, chai tea, mimosas

Serve with: Green salads; braised or roasted vegetable dishes

Wild Rice

After my brother passed away, my dad's commitment to healthier foods became a prevalent part of his dishes. We still ate white rice with dishes such as beans or gumbo. However, for dishes such as broiled chicken or pot roast, wild rice became the norm. I particularly like the fat drippings from the chicken mixed in the rice. It was better than butter because it contained all the seasonings.

Serves 4

1 tablespoon blended olive oil

1 small carrot, diced (about ¼ cup)

1 celery stalk, diced (about ¼ cup)

1 small white onion, diced (about ¾ cup)

1 cup (8 ounces) dry white wine

1¼ cups uncooked wild rice

½ teaspoon dried thyme

½ teaspoon coarsely ground black pepper

2 bay leaves

6 cups (48 ounces) water

1 ¾ teaspoons kosher salt

1 ounce (2 tablespoons) unsalted butter

1. Heat the oil in a stockpot over medium. Add the carrot, celery, and onion; cook, stirring occasionally, until slightly tender, about 4 minutes. Add wine, and cook until the liquid is reduced by half, about 6 minutes.

2. Stir in the rice, thyme, pepper, and bay leaves. Add 6 cups water and 1 teaspoon of the salt. Bring to a simmer; cook, stirring occasionally, until the rice is tender, 35 to 40 minutes. Let stand for 5 minutes, and drain off any excess liquid. Remove and discard the bay leaves.

3. Stir in the butter and remaining ¾ teaspoon salt.

To Drink: Red Bordeaux, Cabernet Sauvignon or Cabernet/Merlot blend, Rioja Reserva, Chianti Classico, Northern Rhône red, amber beers, IPAs, stouts, hard ciders

Serve with: Grilled seafood; grilled meats; poultry, spicy, braised vegetable, or smoked poultry dishes; grilled vegetables

Cheese Rice

Wild rice has a very aromatic, nutty quality that pairs well with cream. Incorporating cheese in the dish also provides another nut-like quality. This rice recipe is made using the same method as risotto and is fantastic as a stand-alone dish, but is perfect with my Leg of Lamb Steak (page 102).

Serves 2

1 tablespoon blended olive oil
1 small carrot, cut into ¼-inch-thick slices (about ⅓ cup)
1 shallot, diced (about ¼ cup)
½ cup (4 ounces) chicken stock
¼ cup (2 ounces) heavy cream
4 ounces cream cheese

2 ounces aged Cheddar cheese, shredded (about ½ cup)
2 cups cooked Wild Rice (opposite page)
½ teaspoon kosher salt
¼ teaspoon freshly ground black pepper
⅛ teaspoon red pepper flakes

1. Heat the oil in a saucepan over medium. Add the carrot and shallot. Cook, stirring often, 4 minutes.

2. Stir in the stock and heavy cream. Bring to a simmer, and cook 5 minutes.

3. Add the cream cheese and Cheddar cheese. Remove from the heat, and stir until the cheese melts. Fold in the Wild Rice, salt, black pepper, and red pepper flakes until incorporated.

To Drink: Chablis, white Burgundy, sparkling wine, Champagne, Chardonnay, dry Riesling, rosé, amber beers, IPAs, stouts, pale ale, hard ciders

Serve with: Grilled seafood; grilled meats; poultry, spicy, braised vegetable, or smoked poultry dishes; grilled vegetables

Red Beans with Smoked Sausage and Shrimp

Red beans were a Monday night favorite in my family. Dad would pour the same amount of seasoning into his hand every time. It wasn't the sort of precise measurement required for baking, but it was always the perfect balance for this dish. The heat from crushed red pepper flakes and spices is perfectly suited to the earthiness of red beans and the bite of the sausage. Variations using smoked turkey are equally satisfying.

Serves 12

2 tablespoons blended olive oil

1 pound smoked sausage

1 pound dried red kidney beans, soaked in water overnight

6 cups (48 ounces) chicken stock

1 yellow onion (about 4 ounces), finely chopped

4 garlic cloves, minced

2 medium-size green bell peppers (about 5 ounces each), finely chopped

2 celery stalks, finely chopped (about ½ cup)

2 teaspoons kosher salt

1 ½ teaspoons red pepper flakes

1 teaspoon coarsely ground black pepper

¼ teaspoon freshly ground black pepper

Pinch of fennel seeds

2 bay leaves

2 tablespoons apple cider vinegar

16 colossal raw shrimp, peeled and deveined (optional)

4 cups buttered cooked white rice

2 scallions, thinly sliced (about ¼ cup)

1. Heat the oil in a saucepan over medium. Add the smoked sausage. Brown on both sides, and remove from the pan. Drain on paper towels. Let the sausage cool about 10 minutes, and slice.

2. Add the kidney beans, chicken stock, onion, garlic, bell peppers, celery, salt, red pepper flakes, coarsely ground black pepper, freshly ground black pepper, fennel seeds, and bay leaves to the pan. Increase the heat to high, and bring to a boil.

3. Reduce the heat to low, and simmer, covered, until the beans and bell peppers are tender, 2 hours to 2 hours and 30 minutes.

4. Add vinegar and sausage to the pan. Place the shrimp on top of the mixture in the pan. Do not stir; cover the pan, and cook for 5 minutes. Remove from the heat, and let stand for 15 minutes.

5. To serve, spoon the beans and sausage over the buttered rice, and sprinkle with the scallions.

Note: Allowing the beans to stand for a period of time brings flavors together. Do not rush to serve this dish.

Seared Snapper with Red Bean Emulsion

The addition of corn to rice dishes is also a part of my family food identity. Frozen corn, reheated with butter, water, seasoning salt, and black pepper, was served as a deliciously simple accompaniment for any main course. I riff off of that family habit by using Pickled Baby Corn (page 166) as an accent for fish served on a creamy red bean puree.

Serves 2

1 cup (about 5 ¾ ounces) plain yellow
   cornmeal
1 teaspoon kosher salt
½ teaspoon coarsely ground black pepper
1 tablespoon blended olive oil
2 (5-ounce) red snapper fillets (less than
   ½ inch thick), skin-on and scored

1 teaspoon unsalted butter
1 thyme sprig
½ lemon
½ cup Red Bean Emulsion (recipe follows)
2 Pickled Baby Corn, cut in half (page 166)
Fresh thyme sprigs

1. Combine the cornmeal, salt, and pepper in a shallow dish.

2. Heat the oil in a sauté pan or skillet over medium. Dredge the snapper in the cornmeal mixture until completely coated. Add the fish to hot oil in the pan, skin sides down, and cook until crispy, about 5 minutes. Turn fish over, and cook 2 more minutes.

3. Add the butter and thyme to the pan. Baste the fish with the butter-oil mixture in the pan, making sure to avoid any darkened cornmeal. Squeeze the lemon over the fish. Remove the fish from pan, and drain on paper towels.

4. Spoon about ¼ cup of the Red Bean Emulsion on each of 2 plates, and place a piece of fish on top. Serve with Pickled Baby Corn, and garnish with thyme sprigs, if desired.

To Drink: Bordeaux, Cabernet Sauvignon, Chianti Classico, honey wine, Northern Rhône red, red blend, Rioja Reserva, amber beers, light beers, hard ciders, coffee beverages, IPAs
Serve with: Green salads; braised or roasted vegetable dishes; smoked meats; roasted meats; rice dishes

red bean emulsion

2 cups cooked Red Beans (page 297)
   (without sausage, shrimp, or rice)
1 cup (8 ounces) chicken stock

1 ounce (2 tablespoons) cold unsalted butter,
   cut into ½-inch pieces

Bring the Red Beans and stock to a simmer in a saucepan over medium heat. Process the beans until smooth using an immersion blender or standard blender, adding the butter, 1 piece at a time, until the butter and beans are emulsified. Makes about 1½ cups

Note: Refrigerate any leftover Red Bean Emulsion in an airtight container for up to 7 days.

Chicken Thighs and BBQ Beans

BBQ beans are a meal unto themselves. They have a meaty quality that absorbs bold ingredients such as Worcestershire sauce and red pepper flakes. Caramelizing the thighs in the same pan you're going to cook the beans is essential to building the flavor of this dish.

Serves 2

4 bone-in, skin-on chicken thighs

4 teaspoons kosher salt

2 teaspoons coarsely ground black pepper

2 tablespoons blended olive oil

1 pound dried white beans, soaked in water overnight

2 cups diced yellow onion (from 2 onions)

1 ¼ cups diced green bell pepper (from 2 bell peppers)

½ cup diced celery (about 2 stalks)

4 garlic cloves, smashed and minced

1 ½ teaspoons red pepper flakes

6 cups (48 ounces) chicken stock

2 bay leaves

⅛ teaspoon fennel seeds

1 cup packed light brown sugar

½ cup ketchup

¼ cup Worcestershire sauce

2 tablespoons coarse-grain mustard

2 tablespoons apple cider vinegar

2 scallions, thinly sliced

1. Sprinkle the chicken thighs with 1 ½ teaspoons of the salt and 1 teaspoon of the black pepper.

2. Heat the oil in a saucepan over medium. Sear the chicken thighs, skin side down, in the hot oil, until golden brown, about 7 minutes. Turn the chicken thighs over, and cook until browned, about 5 more minutes. Remove the chicken from the pan.

3. Add the beans, onions, bell peppers, celery, garlic, red pepper flakes, chicken stock, bay leaves, and fennel seeds to the pan; bring to a boil.

4. Reduce heat to medium-low, and simmer until the beans are tender, about 1 hour and 30 minutes. Stir in the brown sugar, ketchup, Worcestershire sauce, mustard, vinegar, and remaining 2 ½ teaspoons salt into the pan. Return the chicken thighs to the pan, and simmer until the chicken is done, about 10 minutes. Remove and discard the bay leaves.

5. Let stand for 25 minutes. Sprinkle with remaining 1 teaspoon black pepper and scallions before serving.

To Drink: Bordeaux, Cabernet Sauvignon, Chianti Classico, honey wine, Northern Rhône red, red blend, Rioja Reserva, amber beers, light beers, hard ciders, coffee beverages, IPAs
Serve with: Green salads; braised or roasted vegetable dishes; smoked or roasted meats; rice dishes

Oxtails with Boiled
Peanut Stew
(page 304)

Curried Broccoli Salad
with Peanuts (page 305)

Crispy Plantains and
Chocolate-Covered Bacon
with Peanut Sauce
(page 306)

Oxtails with Boiled Peanut Stew and Curried Broccoli Salad with Peanuts

If you look at the components of this dish, what accompaniments naturally come to mind? Oxtails served with rice makes perfect sense. So does broccoli with rice...broccoli with peanuts...and peanuts with hot spices. Building meals can be as simple as weighing what you like and know works well together, with what you have on hand, and then balancing flavors.

Broccoli stems are an overlooked part of the vegetable. Most of the time they are just discarded, but by peeling the stem in the same manner as you would asparagus, it allows the water to enter the stem, and this helps the entire vegetable cook evenly.

Serves 6

3 tablespoons blended olive oil

6 (8-ounce) oxtail pieces

2 ½ teaspoons kosher salt

1 ½ teaspoons coarsely ground black pepper

¾ cup Seasoned Flour (page 352)

2 cups chopped yellow onion

2 cups chopped green bell pepper

2 cups chopped red bell pepper

1 Scotch bonnet chile, stemmed and finely diced (about 1 teaspoon)

¾ cup diced celery (about 2 stalks)

4 garlic cloves, crushed

½ teaspoon red pepper flakes

¼ teaspoon dried thyme

¼ teaspoon ground allspice

2 bay leaves

3 tablespoons all-purpose flour

3 cups (24 ounces) beef stock or chicken stock

1 ½ cups (12 cups) dry red wine

2 tablespoons Worcestershire sauce

1 ½ cups blanched unsalted peanuts

1. Heat the oil in a saucepan over medium-high. Sprinkle the oxtails with 1 teaspoon each salt and black pepper. Place the Seasoned Flour in a shallow dish. Dredge the oxtails, shaking off any excess. Brown the oxtails in hot oil on 1 side for about 6 minutes.

2. Turn the oxtails, and cook until browned, about 8 minutes. Add the onion, bell peppers, Scotch bonnet chile, celery, and garlic. Cook, stirring occasionally, until softened about 3 minutes. Add the red pepper flakes, thyme, allspice, bay leaves, and remaining 1 ½ teaspoons salt and ½ teaspoon black pepper. Cook for 2 more minutes. Add the all-purpose flour, and cook, stirring constantly, 1 minute. Remove from the heat. Add the beef stock, red wine, and Worcestershire sauce.

3. Return the pan to medium-high; bring to a boil. Reduce heat to medium-low. Cover and cook 1 hour and 30 minutes, stirring gently every 30 to 40 minutes. After 1 hour and 30 minutes, add the peanuts. Cook until the oxtails are tender, about 1 hour.

4. Remove from the heat, and let stand for 30 minutes before serving. Skim any fat from the top with a shallow spoon; discard fat.

To Drink: Cabernet Sauvignon, Pinot Noir, Syrah, Zinfandel, amber beers, light beers, Champagne cocktails, hard ciders, IPAs

Serve with: Rice or potato dishes

Curried Broccoli Salad with Peanuts

Serves 4

4 quarts (16 cups) water
1 tablespoon kosher salt
3 medium heads broccoli
1 cup mayonnaise
2 tablespoons rice wine vinegar
1 teaspoon curry powder
½ teaspoon granulated sugar
½ teaspoon sambal oelek

1 tablespoon roasted, salted peanuts, coarsely
  chopped
2 pieces crystallized ginger, coarsely chopped
  (about 2 tablespoons)
1 jalapeño chile, thinly sliced
1 lime, cut into 8 wedges

1. Combine ice and water in a large bowl.

2. Bring 16 cups water and the kosher salt to a rolling boil in a saucepan over medium-high.

3. Add the broccoli, and cook just until a knife can be inserted into the stem, about 5 minutes.

4. Remove the broccoli and transfer to the ice bath to cool for 5 minutes. Remove the broccoli from the ice bath. Remove the florets, and set aside. Cut the broccoli stems into 1-inch pieces.

5. Stir together the mayonnaise, rice wine vinegar, curry powder, sugar, and sambal oelek in a medium bowl.

6. Fold the broccoli florets and the diced broccoli stems into the mayonnaise mixture. Sprinkle with the peanuts, crystallized ginger, and jalapeño slices. Serve with lime wedges.

Crispy Plantains and Chocolate-Covered Bacon with Peanut Sauce

The first bite of any dish dictates whether a person will have another. The last bite is equally important. If a dessert is cloyingly sweet it kills the palate. Mastering the balance of sweet and savory is a hallmark of a talented cook. So is stretching the expectations and having fun with ingredients.

Serves 12 (Makes 4 cups sauce)

PEANUT SAUCE:

1 pound dry-roasted peanuts, finely chopped

1 (13.66-ounce) can coconut milk, well-shaken

1 cup wildflower honey

1 teaspoon sea salt

½ teaspoon vanilla bean paste

½ cup (4 ounces) water (optional)

¾ teaspoon coarsely ground black pepper

2 cups (16 ounces) water

1 ½ cups bittersweet chocolate chips

½ cup unsweetened shredded coconut, toasted

2 cups (16 ounces) vegetable oil

2 ripe plantains, thinly sliced

½ teaspoon lime zest (from 1 lime)

½ teaspoon kosher salt

CRISPY PLANTAINS AND CHOCOLATE-COVERED BACON:

12 bacon slices, cut in half crosswise

1. Simmer the peanuts through vanilla bean paste in a saucepan over medium, stirring, until liquid is syrupy and reduced by half, about 30 minutes. Remove from heat and cool 10 minutes. Process in a food processor until smooth, adding up to ½ cup water as needed to reach desired consistency. Cool about 30 minutes before serving.

2. Preheat the oven to 350°F. Line 2 rimmed baking sheets with foil and arrange the bacon slices in a single layer; sprinkle with pepper. Bake until crispy, 14 to 16 minutes. Remove and transfer the bacon to a wire rack over paper towels. Cool 30 minutes.

3. Heat 2 cups of water in the bottom of a double boiler over low. Add the chocolate chips to the top of the double boiler, and stir until melted. Remove from the heat. Dip 1 end of each bacon slice into the chocolate, allowing any excess to drip off, and place on parchment paper. Sprinkle with the shredded coconut while the chocolate is still warm.

4. Keep remaining melted chocolate warm (about 85°F) in the double boiler over low.

5. Heat the oil to 350°F in a saucepan over medium. Fry the plantains, in batches, in the hot oil until crispy, about 2 minutes. Drain on paper towels.

6. Combine the lime zest and salt in a small bowl. Dip 1 edge of each plantain chip in the melted chocolate, and place on parchment paper. Sprinkle with zest mixture. Serve the crispy plantains and bacon with Peanut Sauce.

Note: Turkey bacon is not a good substitute for this dish.

To Drink: Banyuls, port, late harvest Zinfandel, IPAs, stouts

Serve with: Creamy desserts, fresh fruit

Soul food has always been rooted in the story of our ancestors...and shared with us by our grandmothers. It's what I appreciate the most about the cuisine. Each generation fuels the flame a little differently before passing the torch. And each generation pays homage to the grandmothers—those who are and were the nurturers and sustainers of our souls through delicious food traditions. Cooking together is critical. Passing down the steps and ingredients of a beloved family recipe for spicy red beans and rice or sharing the simple technique for making buttery breakfast porridge is an opportunity to stay connected with our elders and learn from them. They empower us so that when they are no longer here we are fortified to carry on. Keeping our food traditions alive and appreciating their evolution is the most beautiful way I know to honor our roots and souls.

Baked Quail Eggs in Green Pea Soup
with Ham Hocks, Crispy Shallots,
and Parmesan (page 311)

Chilled Green Pea Soup with Ham Hock and Fennel Salad

The grassy sweetness of the peas pairs deliciously with the hammy flavor of the hock meat. Everything is balanced by the bright acidity of the fennel salad, which cuts the richness of the broth and crème fraîche.

Serves 6

CHILLED GREEN PEA SOUP:

3 cups (24 ounces) water

1 smoked ham hock (about 8 ½ ounces)

1 medium-size yellow onion, cut into large pieces (about 1 ½ cups)

2 celery stalks, cut into large pieces (about ½ cup)

4 garlic cloves, smashed and chopped (about 4 teaspoons)

2 bay leaves

1 teaspoon kosher salt

¼ teaspoon black peppercorns

1 pound frozen green peas, thawed

1 tarragon sprig, leaves removed

HAM HOCK AND FENNEL SALAD:

1 braised ham hock (from Chilled Green Pea Soup)

1 shallot, cut into small pieces

¼ cup (2 ounces) white balsamic vinegar

½ teaspoon kosher salt

½ teaspoon blended olive oil, plus more for serving

½ teaspoon Dijon mustard

¼ teaspoon coarsely ground black pepper

1 fennel bulb, fronds reserved, bulb very thinly sliced (about 2 cups)

1 cup crème fraîche

1. Prepare the Chilled Green Pea Soup: Bring the 3 cups water, ham hock, and next 6 ingredients to a boil in a stockpot over medium-high. Reduce the heat to medium-low, and simmer, partially covered, 1 hour or until the ham hock is tender. Remove from the heat, and let stand 20 minutes.

2. Pour mixture through a fine wire-mesh strainer into a bowl. Reserve the ham hock for the salad; discard the remaining solids. Add the peas to the stock, and let stand 2 minutes. Add the tarragon leaves. Process the mixture with an immersion blender until smooth. (Or in batches in a regular blender. Be sure to remove the center of the blender lid to allow steam to escape and to prevent overflowing.) Refrigerate at least 1 hour.

3. Prepare the Ham Hock and Fennel Salad: Remove and discard the skin from the hock. Remove the meat from the bone, and dice.

4. Whisk together the shallot, vinegar, salt, oil, mustard, and pepper in a large bowl. Add the fennel; toss to coat. Add the ham, and toss to combine. Let stand 10 minutes.

5. Whisk the crème fraîche in the chilled soup. Ladle the soup into bowls. Top each serving with some of the salad. Garnish with the fennel fronds and drizzle with oil.

To Drink: Albariño, white Burgundy, Chardonnay, Muscadet, Picpoul, Pinot Noir, amber beers, light beers, Champagne cocktails, hard ciders, IPAs

Serve with: Green salads; braised or roasted vegetables; smoked or roasted meats; rice dishes

Baked Quail Eggs in Green Pea Soup with Ham Hocks, Crispy Shallots, and Parmesan

I'm often inspired by breakfast dishes. Flavors often navigate through salty, sour, and sweet. Dishes can be protein-filled and tend to have a satisfying richness to them. This version of "bacon and eggs" utilizes the simplicity of soup where you would traditionally see grits. The pea soup will reduce and coddle with the egg to create this rich velvet texture, similar to grits but just different enough to understand the inspiration.

Serves 4

Chilled Green Pea Soup (recipe opposite), prepared through step 2
½ teaspoon kosher salt
2 cups plus 1 tablespoon frozen green peas (about 8 ounces), thawed
12 quail eggs
3 ½ ounces braised ham hock (from Chilled Green Pea Soup), skin removed and discarded, meat diced (about ½ cup meat)

Crispy Shallots (page 68)
1 cup pea tendrils or bitter greens such as arugula or curly mustard greens
1 teaspoon olive oil
¼ teaspoon lemon zest, plus ½ teaspoon juice (from 1 lemon)
1 ounce Parmesan cheese, shaved
¼ teaspoon gray sea salt

1. Preheat the broiler. Process the soup, kosher salt, and 2 cups of the peas in a blender until smooth, about 30 seconds. Transfer to a stockpot, and cook over medium, stirring occasionally, until heated through, about 10 minutes.

2. Divide the soup mixture evenly among 4 ovenproof dishes (each about 4 inches wide and at least ¾ inch tall). Cut the tops off the quail eggs, and gently pour 3 eggs into each dish. Broil until the egg whites just begin to set, 4 to 5 minutes.

3. Top the egg whites evenly with the diced ham hock and remaining 1 tablespoon peas. (Do not cover the egg yolks.) Broil until the egg yolks just begin to set, 2 to 4 minutes. Remove from the oven, and top evenly with the Crispy Shallots. (Do not cover the egg yolks.)

4. Toss together the pea tendrils, oil, lemon zest, and lemon juice in a small bowl. Place a small mound of the pea tendril mixture on top of the soup in each dish. Sprinkle evenly with the shaved Parmesan cheese and the gray sea salt.

⊰ CHEF'S TABLE ⊱

What do I serve when I am entertaining at home? My imagination guides me every time. This menu represents how you can express yourself through the bounty of Soul cooking and the amazing flavors available to us today. You can mix basic ingredients with luxurious ones: serve a traditional dish from West Africa with a favorite from your childhood table. There are no limits and there is no wrong or right dish when it comes to your table.

Smoked Catfish Dip with Parmesan
Tuiles (page 125)

Sea Urchin with Smoked Tomato
Broth and West African Spices (page 188)

Rice Porridge (page 291)

Chilled Green Pea Soup with Ham Hock and
Fennel Salad (page 310)

ON THE RADIO

"I Still Can't Get Over Loving You" — *Ray Parker Jr.*
"Let's Make a Promise" — *Peaches & Herb*
"You Can Leave Your Hat On" — *Joe Cocker*
"This Year's Love" — *David Gray*

Sea Urchin with Smoked Tomato Broth and West African Spices (page 188)

Rice Porridge (page 291)

Smoked Catfish Dip with
Parmesan Tuiles (page 125)

Chilled Green Pea Soup
with Ham Hock and Fennel
Salad (page 310)

ROOTS

Easily stored for eating during lean times, roots and tubers were a necessity in colonial larders and a regular feature of slave meals. Long after the growing season ended, these vegetables were a nutrient-dense package of hearty sustenance. Roots and tubers are interchangeable in most dishes with the exception of rhizomes such as ginger and turmeric, which are used in small doses as flavorings. Prior to the slave trade and migration, a wide variety of root vegetables were cultivated and harvested in the Americas. Slaves simply adapted to the ingredients available. They cooked potatoes and yams as they had cassava root in Africa—boiled, roasted, fried, or mashed. Other roots like beets, turnips, and rutabagas were prepared similarly with the addition of pickling as a preservation technique. From crusty hash browns to a heap of mashed potatoes, roots continue to be comfort foods we crave. Beets star in a jewel-toned hash that I pair with chicken thighs braised in sweet tea. I make a potato gratin as comforting as any side of mac-n-cheese. Yukon Golds and vibrant sweet potatoes layered under a crusty blanket of melted smoked Cheddar are irresistible. Modern food technology gave us instant potato flakes, which I find gives fish the crunchiest of coatings. One taste and doubters become converts.

Beet Salad

Beet salad is an earthy avenue for acidity in dishes like the Popcorn-Crusted Scallops on Corn Porridge with Pickled Baby Corn and Beet Salad (page 165). In that dish, having two bright, tart elements to temper the corn's sweetness is key to flavor harmony.

Serves 2 as an entrée or 4 as an appetizer

2 large beets

½ cup (4 ounces) water

½ cup sorghum vinegar (black vinegar)

1 teaspoon kosher salt

2 thyme sprigs

8 black peppercorns

2 tablespoons red wine vinegar

2 tablespoons extra-virgin olive oil

¼ teaspoon sea salt

1. Preheat the oven to 350°F. Combine the beets, ½ cup water, sorghum vinegar, salt, thyme, and peppercorns in a Dutch oven or roasting pan, and cover. Bake in the preheated oven 1 hour and 15 minutes.

2. Let stand 20 minutes. Peel the beets using a paper towel. Discard the cooking liquid.

3. Cut the beets into ½-inch pieces, and place in a serving bowl. Drizzle with the red wine vinegar and oil, and sprinkle with sea salt.

Note: Sorghum vinegar (aka black vinegar) is what I consider molasses vinegar. It is most popular in Chinese dishes and markets. It is very similar to Sherry vinegar but with more grassy notes.

To Drink: Grüner Veltliner, Chablis, white Burgundy, sparkling wine, Champagne, Chardonnay, dry Riesling, rosé, amber beers, IPAs, stouts, pale ale, hard ciders

Serve with: Grilled seafood; grilled meats; poultry or smoked poultry; rice, potato, or pasta dishes

Golden Beet Hash

Beets come in many shapes and shades. Golden beets have a slightly sweet and bitter flavor when served raw. Roasted or caramelized, they become sweet and somewhat tannic. When paired with braised or grilled items, they lend earthy depth of flavor that counterbalances the sweet, meaty flavor of the brined chicken.

There are many different vinegars that work well with golden beets. Aged red wine or balsamic vinegars have oaky tannin flavors so I suggest staying away from them for this recipe. Apple cider vinegar, however, dances well between sweet and bitter.

Serves 4

2 large golden beets
3 tablespoons blended olive oil
2 teaspoons kosher salt
1 shallot, cut into ⅛-inch rings (about ⅓ cup)

2 tablespoons chicken drippings (from Blueberry Sweet Tea-Brined Roasted Chicken Thighs, page 93) or blended olive oil
Pinch of red pepper flakes
1 oregano sprig
1 teaspoon apple cider vinegar

1. Preheat the oven to 375°F. Rub the beets with 2 tablespoons of the oil, and sprinkle with 1 teaspoon of the salt. Wrap the beets loosely with aluminum foil. Bake in the preheated oven until a knife inserts easily, about 50 minutes.

2. Remove from the oven, and let stand 20 minutes. Peel the beets, and cut them into ½-inch pieces.

3. Heat a sauté pan or skillet over medium. Add remaining 1 tablespoon oil to the pan, and swirl to coat pan. Add the beets and shallots, and cook until golden brown on 1 side, about 6 minutes. Stir in the chicken drippings, red pepper flakes, and the remaining 1 teaspoon salt. Add the oregano sprig. Cook, stirring often, until crispy, about 4 minutes. Stir in the vinegar, and serve immediately.

To Drink: Grüner Veltliner, Chablis, white Burgundy, sparkling wine, Champagne, Chardonnay, dry Riesling, rosé, Pinot Noir, Grenache, amber beers, IPAs, stouts
Serve with: Grilled seafood; grilled meats; poultry or smoked poultry; rice, potato, or pasta dishes

Delicious food is the root of happiness. I have little doubt that much suffering in the world is because people do not have access to good food. If you look at the American culinary landscape, there are food deserts even in the most densely populated urban areas. Thousands of people just don't have exposure to quality ingredients or get to experience how life-changing delicious meals can be. They've never tasted a vine-ripened tomato and can't imagine that peppers come in a range of colors beyond anemic bell pepper green. Many view onions as papery globes of white, yellow, or purple and miss out on all the other varieties—leeks, ramps, and shallots—that make dishes taste delicious. I truly believe that creative minds and improved lives center on the availability of quality food and shared sustenance. It's why many of us are drawn to our grandmother's table. We crave the dishes of our youth when food was grown closer to home and eaten more seasonally...when meals were made from scratch and shared around the table. My grandmother's cooking was always authentic. Regardless of what she was making or how basic the elements, you could taste that each dish was built on the best ingredients she could find and that she instinctively knew how to make things delicious. Today the convenience of inexpensive, mass-produced fast foods and shrink-wrapped meals distances us from where food comes from and eliminates any need to know how to prepare ingredients. We are not only sacrificing flavor, nutrition, and fellowship around the table, but the exercise in creativity and expression of love that comes from cooking for ourselves and others.

Beet-Cured Trout with Beet Cream Cheese and Watercress Salad

My mother could've been crowned Pickled Beet Queen. Beets were a mainstay of "Mother Meals" much like tomato, cucumber, and onion were Dad's go-to ingredients. Mom made her pickled beets with jarred cocktail onions, and they were so delicious.

Beet powder is sold as a culinary ingredient and as a health food because it is packed with nutrients. You can easily find it online, often referred to as "beet juice powder" or "beet root powder." It lends concentrated beet flavor to the trout curing mixture that is further complemented by the other components of the dish.

The beauty of this jewel-toned plated dish is jaw-dropping. It is light and fresh, with an earthiness and acidity from the beets that is so satisfying.

Serves 8

4 cups Pickle Brine (page 354)

3 (4-ounce) red beets (about 2 ½ inches in diameter), trimmed and peeled

¼ cup plus 2 teaspoons kosher salt

¼ cup granulated sugar

2 tablespoons beet powder

2 teaspoons fresh thyme leaves

1 teaspoon black peppercorns

½ teaspoon fennel seeds

½ teaspoon ground coffee

8 (4-ounce) skinless trout fillets

2 teaspoons olive oil

8 ounces cream cheese, softened

1 tablespoon prepared horseradish

¼ teaspoon ground white pepper

16 toast points

Watercress Salad (recipe follows)

1. Bring the Pickle Brine, beets, and 2 teaspoons of the salt to a boil in a stockpot over high. Reduce heat to medium-low, and simmer until the beets are tender and a knife can easily be inserted into the beets, about 25 minutes.

2. Remove from the heat. Let the beets stand in the pickling liquid 1 hour. Transfer the beets and liquid to an airtight container. Seal and refrigerate 8 hours or overnight.

3. Combine the sugar, beet powder, thyme leaves, peppercorns, fennel seeds, ground coffee, and the remaining ¼ cup salt in a spice grinder; process until the mixture is finely ground. Spread half of the mixture on the bottom of a rimmed baking sheet. Top with the trout fillets, and cover with the remaining spice mixture. Cover and refrigerate 8 to 12 hours.

4. Rinse the trout under cold running water, and thoroughly pat dry with paper towels. Drizzle the trout with the olive oil, and wrap each fillet in parchment paper. Let the trout fillets stand at room temperature for 1 hour. Remove the trout from the parchment and thinly slice the fillets into ⅛-inch-thick slices.

5. Remove the beets from the pickling liquid and discard the liquid. Cut 1 of the beets into ¼-inch-thick slices. Place the remaining beets in a food processor. Add the cream cheese, horseradish, and white pepper, and process until the mixture is smooth.

6. Serve the trout with the pickled beet slices, beet cream cheese, toast points, and Watercress Salad.

To Drink: Champagne, Chardonnay, Pinot Noir, dry Riesling, rosé, sparkling rosé, Sauvignon Blanc, Sémillon, amber beers, dark beers, hard ciders, IPAs, pale ales

Serve with: Braised greens; beans; rice, bread, tomato, or potato dishes

watercress salad

2 tablespoons olive oil

4 teaspoons fresh lemon juice
  (from 2 lemons)

½ teaspoon sea salt

8 ounces watercress

Whisk together the oil, lemon juice, and salt in a medium bowl. Add the watercress, and toss to coat. Makes about 2 cups

Beet-Cured Trout with Beet
Cream Cheese and Watercress
Salad (page 322)

Smoked Turkey Breast with Pickled Beet Chutney

Though beets and mangoes grow worlds apart, they pair well with smoked or grilled meats, so I like to combine the two. Understanding the flavor profile of proteins makes it easier to understand what may seem like odd ingredient choices. Just know that the more you experiment with flavors, the more you'll be inspired to explore many of the regional influences and ingredients the world has to offer.

Serves 6

1 (3 ½-pound) skin-on turkey breast
6 cups (48 ounces) Sweet Tea Brine
  (page 355)
3 tablespoons olive oil

1 teaspoon freshly ground black pepper
½ teaspoon kosher salt
Pickled Beet Chutney (recipe follows)

1. Crack the breastbone of the turkey so that the turkey breast can be flattened. Combine the turkey breast and the Sweet Tea Brine in a large container. Refrigerate 2 to 8 hours.

2. Remove the turkey from the brine, and let stand 1 hour. Discard the brine. Rub the turkey breast all over with oil, and sprinkle with the pepper and salt.

3. Prepare a smoker according to manufacturer's instructions, bringing the internal temperature to 240°F; maintain temperature 15 to 20 minutes. Place the turkey in the smoker, skin side up. Smoke the turkey, maintaining the temperature inside the smoker at 240°F, for 1 hour and 30 minutes to 2 hours or until a meat thermometer inserted in the thickest portion registers 160°F.

4. Remove the turkey from the smoker, and let stand 30 minutes before slicing. Serve with the Pickled Beet Chutney.

Note: Chutneys can be served with most smoked meats and rice dishes. They can be served with nut dishes as well.

To Drink: Champagne, Chardonnay, Pinot Noir, dry Riesling, rosé, sparkling rosé, Sauvignon Blanc, Sémillon, amber beers, dark beers, hard ciders, IPAs, pale ales

Serve with: Braised greens; beans; rice, bread, tomato, or potato dishes

pickled beet chutney

4 cups Pickle Brine (page 354)

2 medium-size golden beets (about 6 ounces each), trimmed and peeled

1 tablespoon kosher salt

2 tablespoons blended olive oil

1 shallot, cut into rings

4 mangoes, peeled and cut into medium-size pieces

½ cup agave nectar

¼ cup (2 ounces) white wine vinegar

2 tablespoons orange zest, plus ¼ cup juice (from 1 orange)

1 jalapeño chile, stemmed, seeded, and finely minced

1 tablespoon coarse-grain mustard

1 teaspoon ground ginger

Pinch of red pepper flakes

1. Bring the Pickle Brine, beets, and 2 teaspoons of the salt to a boil in a stockpot over high. Reduce the heat to medium-low, and simmer until beets are tender, about 25 minutes. Remove from the heat; let the beets stand in the pickling liquid 1 hour.

2. Transfer the beets and liquid to an airtight container. Seal and refrigerate 8 hours. Drain and dice the beets; return to container. Seal and refrigerate until ready to use.

3. Heat the oil in a saucepan over medium. Add the shallot, and cook, stirring often, until softened, about 2 minutes. Stir in the next 7 ingredients and remaining 1 teaspoon salt. Bring to a boil. Reduce heat to medium-low, and simmer 15 minutes. Remove from the heat, and let stand 1 hour.

4. Transfer the chutney to an airtight container. Seal and refrigerate until cold, about 30 minutes.

5. Remove the chutney and beets from the refrigerator, and fold the beets into the chutney. Stir in the red pepper flakes. Store in the refrigerator up to 1 week. Makes about 2 cups

Mashed Potatoes with Chive Sour Cream

Potatoes are considered an everyday vegetable. I believe they should fall in the luxury category, especially when expertly blended with butter and cream. Prepared this way, they coat the mouth with an almost custard-like, silky texture that is pure pleasure to eat. Perfect mashed potatoes pair well with most any vegetable or protein or are equally delicious by themselves. I turn to waxy instead of starchy varieties of potatoes here for an ideal texture. Leftover mashed potatoes make the best Potato Croquettes (page 330).

Serves 4

2 pounds Yukon Gold potatoes, peeled and cut into 1 ½-inch pieces	¼ cup cold unsalted butter
1 tablespoon kosher salt	½ teaspoon fine sea salt
½ cup heavy cream	½ teaspoon ground white pepper
	Chive Sour Cream (page 330)

1. Fill a stockpot with water, and bring to a boil over high. Add the potatoes and kosher salt; return water to a boil. Reduce the heat to medium. Cover, and simmer until a knife can easily be inserted into the potatoes, about 20 minutes. Remove from the heat, and let the potatoes stand in the cooking water 15 minutes. Remove ⅔ cup of the cooking water, and set aside. Drain the potatoes.

2. Process the potatoes with a food mill into a large bowl until smooth.

3. Bring the heavy cream and reserved cooking water to a boil in a small saucepan over medium-high. Pour over the potatoes, and fold to combine. Fold in the butter, sea salt, and white pepper. Serve immediately with Chive Sour Cream, or refrigerate to make the Potato Croquettes (page 330).

To Drink: When pairing dishes such as mashed potatoes and potato croquettes, follow the lead of the entire dish for suggested pairings. If dishes are light seafood, utilize white wines such as Pinot Gris. If the main part of the dish is intense in flavor, such as oxtails, utilize red wines such as Chianti Classico and Bordeaux.

Serve with: Grilled seafood; grilled meats; poultry or smoked poultry; rice, potato, or pasta dishes

Potato Croquettes

Serves 6

2 cups panko (Japanese-style breadcrumbs)

½ cup chopped fresh flat-leaf parsley

2 teaspoons kosher salt

½ teaspoon granulated onion

2 cups Mashed Potatoes (page 329), refrigerated overnight

½ cup finely chopped cooked bacon (about 2 ounces)

1 cup Seasoned Flour (page 352)

½ cup (4 ounces) water

1 large egg, beaten

Blended olive oil

Chive Sour Cream (recipe follows)

1. Pulse the panko, parsley, salt, and granulated onion in a food processor until thoroughly combined, 6 to 10 times.

2. Stir together the potatoes and bacon in a medium bowl. Scoop the potato mixture by tablespoonfuls, and shape into 2-inch-long cylinders.

3. Place the Seasoned Flour in a shallow dish. Stir together the water and egg in a second shallow dish. Place the panko mixture in a third shallow dish. Roll the potato cylinders in the flour, and dip in the egg wash, shaking off any excess. Dredge in the panko mixture, pressing to coat. Place the coated potato cylinders on a baking sheet, and freeze until slightly firm, about 15 minutes.

4. Pour the oil to a depth of 1 inch in a deep skillet. Heat over medium until the oil reaches 350°F. Gently place the potato croquettes, 7 to 8 at a time, in the skillet. Fry the croquettes until golden brown, turning occasionally if necessary, about 3 minutes. Drain on a plate lined with paper towels. Serve hot with the Chive Sour Cream.

To Drink: When pairing dishes such as mashed potatoes and potato croquettes, follow the lead of the entire dish for suggested pairings. If dishes are light seafood, utilize white wines such as Pinot Gris. If the main part of the dish is intense in flavor, such as oxtails, utilize red wines such as Chianti Classico and Bordeaux.

Serve with: Potato croquettes are a fantastic dish by themselves as a snack or an appetizer. If serving with a meal, follow mashed potato guidelines (page 329).

chive sour cream

1 cup sour cream

1 tablespoon mayonnaise

1 tablespoon plain Greek yogurt

1 teaspoon granulated onion

1 teaspoon Worcestershire sauce

¼ bunch fresh chives, thinly sliced

¼ teaspoon ground white pepper

1 tablespoon lemon zest (from 1 lemon)

Stir together all ingredients in a small bowl. Serve with Mashed Potatoes (page 329) or Potato Croquettes. Makes about 1¼ cups

Smoked Fingerling Sweet Potatoes

Sweet potatoes are a root vegetable that absorb smoky flavors just like pork ribs or brisket do. Finishing the crispy, smoky potato skin with butter gives the potatoes a welcome rich, meaty quality. Experiment with different types of salt to bring out different aspects of the smoke and the potato.

Serves 4 as a side

2 pounds pecan wood chips, soaked in water 30 minutes

8 fingerling sweet potatoes (about 1 inch in diameter)

2 teaspoons blended olive oil

2 teaspoons kosher salt

1 ounce (2 tablespoons) salted butter

4 thyme blossoms or leaves from 1 thyme sprig (about 1 teaspoon leaves)

1. Light charcoal in a charcoal chimney starter. When the charcoal is covered with gray ash, pour into the bottom grate of the grill, and then push to 1 side of the grill. Bring temperature to low (about 275° to 300°F). (If using a gas grill, preheat 1 side of the grill to 210° to 250°F.) Place the wood chips on the hot coals, and close the lid.

2. Rub the sweet potatoes with the oil and kosher salt.

3. When the wood begins to smoke, place the sweet potatoes on the grill grates over the unlit side of the grill. Grill, covered with the grill lid, until tender, 40 to 45 minutes, turning once.

4. Remove the potatoes from the grill, and let stand for 15 minutes.

5. Slice the sweet potatoes, and toss with the butter and thyme.

To Drink: When pairing dishes such as mashed potatoes and potato croquettes, follow the lead of the entire dish for suggested pairings. If dishes are light seafood, utilize white wines such as Pinot Gris. If the main part of the dish is intense in flavor, such as oxtails, utilize red wines such as Chianti Classico and Bordeaux.

Serve with: Grilled seafood; grilled meats; poultry or smoked poultry; braised meats and vegetables; grilled vegetables

Dad's Smothered Potatoes

Smothered potatoes are one of our family's classic Soul food dishes. It is easily the single most favorite dish that my dad prepared for us during the holidays. He served these with chicken and scrambled eggs. They are also terrific with caramelized Brussels sprouts or radishes.

Serves 4

8 cups (64 ounces) water
1 pound Yukon Gold potatoes
1 tablespoon plus 1 teaspoon kosher
  salt
1 cup Seasoned Flour (page 352)
½ cup (4 ounces) blended olive oil

2 small yellow onions, halved and very thinly
  sliced (about 2 ½ cups)
2 thyme sprigs
½ cup (2 ounces) chicken stock
½ small bunch fresh flat-leaf parsley,
  chopped (about ⅓ cup)

1. Bring 8 cups water to a boil in a large stockpot over high. Add the potatoes and 1 tablespoon of the salt; return to a boil. Reduce the heat to medium-low, and simmer until a knife can easily be inserted into the potatoes, about 20 minutes. Remove from heat, and let the potatoes stand in the cooking water 15 minutes.

2. Drain the potatoes, and let stand 30 minutes. Cut the potatoes into ¼-inch-thick slices. Place the Seasoned Flour in a shallow dish. Dredge the potato slices in the flour, tossing to coat completely. Shake off excess flour.

3. Heat 2 tablespoons of the oil in a large skillet over medium. Add the onions, and cook, stirring occasionally, until slightly tender, about 4 minutes. Transfer the onions to a plate.

4. Heat the remaining 6 tablespoons oil in the skillet over medium. Add the potatoes and thyme, and cook, turning occasionally, until golden brown, 10 to 12 minutes. Stir in the cooked onions. Add the chicken stock and remaining 1 teaspoon salt. Stir in the parsley, and cook until the liquid is thickened, about 30 seconds.

Note: Yellow onions will give the potatoes a sweeter flavor. Substituting white onions or red onions will change the flavor of the potatoes. White onions may be preferred for lighter dishes; red onions can be used for heavier dishes.

To Drink: When pairing dishes such as mashed potatoes and potato croquettes, follow the lead of the entire dish for suggested pairings. If dishes are light seafood, utilize white wines such as Pinot Gris. If the main part of the dish is intense in flavor, such as oxtails, utilize red wines such as Chianti Classico and Bordeaux.

Serve with: Grilled seafood; grilled meats; poultry or smoked poultry; braised meats and vegetables; grilled vegetables

Potato-Crusted Flounder

Instant potatoes were an intrinsic part of the TV dinner movement of my childhood. While most chefs tend to thumb their noses at instant potatoes, I embrace them. Using the dry potato flakes as a crust for fish elevates this familiar supermarket staple to new heights. Your family and guests will request this dish again and again. Serve with Okra, Andouille, and Crab Fritters (page 279).

Serves 4

¼ cup (2 ounces) blended olive oil

4 (6- to 8-ounce) skin-on flounder fillets

2 ½ teaspoons kosher salt

1 teaspoon ground white pepper

1 cup instant mashed potatoes

½ lemon

2 thyme sprigs

Lemon slices

1. Heat the oil in a skillet or nonstick skillet over medium. Sprinkle the flounder evenly with the salt and white pepper. Place the instant potatoes in a shallow dish. Dredge the fillets, skin sides up, in the instant potatoes, pressing to adhere.

2. Fry the flounder, skin sides down, in the hot oil until golden brown, about 5 minutes. Carefully turn the flounder, and squeeze the juice from the lemon half over the top. Add the squeezed lemon half and thyme sprigs to the skillet. Cook 1 minute. Drain the flounder on a plate lined with paper towels. Discard the lemon and thyme sprigs.

Note: Different flavored instant potatoes like sour cream and onion or cheese can add an interesting twist to this dish. Note the sodium level of instant potatoes. The higher sodium flakes will require less seasoning on the fish.

To Drink: Champagne, Chardonnay, Pinot Noir, dry Riesling, rosé, sparkling rosé, Sauvignon Blanc, Sémillon, amber beers, dark beers, hard ciders, IPAs, pale ales

Serve with: Egg, bacon, braised greens, or smoked meat dishes; fried chicken

Okra, Andouille, and Crab
Fritters (page 279)
Potato-Crusted Flounder
(opposite)

Potato and Sweet Potato Casserole

Settling may be the most difficult thing to do in a kitchen. Sometimes in commercial kitchens the rhythm of the day is just off, so the simplest way to get out of a rut is to just focus on delicious food. Why serve one type of potato when you can serve two?

Serves 12

2 pounds Korean sweet potatoes or small sweet potatoes, peeled

1 pound Yukon Gold potatoes

1 tablespoon kosher salt

2 tablespoons blended olive oil

2 small yellow onions, halved and thinly sliced (about 2 cups)

6 cups (48 ounces) heavy cream

2 tablespoons hot sauce

1 tablespoon chopped fresh thyme

2 teaspoons fine sea salt

½ teaspoon ground white pepper

¼ teaspoon freshly grated nutmeg

4 large eggs, lightly beaten

2 tablespoons chopped fresh flat-leaf parsley

6 ounces smoked Cheddar cheese, shredded (about 1 ½ cups)

Thyme sprigs

1. Fill a stockpot with water, and bring to a boil over high. Add the potatoes and kosher salt, and return to a boil. Reduce the heat to medium-low, and simmer until a knife can easily be inserted into the potatoes, about 25 minutes. Remove from the heat, and let potatoes stand in the cooking water 15 minutes. Drain and let stand 30 minutes. Cut the potatoes crosswise into slices.

2. Heat the oil in a skillet over medium. Add the onions; cook, stirring occasionally, until caramelized, about 10 minutes. Transfer the onions to a large heatproof bowl.

3. Add the heavy cream and next 5 ingredients to the skillet. Cook 5 minutes. Remove from the heat, and cool 15 minutes. Add the eggs to the cream mixture, and whisk to combine. Pour the mixture over the onions. Add the parsley, and stir to combine.

4. Lightly grease a 13- x 9-inch baking dish. Line the bottom of the dish with parchment paper. Coat the paper with cooking spray. Layer half of the sweet potatoes alternately with half of the Yukon Gold potatoes in the dish. Pour half of the cream mixture over the top. (The liquid should come to the top of the potatoes but not cover them.) Repeat the process with the remaining potatoes and cream mixture. Sprinkle evenly with cheese. Refrigerate 1 hour.

5. Preheat the oven to 325°F. Remove the dish from the refrigerator, and let stand at room temperature 20 minutes. Bake in the preheated oven until the sauce is set and the cheese forms a crust, about 40 minutes. Let stand 15 minutes before serving. Top with fresh thyme sprigs.

Note: Smoked Cheddar cheese gives the dish a smoked cream flavor. Other cheeses that work perfectly too: Gruyère or Muenster or all three together.

To Drink: Champagne, Chardonnay, Pinot Noir, dry Riesling, rosé, sparkling rosé, Sauvignon Blanc, Sémillon, amber beers, dark beers, hard ciders, IPAs, pale ales

Serve with: Meats; fried chicken; braised greens; mixed green or raw vegetable salads

Roasted Sweet Potatoes with Collard Green Butter

Sweet potatoes are most often used in the fall yet are versatile enough to enjoy year-round. Spring potatoes contain a fair bit more starch compared to their fall-harvested counterparts. The earthy qualities of the roasted sweet potatoes in this dish are enhanced by the slightly bitter tang that collard green butter brings.

Serves 4

4 (12-ounce) sweet potatoes
¼ cup Collard Green Butter (page 347)
Freshly grated nutmeg
1 teaspoon gray sea salt

½ teaspoon freshly ground black pepper
4 cups packed curly mustard greens
2 tablespoons olive oil
1 tablespoon aged red wine vinegar

1. Preheat the oven to 350°F. Place the sweet potatoes in a baking pan, and bake in the preheated oven until tender, 30 to 45 minutes. Let stand 10 minutes.

2. Cut the sweet potatoes in half lengthwise, and place 1 tablespoon of Collard Green Butter in each potato. Sprinkle the potatoes with the nutmeg, salt, and pepper.

3. Toss the greens with the oil and vinegar. Top the potatoes evenly with dressed greens, and serve immediately.

Note: Curly mustard greens may be a specialty item. They can be easily substituted with watercress, small and tender mustard greens, or just a salad mix. Don't be fearful of searching a farmers' market to find small tasty greens. They hold up well with the contrasting sweetness of the potato.

To Drink: Champagne, Chardonnay, Pinot Noir, dry Riesling, rosé, sparkling rosé, Sauvignon Blanc, Sémillon, amber beers, dark beers, hard ciders, IPAs, pale ales

Serve with: Egg, bacon, braised greens, or smoked meat dishes; fried chicken

Curried Cauliflower, Crab, and Sweet Potato Gratin

Curries are underutilized in this country. They flavor foods without masking other ingredients. I use them with ingredients that are naturally light in color, like cauliflower and crab. In braises of fattier, stronger meats such as lamb or goat, curry tempers the dominant flavor notes. Try different brands and blends. If using ground curry, know it loses potency after about six months.

Serves 4 to 6

2 to 4 teaspoons kosher salt

1 head white or yellow cauliflower, florets removed, stem reserved

2 (8-ounce) sweet potatoes, peeled and chopped into ½-inch pieces (about 3 cups)

1 ounce (2 tablespoons) unsalted butter

2 ½ tablespoons all-purpose flour

1 ½ cups (12 ounces) heavy cream

¼ cup (2 ounces) dry white wine

1 teaspoon curry powder

¼ teaspoon ground white pepper

¼ teaspoon lemon zest (from 1 lemon)

4 garlic cloves, sliced

1 thyme sprig

2 bay leaves

1 pound fresh jumbo lump crabmeat, drained

¼ teaspoon red pepper flakes

Freshly grated nutmeg

4 ounces smoked Gouda cheese, shredded (about 1 cup)

4 ounces Parmigiano-Reggiano cheese, grated (about 1 cup)

¼ cup crumbled Cornbread (page 149)

1. Preheat the oven to 400°F. Fill a stockpot three-fourths full with water. Add 2 teaspoons salt. Bring to a boil over high. Add the cauliflower and sweet potatoes; cook 6 minutes. Transfer vegetables to a baking sheet and cool about 30 minutes. Reserve ½ cup of the cooking water; discard the remaining water. Return the pot to the stove.

2. Melt the butter over medium; whisk in the flour. Cook, whisking, until the flour is incorporated and it smells nutty, 2 to 3 minutes. Whisk in the reserved ½ cup cooking liquid. Whisk in the cream and wine. Add the cauliflower stem, curry powder, and next 5 ingredients. Bring to a boil; reduce heat to low. Simmer, stirring, until thickened, 5 minutes. Pour through a fine wire-mesh strainer into a large bowl; discard the solids.

3. Pick the crabmeat, removing any bits of shell. Add the vegetables, crabmeat, and red pepper flakes to the cream mixture. Fold in the nutmeg; season to taste with the remaining 2 teaspoons salt. Transfer the mixture to a 11- x 7-inch baking dish. Top with the cheeses. Bake in the preheated oven until the cheese is melted, 25 to 30 minutes.

4. Remove from oven, and top with the Cornbread. Return to the oven, and bake until toasted, 8 minutes. Remove from the oven, and let stand 20 minutes before serving.

To Drink: White Burgundy, Champagne, Chardonnay, Pinot Gris, Pinot Noir, rosé, sparkling rosé, sparkling Shiraz, amber beers, light beers, gin cocktails, vodka cocktails

Serve with: Smoked meats; smoked and baked poultry; grilled and roasted pork dishes; braised greens dishes; spicy vegetable dishes

ESSENTIALS

A well-curated pantry is the hallmark of any successful cook or chef. It is the key to all successful dishes and is essential to fixing dishes that need that something extra. It's where I find my muse, my laughter, and joy. Opening the pantry door reveals my arsenal and piques my creativity. Its offerings set me in a particular direction. My pantry is a representation of the people, places, and flavors that shape my cooking. Closed, it is dark like black pepper. Opened, it is illuminated like sea salt. The pantry is the place where the most delicious dishes start and all the integral basics I use in my cooking are born.

COMPOUND BUTTER

Compound butters have dual purposes. The first is to deliver flavor to the dish, and the second is to enrich the dish with fat. Fat can be flavorful on its own, but it is also the key ingredient for carrying other flavorings—like herbs, citrus zest, and aromatics (shallot, garlic, and onion). The herbs, spices, and other flavors added to a dish often signal a recipe's place of origin. Using shrimp (for salinity) or collard greens (for bitterness) in butter can balance dishes that can be high in acid (lemon butter sauce) or high in sugar (caramelized onions). Finishing sauces or dishes with either can enliven flavors, providing sea-like umami or herbaceous distinction. Freeze leftover compound butter, or enjoy it smeared on hot toast.

crawfish butter

This well-seasoned butter is used in Curried Lamb Ribs with Crawfish Butter-Boiled Potatoes (page 114) but is also delicious melted atop mashed potatoes or slathered on crusty bread for a po'boy sandwich.

1 teaspoon blended olive oil

½ nori (dried seaweed) sheet

1 small shallot, diced

1 garlic clove, minced

2 bay leaves

¼ cup (2 ounces) dry white wine

½ pound peeled, cooked crawfish tails, thawed if frozen

3 tablespoons finely chopped fresh flat-leaf parsley

3 fresh chives, very thinly sliced

½ teaspoon lemon zest (from 1 lemon)

½ teaspoon Worcestershire sauce

½ teaspoon sea salt

⅛ teaspoon chili powder

⅛ teaspoon coarsely ground black pepper

Pinch of celery seeds

Pinch of dry mustard

Pinch of red pepper flakes

8 ounces (1 cup) unsalted butter, softened

1. Heat the oil in a heavy-bottomed saucepan over medium; add the nori sheet. Toast until crispy, about 2 minutes per side. Remove the nori, and chop. Set aside.

2. Add the shallot and garlic to the saucepan; cook, stirring often, 2 minutes. Add the bay leaves. Stir in the wine, and cook until reduced by half. Remove from the heat, and let stand 5 minutes.

3. Remove and discard the bay leaves. Stir in the crawfish, parsley, chives, lemon zest, Worcestershire, salt, chili powder, black pepper, celery seeds, mustard, and red pepper flakes. Stir to combine. Add the butter, and fold to combine. Fold in the chopped nori.

4. Transfer the crawfish butter to an airtight container. Cover with a lid, and refrigerate until firm. The butter can be made 2 or 3 days in advance. Makes 2½ cups

Note: Serve with the Corn Maque Choux (page 162) and Curried Lamb Ribs with Crawfish Butter-Boiled Potatoes (page 114).

shrimp butter

A classic court bouillon, made by sautéing the shrimp shells and simmering with wine aromatics, is blended with butter to highlight flavors of salt and sea. It's less assertive than Crawfish Butter (previous page) but is an ideal accent for my Shrimp and Grits with Grits Crust and Shrimp Butter (page 130).

1 teaspoon blended olive oil

3 ounces shrimp shells (about 1 ½ cups) (from 1 ½ pounds raw shrimp)

1 tablespoon dry white wine

2 garlic cloves, minced

1 thyme sprig

1 pound (2 cups) unsalted butter, softened

1 teaspoon kosher salt

½ teaspoon lemon zest (from 1 lemon)

1. Heat the oil in a heavy-bottomed medium stockpot over medium. Add the shrimp shells, and cook, stirring often, 2 minutes. Add the wine, garlic, and thyme. Cook, stirring constantly, 30 seconds. Remove from the heat. Remove and discard the thyme sprig.

2. Transfer the shrimp shell mixture to the bowl of a heavy-duty electric stand mixer fitted with the paddle attachment. Add the butter and salt. Beat on medium-high speed until the mixture is creamy, about 2 minutes. Press the mixture through a fine wire-mesh strainer into a bowl using the back of a spoon. Discard solids.

3. Stir the lemon zest into the butter mixture. Transfer the shrimp butter to an airtight container, and refrigerate until ready to use. Makes 2 cups

collard green butter

Green butters are typically comprised of herbs, but the bitter tang of collards is another great match. The fat tempers the strong flavor of the greens in a manner similar to pork fat. Try this with Roasted Sweet Potatoes (page 338).

4 cups (32 ounces) water

1 tablespoon kosher salt

2 collard green leaves

1 pound (2 cups) unsalted butter, softened

1 teaspoon fine sea salt

1. Combine ice and water in a large bowl.

2. Bring 4 cups water and the kosher salt to a boil in a medium stockpot over medium-high. Add the collard green leaves, and cook 2 minutes. Transfer to the ice bath, and let cool 10 minutes.

3. Drain the collard green leaves, and pat dry with a paper towel. Transfer leaves to a food processor, and process until smooth. Add the butter and sea salt, and process until smooth. Refrigerate until ready to use. Makes about 2 cups

pickled mushrooms

Meaty mushroooms change texture when marinated and are like sponges for flavors. These make a great cocktail hour snack or to add a bright note to Egg-in-the-Hole with Summer Sausage Croutons (page 255).

2 cups (16 ounces) apple cider vinegar (5% acidity)

1 cup (8 ounces) water

1 cup (8 ounces) apple cider

½ cup raw sugar

1 tablespoon kosher salt

1 tablespoon pickling spice

1 pound fresh shimeji (brown beech) mushrooms, bottom portions of the stems removed (just enough to separate the mushrooms)

2 garlic cloves, thinly sliced

1 shallot, thinly sliced

Bring the vinegar, 1 cup water, cider, sugar, salt, and pickling spice to a boil in a medium saucepan over high. Reduce the heat to medium-low, and simmer 10 minutes. Combine the mushrooms, garlic, and shallot in a large heatproof bowl. Pour the simmering liquid through a fine wire-mesh strainer over mushroom mixture; discard solids. Let stand at least 2 hours, or store in an airtight container in the refrigerator overnight, before serving. Makes 4 cups

chicken stock

Great stock is the backbone of countless recipes and a great way to wring out every ounce of flavor from bones and vegetable trimmings.

2 pounds chicken bones and necks (from 2 [4-pound] chickens)

1 gallon water

2 large carrots, cut into 1-inch pieces (about 2 cups)

2 small yellow onions, cut into 1-inch pieces (about 1½ cups)

2 celery stalks, cut into 1-inch pieces (about ¾ cup)

2 thyme sprigs

½ teaspoon black peppercorns

½ teaspoon kosher salt

1. Rinse chicken pieces with hot water for 3 minutes.

2. Combine all ingredients in large stockpot, and bring to a boil over high. Reduce the heat to medium-low, and simmer until the liquid is reduced by one-third, 2 to 3 hours.

3. Pour the mixture through a fine wire-mesh strainer into a bowl, and discard the solids. Store the stock in airtight containers in the refrigerator up to 1 week, or freeze up to 6 months. Makes about 10½ cups

RUBS

Rubs are pantry essentials for concentrating protein flavors. Usually meats with a high fat content (pork butt, spareribs, and brisket) utilize rubs. The use of rubs with seafood varies with the fat content of the protein as well as the cooking technique. Salmon, hamachi, and trout can be both rubbed and cured (in low temperature smoking) or brined (in high heat searing).

basic dry rub

Add this general all-purpose rub to your repertoire. It's a good match for most any protein. It's my go-to blend for spareribs (page 232).

¼ cup paprika

2 tablespoons kosher salt

2 tablespoons granulated sugar

2 tablespoons granulated garlic

2 tablespoons granulated onion

2 tablespoons chili powder

1 tablespoon ground cumin

1 tablespoon curry powder

1 tablespoon freshly ground black pepper

1 ½ teaspoons ground ginger

Stir together all ingredients in a small bowl. Store in an airtight container up to 3 months. Makes about 1 cup

curried coffee rub

Use a dark roast coffee, such as French roast, for depth of flavor in this rub. Toasting the fennel seeds brings out their distinctive, flavorful oil. This rub works well on most any red meat, but especially Leg of Lamb Steak (page 102).

⅓ cup fennel seeds

½ cup ground coffee

2 tablespoons sea salt

1 tablespoon curry powder

1 teaspoon freshly ground pink peppercorns

1. Heat a heavy-bottomed skillet over medium. Add the fennel seeds, and cook, shaking pan occasionally, until toasted and fragrant, about 5 minutes. Pour into a bowl, and cool 5 minutes.

2. Add the ground coffee, salt, curry powder, and peppercorns to fennel seeds; stir to combine. Store in an airtight container for up to 3 months. Makes about 1 cup

seasoned flour

Every Soul and Southern kitchen has a good all-purpose seasoned flour to use for frying or my Oxtails with Boiled Peanut Stew (page 304). This will keep for months in a cool, dry place or even longer in the freezer.

2 cups (about 8 ½ ounces) all-purpose flour

2 tablespoons kosher salt

1 ½ tablespoons granulated onion

1 tablespoon coarsely ground black pepper

1 tablespoon granulated garlic

1 tablespoon chili powder

1 teaspoon curry powder

1 teaspoon ground ginger

Combine all ingredients in a medium bowl, and store in an airtight container.
Makes about 2 ¼ cups

erika council's piecrust

This basic piecrust is by Erika Council, a talented baker in Atlanta and founder of the blog Southern Soufflé, *where she shares Southern Soul food recipes and her family's legacy. (Her grandmother is the legendary Mildred Council, owner of Mama Dip's, a 40-year-old restaurant in Chapel Hill, North Carolina.) Erika's piecrust recipe can be used for both sweet and savory pies.*

3 cups (about 12 ¾ ounces) all-purpose flour, plus more for dusting

1 tablespoon granulated sugar

1 teaspoon kosher salt

6 ounces (¾ cup) very cold unsalted butter, cut into ½-inch pieces

⅓ cup very cold vegetable shortening

6 to 8 tablespoons ice water

1. Place the flour, sugar, and salt in the bowl of a food processor, and pulse a few times until combined. Add the butter and shortening, and pulse until the mixture resembles small peas, 8 to 12 times.

2. With the processor running, drizzle 6 tablespoons of the ice water through the food chute, and process until the dough begins to form a ball. (Add up to 2 more tablespoons, 1 tablespoon at a time, if needed, to reach desired consistency.)

3. Turn the dough out on a lightly floured work surface, and shape into a ball. Wrap in plastic wrap, and refrigerate at least 30 minutes or up to 2 days.

To use: Cut the dough in half. Roll each half into 1⅛-inch-thick round on a well-floured surface. Makes enough for 2 (9-inch) piecrusts

BRINES

Brining is a traditional preservation method that absolutely must be mastered in order to impart the delicious flavors found in Soul cuisine. Yes, brining requires ample time to make the magic happen. However, the time spent in preparing the protein can be minimal since you are essentially letting the salt do the work of enhancing flavor and texture.

citrus brine

This citrusy brine channels flavors of Asia with an ample dose of umami that comes from soy sauce and the astringency of steeped pekoe tea leaves. Adding the citrus after the liquid is removed from the heat prevents the brine from becoming bitter. I submerge the fish for my Salmon Croquettes (page 126) in this brine before cooking. It works well with poultry and pork too.

1 gallon water

½ cup kosher salt

½ cup (4 ounces) soy sauce

¼ cup packed light brown sugar

½ tablespoon black peppercorns

1 regular-size orange pekoe black tea bag

1 thyme sprig

3 bay leaves

1 orange, cut in half

1 lemon, cut in half

½ grapefruit

1. Bring 1 gallon of water, salt, soy sauce, brown sugar, peppercorns, tea bag, thyme, and bay leaves to a simmer in a heavy-bottomed stockpot over medium heat, stirring every few minutes to dissolve the salt and brown sugar, about 5 minutes.

2. Remove from the heat, and add the orange, lemon, and grapefruit. Let stand until cool, about 30 minutes. Remove and discard the citrus. Makes about 1 gallon

pickle brine

Whether you have a bumper crop of cucumbers or hate to see the rind of a summer watermelon go to waste, turn to this versatile pickling liquid to preserve firm, homegrown vegetables and fruits like Pickled Carrots and Turnips (page 109) and watermelon rind.

8 cups (64 ounces) water

4 cups (32 ounces) apple cider vinegar
    (5% acidity)

2 cups granulated sugar

1 cup kosher salt

2 tablespoons pickling spice

Bring all ingredients to a boil in a heavy-bottomed saucepan over medium-high, stirring often to dissolve sugar and salt. Remove from the heat, and cool completely, about 45 minutes. Refrigerate in an airtight container up to 1 week. Makes about 3 quarts

sweet tea brine

Warm spices such as cloves, star anise, and peppercorns infuse this sweet tea brine with lots of flavor that takes fried chicken (page 256) to another level. Lose the salt and you could enjoy this herb-and-spice sweet tea over ice.

8 cups (64 ounces) water

8 regular-size orange pekoe black tea bags

1 cup granulated sugar

1 cup kosher salt

1 tablespoon black peppercorns

¼ teaspoon red pepper flakes

4 garlic cloves

4 star anise pods

4 bay leaves

2 large thyme sprigs

2 medium-size oranges, cut into quarters

1 large lemon, cut into quarters

Bring the water just to boiling in a large saucepan over medium-high. Remove from the heat, and add the tea bags. Let stand 5 minutes; remove and discard the tea bags. Add the sugar, salt, black peppercorns, red pepper flakes, garlic, star anise, bay leaves, thyme sprigs, and orange and lemon quarters, squeezing the citrus juice into the pan as you add them. Return to medium-high, and bring to a simmer. Remove from heat, and let stand 1 hour. Remove the solids, and store in an airtight container in refrigerator up to 5 days. Makes about 2 quarts

Variation: Blueberry Sweet Tea Brine: Substitute the Blueberry Sweet Tea (page 92) for the water and tea bags called for here, and proceed with recipe as directed.

EMULSIFIED SAUCES

Emulsified sauces provide not only flavor, but also much-needed texture and creaminess. Aioli and mayonnaise are both emulsified sauces. Classic, by-the-book aioli is an emulsification of garlic and olive oil, while mayonnaise is an emulsification of egg yolk and olive oil. Spanish aioli is often seasoned with saffron threads, giving it a sunny hue. Mayonnaise is often called aioli, despite containing no garlic. I use the labels interchangeably.

chive aioli

This whisk-free recipe for herb mayo is great on sandwiches, in chicken salad, or with Salmon Croquettes with Grits Croutons (page 126).

2 garlic cloves, thinly sliced

½ cup plus 1 teaspoon (about 4 ounces) blended olive oil

8 long, fresh chives (if packaged chives are used, use 16 chives)

2 large pasteurized egg yolks

1 ½ tablespoons fresh lemon juice (from 1 lemon)

1 teaspoon Dijon mustard

¼ teaspoon kosher salt

Pinch of fine sea salt

Pinch of cayenne pepper

Pinch of coarsely ground black pepper

1. Heat the garlic and 1 teaspoon of the oil in a small sauté pan over medium. Cook, stirring, 1 to 2 minutes. Remove the garlic; set aside. Add the chives. Cook 30 seconds. Remove from the pan.

2. Process the egg yolks, lemon juice, mustard, garlic, and chives in a blender until almost smooth, 1 minute. Add the seasonings. With blender running, drizzle in the remaining ½ cup oil through the food chute. Let stand 5 minutes before serving. Makes ⅔ cup

lemon aioli

Super easy and delicious...especially on Broiled Lake Perch and Tomato Aspic in Lettuce Wraps (page 134).

1 teaspoon blended olive oil

2 garlic cloves, thinly sliced

1 tablespoon Dijon mustard

1 ½ teaspoons lemon zest, plus 2 tablespoons juice (from 1 medium lemon)

½ cup mayonnaise

1. Heat the oil in a small sauté pan over medium. Add the garlic, and cook, stirring, until golden, 1 to 2 minutes. Remove from the heat. Transfer to a bowl; stir in the Dijon.

2. Stir in the lemon zest and lemon juice.

3. Stir in the mayonnaise. Let stand at room temperature 10 minutes before serving. Makes about ½ cup

METRIC EQUIVALENTS

COOKING/OVEN TEMPERATURES

	Fahrenheit	Celsius	Gas Mark
Freeze Water	32° F	0° C	
Room Temp.	68° F	20° C	
Boil Water	212° F	100° C	
Bake	325° F	160° C	3
	350° F	180° C	4
	375° F	190° C	5
	400° F	200° C	6
	425° F	220° C	7
	450° F	230° C	8
Broil			Grill

LIQUID INGREDIENTS BY VOLUME

¼ tsp					=	1 ml	
½ tsp					=	2 ml	
1 tsp					=	5 ml	
3 tsp	=	1 Tbsp	=	½ fl oz	=	15 ml	
2 Tbsp	=	⅛ cup	=	1 fl oz	=	30 ml	
4 Tbsp	=	¼ cup	=	2 fl oz	=	60 ml	
5 ⅓ Tbsp	=	⅓ cup	=	3 fl oz	=	80 ml	
8 Tbsp	=	½ cup	=	4 fl oz	=	120 ml	
10 ⅔ Tbsp	=	⅔ cup	=	5 fl oz	=	160 ml	
12 Tbsp	=	¾ cup	=	6 fl oz	=	180 ml	
16 Tbsp	=	1 cup	=	8 fl oz	=	240 ml	
1 pt	=	2 cups	=	16 fl oz	=	480 ml	
1 qt	=	4 cups	=	32 fl oz	=	960 ml	
				33 fl oz	=	1000 ml	= 1 l

DRY INGREDIENTS BY WEIGHT

(To convert ounces to grams, multiply the number of ounces by 30.)

1 oz	=	¹⁄₁₆ lb	=	30 g
4 oz	=	¼ lb	=	120 g
8 oz	=	½ lb	=	240 g
12 oz	=	¾ lb	=	360 g
16 oz	=	1 lb	=	480 g

LENGTH

(To convert inches to centimeters, multiply inches by 2.5.)

1 in				=	2.5 cm	
12 in	=	1 ft		=	30 cm	
36 in	=	3 ft	= 1 yd	=	90 cm	
40 in				=	100 cm	= 1 m

EQUIVALENTS FOR DIFFERENT TYPES OF INGREDIENTS

Standard Cup	Fine Powder (ex. flour)	Grain (ex. rice)	Granular (ex. sugar)	Liquid Solids (ex. butter)	Liquid (ex. milk)
1	140 g	150 g	190 g	200 g	240 ml
¾	105 g	113 g	143 g	150 g	180 ml
⅔	93 g	100 g	125 g	133 g	160 ml
½	70 g	75 g	95 g	100 g	120 ml
⅓	47 g	50 g	63 g	67 g	80 ml
¼	35 g	38 g	48 g	50 g	60 ml
⅛	18 g	19 g	24 g	25 g	30 ml

CREDITS

Food Photographers: Caitlin Bensel, Greg Dupree, Victor Protasio **Prop Stylists:** Thom Driver, Lindsey Lower, Mindi Shapiro, Claire Spollen **Food Stylists:** Torie Cox, Margaret Monroe Dickey, Anna Hampton **Assistant Food Stylists:** Mary Claire Britton, D'mytrek Brown, Blakeslee Giles, Rishon Hanners, Elise Mayfield **Recipe Developers and Testers:** Robin Bashinsky, Adam Dolge, Paige Grandjean, Emily Hall, Adam Hickman, Robby Melvin **Location Photographer:** Angie Mosier **Headshot, page 11:** Eric Vitale Photography **Pages 107, 221:** Robbie Caponetto **Page 136:** Hector Sanchez

INDEX

SOUL

TODD'S PLAYLIST

"Loran's Dance" — Idris Muhammad

"Groove Is In the Heart" — Deee-Lite

"Badia" — Weather Report

"Handa Wanda" — Bo Dollis and The Wild
Magnolias

"Funky President (People It's Bad)"
— James Brown

"Peace Piece" — Bill Evans

"Ain't No Love In the Heart of the City"
— Bobby "Blue" Bland

"Black is Beautiful" — Flavour

"Fame" — David Bowie

"One Day" — Star Cast

"Mas Que Nada" — Sergio Mendes & Brasil '66

"Welcome to the Club" — Blue Magic

"Everyday" — Lucy Pearl

"Soweto" — Abdullah Ibrahim

"So What's New" — Sergio Mendes

"Sunset Lover" — Petit Biscuit

"Brand New Day" — Brainstorm

"Mr. Bojangles" — Sammy Davis Jr.

"Sea Groove" — Big Boss Man

"You Haven't Done Nothin'" — Stevie Wonder

"Can't Find My Way Home" — Steve Winwood

"Not Gonna Let You Walk Away" — LOLO

"Lift Every Voice and Sing" — Ray Charles

"Peaches & Prunes" — Nightlife Unlimited

"Ain't Nobody" — Rufus and Chaka Khan

"Do You Like the Way" — Santana

"Street Life" — The Crusaders

"People Hold On" — Lisa Stansfield

"Blessin' Me" — Avery Sunshine

"Strictly Reserved for You" — Charles Bradley

"Maps (Star Slinger Sunrise
Edit)" — Emancipator

"Nights On Broadway" — Candi Staton

"It Seems to Hang On" — Ashford & Simpson

"It'll Never Happen Again" — Tim Hardin

"Keep It Up" — Milton Wright

"Organic Architecture" — Headphone Activist

"Crush" — Foxgluvv

"We Supply" — Stanley Clarke

"Nothings Into Somethings" — Drake

"I Remember" — Leela James

"Cranes in the Sky" — Solange

SPECIAL THANKS

Tremendous gratitude to all collaborators for the generous
sharing of their skills and talent:

Angie Mosier, for her location photography.

The dedicated team at The Lisa Ekus Group & Time Inc.

The Edna Lewis Foundation, The Southern Foodways Alliance and
Atlanta Food & Wine Festival.

A special gratitude to Shaun Chavis: Her contributions are
far-reaching and a driving force of SOUL.

To Sid Evans & Katherine Cobbs, my family is forever grateful.

HYDE PARK CAREER ACADEMY
Commencement
June 18, 1989